Fodor's

LOS CABOS

FODOR'S LOS CABOS

Writers: Bob Fagan, Marie-Elena Martinez, Jeffrey Van Fleet

Editor: Eric Wechter

Production Editor: Elyse Rozelle
Maps & Illustrations: Mark Stroud, Moon Street Cartography; David Lindroth, Inc, *cartographers;* Rebecca Baer, *map editor;* William Wu, *information graphics*
Design: Fabrizio La Rocca, *creative director;* Tina Malaney, Chie Ushio, Jessica Ramirez, *designers;* Melanie Marin, *associate director of photography;* Jennifer Romains, *photo research*
Cover Photos: Front cover: (Cabo San Lucas) Philip & Karen Smith/SuperStock. Back cover (from left to right): nicksan; csp/Shutterstock; Solmar Hotels & Resorts. Spine: Cabo San Lucas by Jeff Gunn http://www.flicker.com/photos/jeffgunn/5322963020/ Attribution Licence.
Production Manager: Angela L. McLean

3rd Edition

ISBN 978–0–89141–982–2

ISSN 1941–028X

SPECIAL SALES

This book is available at special discounts for bulk purchases for sales promotions or premiums. Special editions, including personalized covers, excerpts of existing books, and corporate imprints, can be created in large quantities for special needs. For more information, write to Special Markets/Premium Sales, 1745 Broadway, MD 3-1, New York, NY 10019, or e-mail specialmarkets@randomhouse.com.

AN IMPORTANT TIP & AN INVITATION

Although all prices, opening times, and other details in this book are based on information supplied to us at press time, changes occur all the time in the travel world, and Fodor's cannot accept responsibility for facts that become outdated or for inadvertent errors or omissions. So **always confirm information when it matters**, especially if you're making a detour to visit a specific place. Your experiences—positive and negative— matter to us. If we have missed or misstated something, **please write to us.** Share your opinion instantly through our online feedback center at fodors.com/contact-us.

PRINTED IN COLOMBIA

10 9 8 7 6 5 4 3 2 1

CONTENTS

Fodor's Features

MAPS

ABOUT THIS GUIDE

Fodor's Ratings

Everything in this guide is worth doing— we don't cover what isn't—but exceptional sights, hotels, and restaurants are recognized with additional accolades. **Fodor'sChoice★** indicates our top recommendations; **★** highlights places we deem highly recommended. Care to nominate a new place? Visit Fodors.com/contact-us.

Trip Costs

We list prices wherever possible to help you budget well. Hotel and restaurant price categories from $ to $$$$ are noted alongside each recommendation. For hotels, we include the lowest cost of a standard double room in high season. For restaurants, we cite the average price of a main course at dinner or, if dinner isn't served, at lunch. For attractions, we always list adult admission fees; discounts are usually available for children, students, and senior citizens.

Hotels

Our local writers vet every hotel to recommend the best overnights in each price category, from budget to expensive. Unless otherwise specified, you can expect private bath, phone, and TV in your room. For expanded hotel reviews, facilities, and deals visit Fodors.com.

Restaurants

Unless we state otherwise, restaurants are open for lunch and dinner daily. We mention dress code only when there's a specific requirement and reservations only when they're essential or not accepted. To make restaurant reservations, visit Fodors.com.

Credit Cards

The hotels and restaurants in this guide typically accept credit cards. If not, we'll say so.

Ratings

- ★ Fodor's Choice
- ★ Highly recommended
- ᕕ Family-friendly

Listings

- ⊠ Address
- ✉ Branch address
- ☎ Telephone
- 🖷 Fax
- ⊕ Website
- ✉ E-mail
- ✑ Admission fee
- ☉ Open/closed times
- Ⓜ Subway
- ⊹ Directions or Map coordinates

Hotels & Restaurants

- ⛨ Hotel
- ↯ Number of rooms
- 🍽 Meal plans
- ✗ Restaurant
- ✑ Reservations
- 👗 Dress code
- ▭ No credit cards
- $ Price

Other

- ⇨ See also
- ☞ Take note
- 🏌 Golf facilities

Experience
Los Cabos

WHAT'S NEW IN LOS CABOS

San José del Cabo Grows Up

The same gnawing question has always confronted visitors planning a trip to Los Cabos: Do I stay in San José del Cabo or Cabo San Lucas? Most visitors have always opted for the flash and glitter of the latter. San José's hoteliers and restaurateurs have stopped trying to compete on San Lucas's terms, opting instead to market their community for what it is.

The city has truly come into its own. San José's zócalo (central plaza) has been jazzed up with a lighted fountain and gazebo; old haciendas have been transformed into trendy restaurants and charming inns. And the city's art scene is thriving with a high-season **Thursday Night Art Walk,** where those interested in art can visit participating galleries and enjoy free drinks and live music.

The Rise of Todos Santos

Once the province of surfers—the undertow is wicked here, making for some amazing waves, but risky swimming— this town overlooking the western cape about an hour north of Cabo San Lucas is home to a growing artists' community. Just don't call Todos Santos Baja's "hot" new destination, because folks here aren't interested in becoming another Los Cabos, thank you very much. But "genteel" and "refined" and "preserving Mexican culture"? Absolutely, those descriptions apply.

Baja's Boomtown

People always ask, "Is Los Cabos the next Cancún?" And that's not exactly a compliment, as potentially negative repercussions for the environment and local culture are implied. Perversely, Los Cabos did benefit from 2005's Hurricane Wilma, which battered Cancún and the Mayan Riviera, as visitors canceled plans to vacation there in the storm's aftermath. The next three years were boom times unlike Los Cabos had ever seen.

The east–west balance has been restored and the world economy has slowed. The flurry of new construction, especially in Cabo San Lucas, has abated, but only somewhat. Even if the number of new hotels opening has subsided, many are still being remodeled and refurbished.

New Terminal at SJD

Anyone who's recently flown into Aeropuerto Internacional de Los Cabos—SJD in airport-code lingo—can tell you that the infrastructure at Mexico's seventh-busiest airport has not kept pace with the ever-rising number of visitors coming here. Relief is on the way in the form of a new terminal, which was still under construction at this writing. The 10 additional gates should greatly ease congestion for the nearly 3 million passengers who pass through annually.

Border Crossing 2013

U.S. citizens need to have their paperwork in order to return to the United States from Mexico by land or sea. Those aged 16 years and older need to carry a passport or passport card. Children 15 and under are only required to provide a birth certificate if traveling with their parents or an organized group.

Note that if you return from a cruise and your itinerary also took you beyond Mexico, a full-fledged passport is necessary for reentry to the United States. All travelers, regardless of age, require a passport when returning by air from Mexico. See the U.S. Department of Homeland Security's website (⊕ *www. dhs.gov*) for more information.

LOS CABOS PLANNER

Getting Here

Once upon a time, the majority of Cabo's visitors were anglers primarily from Southern California and the West Coast.

These days, however, they fly in nonstop to Los Cabos from all over the United States, and to La Paz from some U.S. cities. Via nonstop service, Los Cabos is about 2½ hours from Los Angeles, 2¾ hours from Houston, 2¾ hours from Dallas/Fort Worth, and 2 hours from Phoenix.

Flying time from New York to Mexico City, where you must switch planes to continue to Los Cabos, is five hours. Los Cabos is about a two-hour flight from Mexico City.

Safety

Although Los Cabos is one of the safest areas in Mexico, it's still important to be aware of your surroundings and to follow standard safety precautions. In Los Cabos, pickpocketing and petty thievery are usually the biggest concerns.

Standard precautions always apply: Distribute your cash, credit cards, and IDs between a deep front pocket, an inside jacket pocket, and a hidden money pouch. Don't carry more money in your wallet than you plan on spending for the day or evening. And, most important, leave your passport behind, with your other valuables, in your in-room safe—and be sure to make copies of your passport.

When to Go

Although Los Cabos hotels are often busiest starting in mid-October for the sport-fishing season, the high season doesn't technically begin until mid-December, running through the end of Easter week. It's during this busy period that you'll pay the highest hotel and golf rates. Spring break, which can stagger over several weeks in March and April, is also a particularly crowded and raucous time. Downtown Cabo gets very busy, especially on weekend nights, throughout the year. Whale-watching season (December–April) coincides with high season, but whale-watchers tend to stay in La Paz, not Los Cabos.

The Pacific hurricane season mirrors that of the Atlantic and Caribbean, so there is always a slight chance of a hurricane from August through late October. Although hurricanes rarely hit Los Cabos head-on, the effects can reverberate when a large hurricane hits Mexico's Pacific coast. Though much less frequent than Atlantic hurricanes, Pacific hurricanes do occur and can cause significant damage. Still, most summer tropical storms pass through quickly, even during the so-called short "rainy" season, from July through October.

WHAT'S WHERE

1 San José del Cabo.
Thirty-two kilometers (20 miles) east of Cabo San Lucas, San José, the elder sister, has remained the smaller, quieter, and more traditional of the two siblings. Its 18th-century colonial architecture, artsy vibe, and quality restaurants are great for those who like to be within driving distance, not right in the middle, of the happening spots.

2 The Corridor.
Along this stretch of road, which connects San José to Cabo, exclusive, guard-gated resort complexes have taken over much of the waterfront with their sprawling villas, golf courses, and shopping centers such as **Las Tiendas de Palmilla,** an upscale, open-to-the-public mall.

3 Cabo San Lucas.
Cabo San Lucas is located to the west of the Corridor at the very end of the Carretera Transpeninsular (Highway 1). Cabo has always been the more gregarious, outspoken, and, dare we say, rowdy of the sisters. The sportfishing fleet is anchored here, and cruise ships anchored off the marina tender passengers into town. Trendy restaurants and bars line the streets and massive hotels have risen all along the beachfront. Here, you'll find Bahía Cabo San Lucas (Cabo Bay), the towering Land's End Rocks, and the famed arched landmark, El Arco.

4 Todos Santos.
Only an hour north of Cabo San Lucas, Todos Santos lies close enough to be part of the Los Cabos experience— but still be that proverbial world away. This *típico* town on the West Cape is home to a growing expat community, as well as some cozy lodgings and restaurants.

5 La Paz. The capital of southern Baja is a "big little" city, one of the most authentic on the peninsula. La Paz is a laid-back community with excellent scuba diving and sportfishing in the Sea of Cortez. It's lovely ocean-front *malecón* features a number of good restaurants and hotels.

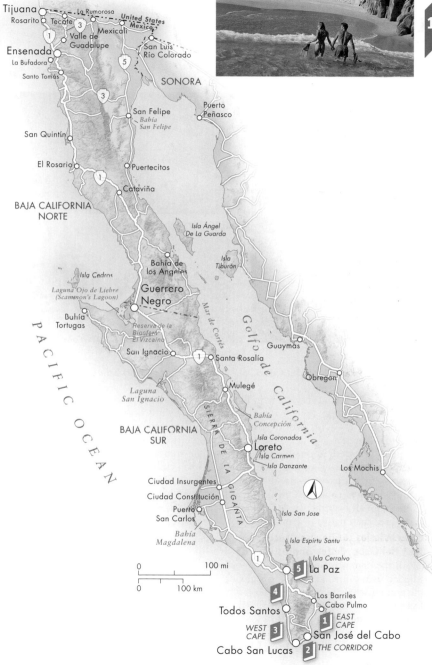

Tijuana
La Rumorosa
Rosarito Tecate
United States
Mexico
Mexicali
Valle de
Guadalupe
Ensenada
San Luis
Río Colorado
La Bufadora
Santo Tomás
SONORA
San Felipe
Bahía
San Felipe
Puerto
Peñasco
San Quintín
El Rosario
Puertecitos
BAJA CALIFORNIA
NORTE
Cataviña

Isla Ángel
De La Guarda

Isla
Tiburón

Bahía de
los Angeles

Isla Cedros

Laguna Ojo de Liebre
(Scammon's Lagoon)

Guerrero
Negro

Bahía
Tortugas

Reserva de la
Biosfera
El Vizcaíno

Mar de Cortés

Golfo de California

Guaymas

San Ignacio
Santa Rosalía
Mulegé
Obregon

Laguna
San Ignacio

BAJA CALIFORNIA
SUR

Bahía
Concepción

Isla Coronados
Loreto
Isla Carmen

Isla Danzante

Los Mochis

Ciudad Insurgentes
Ciudad Constitución
Puerto
San Carlos

Isla San Jose

Bahía
Magdalena

Isla Espíritu Santo

Isla Cerralvo

PACIFIC OCEAN

SIERRA DE LA GIGANTA

0   100 mi
0   100 km

5 La Paz

4

Los Barriles
Cabo Pulmo

Todos Santos

1 EAST CAPE

WEST CAPE 3

San José del Cabo

Cabo San Lucas

2 THE CORRIDOR

1

LOS CABOS TOP ATTRACTIONS

Cacti Mundo, San José del Cabo, Los Cabos

(A) You've seen them everywhere in Baja, but may not know their names. The Cacti Mundo ("Cactus World") botanical gardens in San José del Cabo collect this plant group all in one place and are just the ticket for everything you want to know about cacti and succulents. The facility displays nearly 5,000 species of plants from all over the world, including many rare cacti native to Baja.

Gray Whales, Cabos San Lucas, San José del Cabo, Todos Santos, La Paz

(B) All the commercialism of this part of Mexico evaporates at stunning sight of the annual whale migration—seasonally, December through April—down Baja's west coast and up the east. You arrived by plane, RV, or cruise ship; these 45-ton creatures swam all the way from Alaska.

Land's End, Cabo San Lucas, Los Cabos

(C) This is it. It's the end of the line. The sight of the towering granite formations here lets you know that you've arrived at the tip of the Baja Peninsula. El Arco ("the arch") has become Los Cabos' most iconic symbol—an odd choice, perhaps, for something so stark and natural to represent a place so entrenched in commerce. Yet all the sleek hotels and shopping malls nearby can't deflect from the end-of-the-world feel you get when you arrive.

Malecón, La Paz, Baja Sur
(D) What's Baja's best ocean-side walk? The marina boardwalk in Cabo San Lucas gets most votes, but for a far more authentic Mexican experience, head three hours north to the seaside promenade in southern Baja's largest city. This is urban renewal at its best, with attractive landscaping for the entire 5 km (3 miles) of the malecón's length. The walkway comes alive as evening approaches and residents throng the walkway for their evening paseo.

Parque Nacional Marino Cabo Pulmo, Cabo Pulmo, Baja Sur
(E) The 25,000-year-old coral reef here is the only living coral reef on North America's west coast. Its eight reef fingers attract more than 2,000 different kinds of marine organisms, including almost 250 species of tropical fish. Toss in the sunken wreck of a tuna boat nearby and you have one of Baja's top snorkeling and diving destinations.

Boulevard Mijares San José del Cabo
(F) Shops, trendy restaurants, and a couple boutique hotels line this pleasant street/pedestrian mall, running south from San José's expansive central plaza. As the heat of the day dissipates, locals—usually after evening mass at the 1730 mission church—and visitors alike emerge to partake of the boulevard's attractions.

LOS CABOS
TOP EXPERIENCES

Catch and Release a Marlin

Let's start with the sport that originally put Los Cabos on the map, and keeps it there—fishing! Even for someone who has never been fishing, plying the indigo seas while savoring the stunning scenery from a new perspective makes for an amazing day. Boats from 23 to 110 feet long are available, and you can pay from $250 to $5,000 for the experience. Everyone, even non-anglers, will get excited when the line goes screaming out behind a jumping marlin, as it "greyhounds" off into the ocean. Catch (and, of course, release) all billfish—e.g. marlin and sailfish—but enjoy telling your tale.

"Under the Boardwalk, Down by the Sea"

If you arrive in Cabo San Lucas on a cruise, you'll disembark at its marina boardwalk. Approach from any other direction and you'll still find your way here. Lined with restaurants and bars that are terrific for people-watching, and complete with an air-conditioned shopping mall to pop into when the afternoon heat gets you down, perhaps no place in Baja pulses to the tourist beat quite the way Cabo's marina does. Yes, it's undeniably touristy, but we look at it this way: can all those visitors possibly be wrong?

Go Whale-Watching

The giant gray whales are snowbirds, too. Thousands of these mammoth cetaceans make their lengthy migrations between December and April, swimming nearly 10,000 km (6,000 miles) from Alaska and Canada to mate and give birth in Baja's warm(ish), west-coast lagoons; they make the trip without even stopping to eat, they're in such a rush to get to Mexico (we know how they feel).

Once the whales arrive, they cavort, spyhop (poking their heads straight out of the water), and generally enjoy the seas of Baja, just like their human counterparts. A number of whale-watching tours are available, most of them centered around Scammon's Lagoon, San Ignacio Lagoon, and Magdalena Bay, where tourists go in *pangas* (small boats) out into the lagoons. Oftentimes, the whales and their new babies will approach the boat, rubbing against it, and looking with their sweet brown eyes at the people inside.

Enjoy a Maya Temazcal

Los Cabos has the spas, where giving yourself up to utter pampering and exotic treatments is just another day's vacation, but don't forget about the *temazcal*. This Maya sweat-lodge experience, at the Pueblo Bonito Pacífica Holistic Retreat and elsewhere, is spiritual in nature, working over your psyche as much as your body. Lead by a *temazcalero*, this ritual is a group experience, within a traditional enclosure, and incorporates bathing, steam at high temperatures, and medicinal plants. It requires an almost meditative commitment because extreme emotions often surface in these conditions. Your reward? A feeling of having been completely cleansed and renewed.

View Art and Wine in San José del Cabo

Art lovers unite on Thursday evenings in San José del Cabo, where the Art District Association is behind the Thursday Night Art Walk. With at least 15 impressive art galleries to visit in several square blocks, the district is located north and west of the town's centuries-old church. The art walk takes place from 5 to 9 pm, November through June. The informal, unguided tour makes for a fun

opportunity to drink (free) wine, and be amazed by all forms and variations of art, from amber jewelry, photography, and Huichol beadwork to very pricey sculptures from top Mexican artists.

Hit the Surf

It's during the hot summer months, when tropical storms kick up giant waves, that you'll find the best surfing in these parts. If you are inspired to learn the sport, a number of tour operators offer lessons. By far, though, the easiest way to make this happen is to book a room at the boutique **Cabo Surf Hotel**, with perhaps the most prime Los Cabos surf location. Right out in front of the hotel are three top breaks, Old Man's, La Roca, and Acapulquito, all gentle, forgiving, feathering waves. The Mike Doyle Surf School has taken up residence in the hotel, and has 60 boards of all sizes, shapes, lengths, and compositions to encourage the beginner as well as outfit more advanced surfers.

Tequila Tasting

What better place to enjoy and learn about tequila than in festive Los Cabos? Tequila tasting options abound: Toss down a couple of 70¢ shots of Cuervo. Order $2.80 shots of Don Julio with your lobster omelet at the open-air Crazy Lobster restaurant. Take a tequila class at Pancho's Restaurant & Tequila Museum from a certified "Tequila Ambassador." Enjoy the world's finest tequilas in the exclusive ambience of Las Ventanas al Paraíso resort. Los Cabos is *the* place to put tequila to the test.

Without a doubt, every bar and restaurant in Los Cabos offers a great selection; there are at least four "local" Cabo tequilas (though they're not grown or bottled in Baja but on Mexico's mainland, and then given company labels). Cabo Wabo makes a famed line of tequilas, the Cabo Surf Hotel has its own namesake in the tequila world, as has the Hotel California in Todos Santos. Las Varitas, a popular Cabo dance club located near ME Cabo Hotel by Meliá, also slapped its name on the stuff.

Enjoy the Fiestas

Festivals include Carnaval (February or March, before Lent); Semana Santa (March or April, the week before Easter Sunday); Día de Nuestra Señora de Guadalupe (December 12); and Las Posadas (December 16–25). Don't expect to see much folkloric tradition in avowedly secular Cabo San Lucas or the Corridor. For that festival flavor of old Mexico, head to San José del Cabo, Todos Santos, La Paz, or other smaller, more traditional communities.

GREAT ITINERARIES

Each of these fills one day. Together they touch on some of Los Cabos' most quintessential experiences from boating out to El Arco to visiting the blown-glass factory, and from grabbing a beer at a local brewpub to discovering Cabo's "Fiesta Zone."

Learn the Lay of the Land

On Day 1 take it easy, enjoy your hotel, take a swim in the pool, and get to know the beach in your general area. If staying in Cabo, meander around town, mentally noting the many restaurants and shops on the way that you might wish to sample later. Walking the length of the marina boardwalk will introduce you to Cabo's notorious party central: From the boardwalk's western end beginning near the **Marina Fiesta Hotel,** you'll pass through the marina's "Fiesta Zone" (along which is the infamous **Nowhere ¿Bar?**). If you make it all the way to **Wyndham Hotel,** you've essentially completed the marina walk. Note that it's here where you can catch a boat for sunset cruises, whale-watching, and sportfishing.

Traversing the Corridor

To see the Corridor and make it over to San José del Cabo from Cabos San Lucas, it's most convenient and least expensive if you rent a car for a couple of days. (Taxis are frightfully expensive, and buses limit you to their schedule and stops.) Shop around for rentals and you'll be amazed at the range. Take your time driving along the Corridor, both to enjoy the sights of the coast, as well as to become accustomed to the unique traits of this quirky highway. On and off ramps are challenging, as you'll see. About mid-Corridor you pass **Playa Santa María** and **Chileno Bay,** fun for stops to sun, swim, and snorkel. Bring your own equipment and refreshments.

As you near San José del Cabo, you can't miss the **Tiendas de Palmilla** (Palmilla Shopping Center) across from the **One&Only Palmilla Resort.** "Tiendas" comprises upscale shops and some excellent restaurants, including Nick-San. (Walmart, Costco, and Sam's Club have also set up shop along Highway 1 for more basic shopping needs.) Heading farther east, you'll shortly see a turn-out and large parking lot—a great panoramic overlook of the Sea of Cortez. It's a lovely spot to watch the surf at the **Old Man's** break, to your right, in front of the **Cabo Surf Hotel.**

Beachy, Happy People

For a small deposit, many hotels provide beach towels, coolers, and umbrellas, or you can rent these from **Trader Dicks,** just west of La Jolla de los Cabos Resort near the Costa Azul beach. Dicks also fixes good box lunches. To get to the most pristine beaches along the Sea of Cortez, head east out of San José del Cabo by car. At the corner of Boulevard Mijares and Calle Benito Juárez in San José, turn east at the sign marked "pueblo la playa." The paved street soon becomes a dirt road that leads to the small fishing villages of **La Playa** (The Beach) and **La Playita** (The Little Beach), about 1½ km (½ mile) from San José. As of this writing, construction of a marina resort complex is underway here; watch for road detours.

From La Playita, drive 60 km (37 miles) up the coast to the ecological reserve **Cabo Pulmo,** home of Baja Sur's largest coral reef. Water depths range from 15 to 130 feet, and colorful marine animals live among the reef and many shipwrecks. When hunger pangs call, stroll up the beach from Cabo Pulmo to **Tito's**

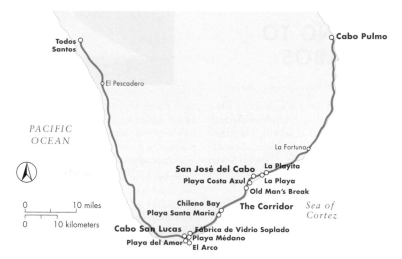

for a fish taco and an ice-cold *cerveza*. Try to get back to La Playa by late afternoon to avoid driving the East Cape's dirt road at night. Stop for some fresh seafood and a frozen margarita at **Buzzard's Bar and Grill** right near the beach just north of La Playa. San José is 10 minutes away.

Artsy Los Cabos
Set out from Cabo San Lucas for the **Fábrica de Vidrio Soplado** (Blown-Glass Factory)—a bit hard to find if you're driving yourself. First head toward San José on Avenida Lázaro Cárdenas, which becomes Highway 1. Turn left at the stoplight and signs for the bypass to Todos Santos; then look for signs to the factory. It's in an industrial area two blocks northwest of Highway 1. At the factory, you can watch the talented artisans use a process little changed since it was first developed some 4,000 years ago.

From the factory, head east for the 20-minute drive to San José del Cabo. Park at the south end of Boulevard Mijares near the Tropicana Inn, since traffic tends to get congested from here on in. Grab some lunch at **Baja Brewing Company**, located on Avenida Morelos. The pub has a tasty San José Especial *cerveza*, and offers international fare to

go along with it. Then stroll through the central plaza, or *zócalo*, directly in front of the **Iglesia San José** (mission church) and take in the several art galleries north and west of the church.

For dinner, try Deckman's, just outside of San Jose proper on Highway 1, where American-born chef Drew Deckman is elevating the presentation of local ingredients and Mexican wines.

Alternatively, from the glass factory, head north on Highway 19 for the one-hour drive to the laid-back town of Todos Santos. Lunch at **El Gusto!** restaurant in the Posada La Poza hotel promises to be one of the most sumptuous you'll get in Baja. (Reservations are a must.) Spend the afternoon visiting in-town galleries near the **Misión de Nuestra Señora de Pilar** (Mission of Our Lady of Pilar) church.

CRUISING TO LOS CABOS

Cruise lines with itineraries to Los Cabos and Baja California include Carnival, Celebrity, Crystal, Cunard, Holland America, Lindblad Expeditions, Norwegian, Oceania, Princess, Regent Seven Seas, Royal Caribbean, Seabourn, and Silversea. Most depart from Los Angeles (Long Beach), San Diego, San Francisco, Seattle, Fort Lauderdale, Miami, New York, San Juan, Vancouver, and even Southampton, England, or Bridgetown, Barbados. Most cruises to Baja dock at Cabo San Lucas, with a few calling at Ensenada, La Paz, and Loreto.

Terrific shopping, dining, beaches, and shore excursions and the unforgettable view of Los Arcos upon approach make Cabo San Lucas a crowd-pleaser among cruise ports. Ships need to drop anchor and tender passengers to the marina, about a 10-minute trip. Ensenada is a favorite stop on shorter Baja cruises. Its modern Cruise Port Village terminal berths two full-size ships at a time. La Paz, on the Sea of Cortez, wins rave reviews as being the most "authentically Mexican" of Baja's cruise destinations. A few large ships dock at its port of Pichilingue, about 16 km (10 miles) north of town. Smaller boats can berth at La Paz itself. It's back to the need for tenders at the port of Loreto, north of Pichilingue.

Carnival. Carnival is known for its large-volume cruises and template approach to its ships, two factors that probably help keep fares accessible. Boats in its Mexican fleet have more than 1,000 staterooms; the newest ship, *Splendor,* was inaugurated in 2008. Seven-night Mexican Riviera trips out of Los Angeles or San Diego hit Cabo San Lucas and, occasionally, La Paz, among other Pacific ports in Mexico. Carnival wrote the book on Baja-only cruises,

with three- or four-day itineraries out of Los Angeles or San Diego to Ensenada. Las Vegas–style shows and passenger participation is the norm. ☎ 888/227–6482 ⊕ *www.carnival.com.*

Celebrity. Spacious accommodations and the guest-lectured Enrichment Series are hallmarks of Celebrity cruises. Its *Millennium, Infinity,* and *Century* ply the Panama Canal east- and westbound on 13- to 17-day itineraries, hitting Cabo San Lucas along the way, with an extensive choice of departure ports (Fort Lauderdale, Los Angeles, Miami, San Diego, San Juan, or Seattle). ☎ 800/647–2251 ⊕ *www.celebritycruises.com.*

Crystal. Crystal is known for combining large ships with grandeur, opulence, and impeccable service. Its *Crystal Symphony* calls at Cabo San Lucas on a variety of itineraries from New York (18 days) and Los Angeles (10 days). ☎ 800/722–0021 ⊕ *www.crystalcruises.com.*

Cunard. It's an infrequent, but festive, occasion when Cunard's luxury liner *Queen Victoria* calls at Cabo San Lucas on select 16-day Panama Canal itineraries that begin in Los Angeles and end in Fort Lauderdale. The port also features in a 40-day cruise from Los Angeles to Southampton. A return 40-day itinerary that begins in England calls at Ensenada before arrival in Los Angeles. ☎ 800/728–6273 ⊕ *www.cunard.com.*

Holland America. The venerable Holland America line leaves from and returns to San Diego or Fort Lauderdale. Panama Canal cruises spanning 14-, 17-, 20-, 28- and 29-day itineraries on the MS *Statendam* include stops in Cabo San Lucas, while a 21-day Hawaii-Mexico on the *Veendam* calls at Cabo San Lucas and

other Mexican ports. ☎ 877/932–4259 ⊕ www.hollandamerica.com.

Lindblad Expeditions. Lindblad's smaller *Sea Lion* and *Sea Bird* take you where the other guys can't go, for an active, nature-themed Baja cruise experience. Eight- to 15-day excursions embark in La Paz and nose around the islands of the Sea of Cortez. Its kayaks and Zodiacs launch from the ship to provide you with unparalleled opportunity to watch whales, dolphins, and seabirds. ☎ 800/ EXPEDITION ⊕ www.expeditions.com.

Norwegian Cruise Lines. Its tagline is "whatever floats your boat," and Norwegian *is* known for its relatively freewheeling style and variety of activities and excursions. Seven-day cruises on the *Star* depart from San Francisco or Los Angeles, with full days in Cabo San Lucas, and Panama Canal cruises on the *Jewel*, *Sun*, and *Pearl* from 14 to 17 days all call on Cabo San Lucas. ☎ 866/234–7350 ⊕ www.ncl.com.

Oceania. "Intimate" and "cozy" are terms that get bandied about to describe the ships of Oceania, a relative newcomer to the cruise scene. Before arrival at Cabo San Lucas or any port, you can attend a lecture to acquaint you with its history, culture, and tradition. The *Regatta* stops here on a 16-day cruise out of Miami. ☎ 800/531–5619 ⊕ www.oceaniacruises.com.

Princess Cruises. Not so great for small children but good at keeping tweens, teens, and adults occupied, Princess strives to offer luxury at an affordable price. Its cruises may cost a little more than others, but you also get more for the money: large rooms, varied menus, and personalized service. Seven- to 11-day Mexican Riviera cruises aboard the *Sapphire Princess*, *Grand Princess*, *Coral Princess*, or *Star Princess* start in Los Angeles or San Francisco and hit Los Cabos and other Pacific ports. Shorter three- or four-day trips out of Los Angeles call at Ensenada. ☎ 800/774–6237 ⊕ www.princess.com.

Regent Seven Seas Cruises. RSSC's luxury liner the *Navigator* offers trips that originate in Miami and San Francisco and call at Cabo San Lucas on select Panama Canal and transpacific itineraries. Some stop here for a half day; others stay in port longer, making RSSC a rare cruise company that lets you sample Los Cabos' evening diversions. ☎ 877/505–5370 ⊕ www.rssc.com.

Royal Caribbean. Royal Caribbean's 14-night Panama Canal cruises on *Vision of the Seas* or *Legend of the Seas* originate in Fort Lauderdale and San Diego and call at Cabo San Lucas, among other Mexican Pacific ports. Striving to appeal to a broad clientele, the line offers lots of activities and services as well as many shore excursions. ☎ 866/562–7625 ⊕ www.royalcaribbean.com.

Seabourn. Think megayachts with sophisticated, personalized service when you hear the name "Seabourn." The line's newest ships, *Odyssey* (2009) and *Sojourn* (2010), call at Cabo San Lucas after departing from Fort Lauderdale on a 18-day Panama Canal itinerary. ☎ 866/755–5619 ⊕ www.seabourn.com.

Silversea. Loads of activities, including guest lectures, are the hallmark of a cruise aboard Silversea's luxury liners. Its *Silver Spirit and Silver Whisper* call at Cabo San Lucas on 15- to 17-day itineraries from Los Angeles and Fort Lauderdale. ☎ 877/276–6816 ⊕ www.silversea.com.

WEDDINGS AND HONEYMOONS

Choosing the Perfect Place. Los Cabos is growing in popularity as a Mexican wedding and honeymoon destination. Many couples choose to marry on the beach, often at sunset because it's cooler and more comfortable for everyone; others chuck the whole weather conundrum and marry in an air-conditioned resort ballroom.

The luxury of enjoying your wedding and honeymoon in one place has a cost: you may find it hard to have some alone time with your sweetie with all your family and friends on hand for days before and days after the main event. Consider booking an all-inclusive, which has plenty of meal options and activities to keep your guests busy. This will make it easier for them to respect your privacy and stick to mingling with you and your spouse at planned times.

Wedding Attire. Some women choose a traditional full wedding gown with veil, but more popular and comfortable—especially for an outdoor wedding—is a simple sheath or a white cotton or linen dress that will breathe in the tropical heat. Some brides opt for even less formal attire: anything from a sundress to shorts or a bathing suit.

Weddings on the beach are best done barefoot, even when the bride wears a gown. Choose strappy sandals for a wedding or reception that's not on the sand; forget the notion of stockings: it's usually too hot and humid. Whatever type of attire you choose, purchase it and get any alterations done before leaving home. (There's virtually no place here to do either.) Buy a special garment bag and hand-carry your dress on the plane. Don't let this be the one time in your life that your luggage goes missing.

The groom and any groomsmen can take their what-to-wear cue from the female half of the wedding party, but know that Los Cabos has no place to rent formal attire.

Time of Year. Planning according to the weather can be critical for a successful Los Cabos wedding. If you're getting married in your bathing suit, you might not mind some heat and humidity, but will your venue—and your future mother-in-law—hold up under the summer heat? We recommend substituting the traditional June wedding that's so suitable for New England with one held between November and February. March through June is usually dry but extremely warm and humid.

By July, the heat can be unbearable for an outdoor afternoon wedding. Summer rains, rarely voluminous in Los Cabos, begin to fall here in July. Although hurricanes are rarer along the Pacific than the Caribbean, they can occur August through late October and even early November. For an outdoor wedding, establish a detailed backup plan in case the weather lets you down.

Finding a Wedding Planner. Hiring a wedding planner will minimize stress for all but the simplest of ceremonies. The slogan of one firm here is: "if you have the groom and the dress, we can do the rest." And a planner really can. A year or more in advance, the planner will, among other things, help choose the venue, find a florist, and arrange for a photographer and musicians.

The most obvious place to find a wedding planner is at a resort hotel that becomes wedding central: providing accommodations for you and your guests, the wedding ceremony venue, and the restaurant or ballroom for the reception. But you can

also hire an independent wedding coordinator; just Google "Los Cabos wedding" and you'll get tons of hits. Unless you're fluent in Spanish, make sure the person who will be arranging one of your life's milestones speaks and understands English well. (Most here do.) Ask for references, and check them.

When interviewing a planner, talk about your budget, and ask about costs. Are there hourly fees or one fee for the whole event? How available will the consultant and his or her assistants be? Which vendors are used and why? How long have they been in business? Request a list of the exact services they'll provide, and get a proposal in writing. If you don't feel this is the right person or agency for you, try someone else. Cost permitting, it's helpful to meet the planner in person.

Requirements. Getting a bona fide wedding planner will obviously facilitate completing the required paperwork and negotiating the legal requirements for marrying in Mexico. Blood tests must be done upon your arrival, but not more than 14 days before the ceremony. All documents must be translated by an authorized translator from the destination, and it's important to send these documents certified mail to your wedding coordinator at least a month ahead of the wedding.

You'll also need to submit an application for a marriage license as well as certified birth certificates (bring the original with you to Los Cabos, and send certified copies ahead of time). If either party is divorced or widowed, official death certificate or divorce decree must be supplied, and you must wait one year to remarry after the end of the previous marriage. (There's no way around this archaic requirement, still on the books,

designed to ensure that no lingering pregnancy remains from a former marriage. It doesn't matter whether you're 25 or 75.) The bride, groom, and four witnesses will also need to present passports and tourist cards. Wedding planners can round up witnesses if you don't have enough or any.

Since religious weddings aren't officially recognized in Mexico, a civil ceremony (*matrimonio civil*) is required, thus making your marriage valid in your home country as well. (It's the equivalent of being married in front of a justice of the peace.) Cabo San Lucas and San José del Cabo each have one civil judge who performs marriages, a good reason to start planning months in advance. Often for an extra fee, the judge will attend the site of your wedding if you prefer not to go to an office. Civil proceedings take about 10 minutes, and the wording is fixed in Spanish. Most wedding planners will provide an interpreter if you or your guests don't speak the language. For a Catholic ceremony, a priest here will expect evidence that you've attended the church's required pre-wedding sessions back home. If you're planning a Jewish wedding, you'll need to bring your rabbi with you: Los Cabos has no synagogues. Another option is to be married (secretly?) in your own country and then hold the wedding event without worrying about all the red tape.

Although same-sex civil unions are now legal in Mexico City and the northern state of Coahuila, and measures are likely or pending in six other Mexican states, Baja California Sur, where Los Cabos is located, is not one of them. A few Los Cabos wedding planners have organized same-sex commitment ceremonies, but these have no legal standing.

SNAPSHOT LOS CABOS

Where Desert Meets Sea

A visitor flying into Los Cabos will readily observe the peninsula's stark, brown terrain—indeed, it feels like you're arriving in middle of nowhere. You'll realize soon after landing that even though the tip of Baja once also resembled the rest of the dry, inhospitable, stark desert, it has been transformed into an inviting desert oasis. The desert topography, where once only cacti and a few hardy palms resided, is now punctuated by posh hotels, manicured golf courses, and brimming swimming pools. As shown by the thousands of sun-worshipping, partying people seemingly oblivious to the fact that true desert lies, literally, across Highway 1 from their beachfront hotel, Los Cabos has successfully beaten back the drylands. Pay some respect to the area's roots by taking a hike or tour around the surrounding desert landscape.

A similar phenomenon exists in the northern sector of the peninsula, with the metro area anchored by Tijuana, in reality just a continuation of U.S. Southern California. Irrigation has turned this desert into one of Mexico's prime agricultural regions.

In between far-northern Baja and Los Cabos—the peninsula logs a distance of just over 1,600 km (1,000 miles), which compares to the north–south length of Italy—expect mostly desert scrubland. Two-thirds of the land mass is desert—a continuation of the Sonora Desert in the southwest United States—and receives about 10 inches of rain per year. The remaining third of the peninsula forms a mountainous spine, technically four mountain ranges. The northernmost of these mountains are pine-forested and might make you think you've taken a wrong turn to Oregon. East of San Felipe,

Baja's highest peak, the Picacho del Diablo ("Devil's Peak"), measures 10,150 feet and is snowcapped in winter.

The Bajacalifornianos

Geography, history, and economics have conspired to give Baja California a different population mix than the rest of Mexico. The country as a whole is the quintessential *mestizo* (mixed indigenous and white-European descent) culture, but only half of *Bajacalifornianos*—the name is a mouthful—can point to any indigenous ancestry. Historically, the peninsula was a land apart, a Wild West where only the intrepid dared to venture to seek their fortunes—many Mexicans still view Baja through that prism—and has drawn a more international population. The indigenous population that does live here is a recent addition of migrants from the poorer southern states of Oaxaca and Chiapas drawn to jobs in the border cities.

Baja's population is just over 3 million, but nearly two-thirds of that number lives near the U.S. border. The 1,600-km (1,000-mile) drive from north to south confirms this is a sparsely populated region of Mexico. The state of Baja California Sur, the southern half of the peninsula, is the country's least populous.

U.S. citizens make up around 10% of the population, with retirees, business owners who have set up shop here, or commuters who live in Mexico but work in the San Diego metro area among them.

A Multifaceted Economy

By Mexican standards, the Baja Peninsula is prosperous, but things were not always so. It was only some six decades ago that Mexico even deemed part of the region to be economically viable enough for statehood, creating the state of Baja California north of the 28th parallel in 1953. Baja

California Sur became Mexico's newest state in 1974. Prior to that, the region, once considered far-off and neglected, was administered as a territory directly from Mexico City.

This is Mexico, however, and all is relative, even today. Wages here may be double, triple, or quadruple those in the rest of the country, but you pause when you realize that $5 a day is still the national average. The presence of the maquiladora economy has brought up the on-paper average level of prosperity to the peninsula. This industry of tariff-free, export-geared manufacturing congregates on the U.S. border with more than 900 factories providing employment for more than 300,000 people, but critics decry the sweatshop conditions. Urban magnet Tijuana—whose population now stands at 1.5 million—attracts people from all over the country looking for jobs.

Agriculture and fishing contribute to Baja's economy, too. Cotton, fruit, flowers, and ornamental plants grow in the irrigated northern region. (Most of the rest of Baja California is too arid and inhospitable to support much agriculture.) Large populations of tuna, sardines, and lobster support the fishing industry.

And it goes without saying that tourism is a huge business in Baja, with an impressive $1 billion flowing into Los Cabos annually. Historically, the border region has tallied those kinds of numbers as well, but fears of drug-cartel violence have greatly eaten into tourism revenues for that area. The U.S. recession—Mexico's northern neighbor provides the bulk of Baja visitors—has dampened peninsula-wide figures somewhat, but increased summer 2012 visitor numbers have sparked optimism.

Livin' la Vida Buena

Living the good life in Mexico—specifically in and around Los Cabos—seems to get easier year after year. Americans and Canadians are by far the biggest groups of expats, not only at the peninsula's southern tip, but in communities such as Ensenada, Rosarito, Loreto, and La Paz. In addition to those who have relocated to make Mexico their home, many foreigners have part-time retirement or vacation homes here.

Do not fall prey, though, to the dreaded "Sunshine Syndrome" that afflicts countless visitors to Los Cabos and Baja. Pause and take a deep breath if you find yourself on vacation here and starting to utter the words: "Honey, we met that nice real estate agent in the hotel bar. You know, we should buy a house here." Many succumb to the temptation, go back home and sell the farm, and return, only to find that living in Baja bears little resemblance to vacationing here. Experts suggest doing a trial rental for a few months. See if living the day-to-day life here is for you.

The sheer number of foreigners living in Los Cabos and the larger communities of Baja means that contractors and shopkeepers are used to dealing with gringos; most speak good to excellent English. Los Cabos, especially, is rich with English-language publications and opportunities for foreigners to meet up for events or volunteer work.

FLAVORS OF LOS CABOS

"Me sube el colesterol, mi amorcita," goes the chorus to a bouncy, popular song here. "My cholesterol's going up, my love," laments the singer about the heavy, fried Mexican food he gets at home. We take it he's never been to Baja and seen how innovative chefs here are playing around with traditional Mexican fare. Not too long ago the dining options in the Cape were pretty limited, though tastily so, with mostly tacos *de pescado y cerveza* (fish tacos and beer) or *pollo y cerveza* (chicken and beer). No longer, amigos. Walking the streets of Cabo and San José, travelers will be pleased to find grand, innovative dining experiences. Things will never go completely highbrow here because, some days, nothing beats tacos and beer.

Sibling Rivalry

The friendly inter-Cabo rivalry infuses everything—the dining scene included. Historically, it's been a comparison of quantity vs. quality: Cabo San Lucas wins hands down in sheer volume and variety of dining places. What San José del Cabo lacks in numbers, it makes up for with the finesse and intimacy of its dining experience. The Golden Rule of Cabo San Lucas restaurateurs was once: "As long as you keep the margaritas coming, the customer will be happy." (The mass-market eateries still adhere to this rule.) But a growing number of San Lucas dining spots have followed San José's lead and have begun to offer intimate, cozy dining experiences.

Nuevo Mexican

The terms get bandied about: "Nouveau Mexican," "Contemporary Mexican," *"Nueva Mexicana."* Ask a dozen Los Cabos chefs for a definition of today's Mexican cuisine, and you'll get a dozen different answers. Many prefer the description "Baja chic," to emphasize the peninsula's uncanny ability to find the right mix of fashionable and casual. Major changes have come to Mexican gastronomy in the past decade. Traditionally heavy cuisine is being altered and reinterpreted. The trend is moving toward using quality local ingredients and combining traditional Mexican fare with elements of other cuisines, all the while asserting one's own interpretation. All chefs are quick to point out that they're not abandoning Mexican cooking entirely. "People visit Mexico. They do expect Mexican food," one chef told us. The rise in popularity of north Baja's steadily growing wine region can also be found on many of Los Cabos' menus, so be sure to try some of quality Mexican varietals that you can't yet obtain the United States.

Seafood

With 4,025 km (2,500 miles) of coastline and no point more than 110 km (70 miles) from the ocean, seafood figures prominently in Baja's cuisine. Baja's signature dish is the ubiquitous *taco de pescado*, or fish taco: take strips of batter-fried fish (frequently halibut or mahi mahi), wrap them, along with shredded cabbage, in a corn tortilla, and top it all off with onions, lime juice, and a dollop of sour cream. You'll find as many recipes for Baja-style seafood stew as there are cooks, who refer to the dish as or paella or *zarzuela*. (Ensenada is Baja's most famous spot for paella.) Any mix-and-match combination of clams, crab, shrimp, cod, sea bass, red snapper, or mahi mahi could find its way into your dish, along with requisite white wine, garlic, and spices. Shellfish is frequently served here as a *coctel*, steamed with sauce and lime juice.

Beaches

WORD OF MOUTH

"Medano [is] lined with cute beach bars where you can sit under an umbrella and have food/drinks served (similar to Playa Los Muertos in PV)."

—suze

Updated by
Marie Elena
Martinez

Along the rocky cliffs of the Pacific Ocean and the Sea of Cortez lie many bays, coves, and some 80-odd km (50-odd miles) of sandy beach. The waters range from translucent green to deep navy (and even a stunning turquoise on some days of the year).

Playa Médano, in Cabo San Lucas, is the most visited and active stretch of sand. Gorgeous and somewhat secluded, but by no means free of people, Playa del Amor (Lover's Beach) is five minutes across the bay by *panga* (water taxi, $7–$10). It's a great spot for swimming, although the waters can be somewhat busy with all the panga traffic. Just southwest of San José, the most popular beaches are Costa Azul and Playa Palmilla.

Most beaches in the area are seldom crowded, with the one major exception being the 3-km (2-mile) Playa Médano in Cabo San Lucas. Most people on this beach are here for the crowds, though, and there is no better place to people-watch. No other beaches are within walking distance of either Cabo San Lucas or San José del Cabo; some can be accessed by boat, but most require a car ride (unless you're staying at a Corridor hotel nearby). You can reach nearly all the beaches by bus. Taking the local public bus in Los Cabos is a safe and affordable way to access the beaches, but it takes time and it is imperative that you lug extra water if your adventuring is going to take place during the searing summer months.

PLANNING

WHEN TO GO

Nearly 360 warm and sunny days per year, few bugs, and fantastic water temperatures (70s in winter and 80s in summer) allow visitors to enjoy this natural wonderland year-round. The winter holiday season is busy, and people often book months in advance. Spring break is another busy time. Late May through September is when it's hottest, and the least crowded.

2

SUN AND SAFETY

If swimming in the ocean or the sea is important to you, be sure to research beachside resorts, as many in this region are on stretches of beach where swimming is dangerous or forbidden due to strong currents. Barely visible rocks and strong undertows make many of the beaches unsuitable for swimming. Take care when you go swimming—it can be serenely calm or dangerously turbulent, depending on the day or even the hour. The Pacific side is notorious for rogue waves and intense undertows. Also, the sun here is fierce: don't underestimate the need for waterproof sunscreen and a wide-brimmed hat.

BEACH ETIQUETTE

As on most beaches in Mexico, nudity is not permitted on Los Cabos beaches. If you head to a beachside bar, it's appropriate to put on a cover-up, although you'd be hard-pressed to find a strict dress code at any of these places unless you're at one of the more posh resorts. As tempting as it is to pick up seashells from the beach, be advised that U.S. Customs commonly seizes these items upon reentry to the United States. Packing a picnic or cooler for a day at the beach is a great idea, as few of the public beaches have restaurants or food vendors. A few beaches have vendors offering umbrella rentals, but if you're really keen on having one for shelter, it's best to take your own.

BEACH FACILITIES

As a general rule, Los Cabos beaches are no-frills, with very few facilities. There is no established lifeguard program in the entire Los Cabos region. Hotels will often post a red flag on the beach to alert swimmers to strong currents and undertows, but you won't see such warnings on the stretches of public beach along the coasts.

More and more of the public beaches have toilets, but you'll still be hard-pressed to find a shower. The picnic tables, grills or fire pits, playgrounds, and other amenities common at U.S. beaches simply aren't part of the scene in Los Cabos. If you want or need anything for your day at the beach, it's best to pack it yourself. If any of the following facilities are present at a beach, we'll list it: lifeguard, toilets, showers, food concession, picnic tables, grills or fire pits, playground, parking lot, camping.

Mexican beaches are free and open to the public, although some of the resort developments along the Corridor are doing their best to keep everyone but their guests off the beaches in front of the resorts. Resort boundaries are usually very well marked; any beach after that is free for all.

SAN JOSÉ DEL CABO

Oh, the madness of it all. Here you are in a beach destination with gorgeous weather and miles of clear blue water, yet you dare not dive into the sea. Most of San José's hotels line Playa Hotelera on Paseo Malecón San José, and brochures and websites gleefully mention beach access. But here's the rub—though the long, level stretch of coarse brown sand is beautiful, the currents can be dangerously rough, the

IF YOU LIKE:	IN CABO SAN LUCAS	ALONG THE CORRIDOR	IN SAN JOSÉ DEL CABO OR BEYOND
Crystal-clear water	El Médano, Playa del Amor	Bahía Santa María	San José del Cabo's main beach (aka Playa del Sol)
Snorkeling/ Swimming	Playa del Amor (near the Sand Falls area)	Bahía Santa María, Bahía Chileno	For snorkeling, keep going to the East Cape and Cabo Pulmo area
Surfing	Monuments Beach (at eastern end of El Médano Beach)	Costa Azul stretch, Acapulquito Beach (at the Cabo Surf Hotel)	Shipwreck, 14½ km (9 miles) northeast of San José; Nine Palms, just beyond
Beachside or ocean-view bars	The Office, Mango Deck, Billygan's at El Médano Beach	Zipper's at Costa Azul, 7 Seas at Cabo Surf Hotel	Buzzard's Bar & Grill (east of La Playita)
Undiscovered beaches	El Faro Viejo Beach is difficult to access, with dangerous waves, but is a gem for sunbathing	A drive along the highway will reveal many "acceso a playa" signs—be wary of waves!	Cabo Pulmo is distant—a full day's adventure—but pristine for water activities and well worth the time

drop-offs are steep and close to shore, and the waves often pound brutally up onto the shore. While surfers love this type of water and flock here in droves, it's extremely dangerous for the casual swimmer. Warning signs are posted up and down the beach, just in case you happen to forget. Feel free to walk along the beach to the Estero San José, play some beach volleyball, or enjoy a horseback ride along the shore. But for swimming, head to protected Playa Palmilla just a few miles west, in the Corridor.

Playa Estero. A sandy beach can be enjoyed at the mouth of the Estero San José, the lush estuary that starts just east of the Holiday Inn hotel. This oasis is home to more than 350 species of wildlife and vegetation (200-plus species of birds alone), and can be explored on foot, or via kayaks rentable at Tio Sports, next to the Holiday Inn. Not recommended for swimming, it is nevertheless a worthwhile trip in an area that is otherwise not known for its lushness. Public parking is available just beyond the Holiday Inn. **Amenities:** Parking lot. **Best for:** walking; sunrise. ⊠ *San José del Cabo.*

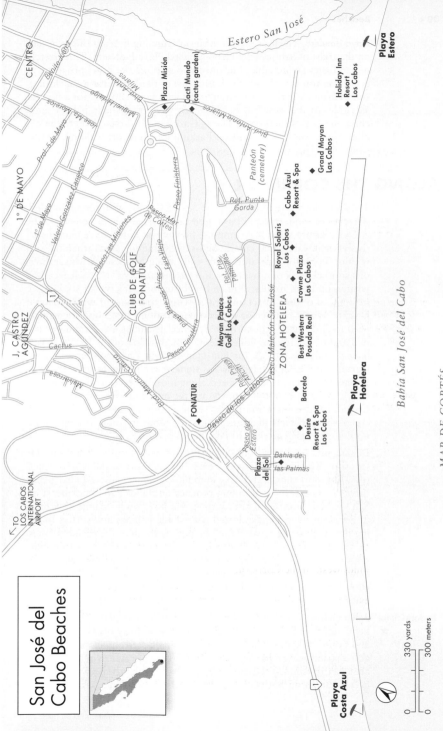

San José del Cabo Beaches

MAR DE CORTÉS

Bahía San José del Cabo

Playa Estero

Holiday Inn Resort Los Cabos

Estero San José

Plaza Misión

Cacti Mundo (cactus garden)

CENTRO

Bahía Juárez

Blvd Antonio Mijares

Miguel Hidalgo

José Ma. Morelos

Prol. 5 de Mayo

1° DE MAYO

1° de Mayo

Valerio González Canseco

Paseo Las Misiones

Paseo Mar de Cortés

Paseo Finisterra

CLUB DE GOLF FONATUR

Paseo los Aires

Faro Viejo

Paseo Finisterra

Ret. Los Palmas

Panteón (cemetery)

Ret. Punta Gorda

Grand Mayan Las Cabos

Cabo Azul Resort & Spa

Royal Solaris Los Cabos

Crowne Plaza Los Cabos

ZONA HOTELERA

Best Western Posada Real

Mayan Palace Golf Los Cabos

Paseo Malecón San José

Blvd Antonio Mijares

J. CASTRO AGÚNDEZ

Cactus

Malecón

Blvd Mauricio Castro

FONATUR

Paseo de los Cabos

Playa Ret. Playa

Paseo del Estero

Barcelo

Desire Resort & Spa Los Cabos

Plaza del Sol

Bahía de las Palmas

TO LOS CABOS INTERNATIONAL AIRPORT

Playa Hotelera

Playa Costa Azul

330 yards

300 meters

0

0

Ⓒ **Playa Hotelera.** The long stretch of beach running in front of the hotels
on the coast of San José del Cabo is called Playa Hotelera. This stretch
of sand isn't swimmable, but once you step off the hotel property, it
is public. You can always duck into one of the hotels for a snack or a
sunset drink, and there are often locals with horses to rent for a beachside ride. At the west end of the beach you'll find shade palapas and
children's play structures at Plazas Garuffi and Caracol, where there's
also public parking. **Amenities:** Parking lot. **Best for:** walking. ⊠ *San
José del Cabo.*

ALONG THE CORRIDOR

The Corridor's coastline edges the Sea of Cortez, with long, secluded
stretches of sand, tranquil bays, golf fairways, and huge resorts. Only
a few areas are safe for swimming, but several hotels have man-made
rocky breakwaters that create semi-safe swimming areas when the sea
is calm. Look for blue-and-white signs along Mexico 1 with symbols
of a snorkel mask or a swimmer and "*acceso a playa*" ("beach access")
written on them to alert you to beach turnoffs. It's worth studying a
map ahead of time to get an idea of where your turnoff will be. Don't
hesitate to ask around for directions, and don't lose hope if you still
need to circle back around once or twice. Facilities are extremely limited and lifeguards are nonexistent, though many of the beaches now
have portable toilets. ⚠ **The four-lane Highway 1 has more-or-less well-
marked turnoffs for hotels. Be wary: signage as a rule appears at the very
last minute.** Drivers tend to speed along most of the Corridor highway,
which makes for a lot of business for the police officers who patrol the
Corridor. Slow buses and trucks seem to appear out of nowhere, and
confused tourists switch lanes with abandon. If you're driving, wait
until you're safely parked to take in Sea of Cortez views.

Bahía Santa María and **Bahía Chileno** are two beautiful strands in the
Corridor. Bahía Santa María is the less busy of the two, and both beaches
offer fun snorkeling and safe swimming. For some truly secluded gems,
drive northeast to the stunning beaches on the dirt road northeast of
San José del Cabo. Soon after leaving San José you'll see mile after mile
of gorgeous white sands, dotted with shade palapas and surfers looking for the next big break. Don't be put off by all of the private homes
or "no trespassing" signs—beaches are plentiful and access to public
ones is clear. The dirt road is well maintained and fine for passenger
cars (despite dire-sounding warnings from locals who will tell you that
you must have a four-wheel-drive vehicle)—but the dirt roads are best
avoided if it's raining.

Fodor'sChoice **Bahía Chileno.** A private enclave—with golf courses and residences—is
★ being developed at Bahía Chileno, roughly midway between San José
and Cabo San Lucas. The beach skirts a small, crescent-shape cove with
aquamarine waters that are perfect for snorkeling and swimming (there
are even restrooms). Getting here is easy, thanks to the well-marked
access ramps on both sides of the road. The Chileno Bay project, a

Continued on page 37

SURFING
CABO STYLE

by Larry Dunmire

From the gentlest of beginner waves at Old Man's surf spot to the gnarliest winter waves at Los Cerritos, Los Cabos has surf for everyone. The tip of the Baja Peninsula has three key areas: the Pacific coast (often called "the Pacific side"), the East Cape, and the Cabo Corridor between them. This means that there are east-, west- and south-facing beaches taking waves from just about every direction.

There are also warm, crystalline seas and great surf schools. Friendly instructors make lessons fun and are more than willing to tailor them to the needs of anyone—from tots to retirees, aspiring surfers to experts. Schools also offer surf tours so you can benefit from insider knowledge of the local waves and quirky surf spots before heading out on your own.

LOS CABOS SURF FINDER

Surfer at a right-hand point break

Punta Conejo
Todos Santos
Punta Lobos
Playa San Pedrito
El Pescadero
El Pescadero
Playa Los Cerritos

Gentle waves during summer time.

PACIFIC SIDE

In winter, the Pacific from Cabo San Lucas town north to Todos Santos, often roils with rough, thundering swells. Surf spots here are only for the most accomplished although Los Cerritos, home to the Costa Azul Surf Shop and school, can have gentle waves in summer. Pacific-side beaches face essentially west and slightly north. Hence, winter swells coming from these directions (thanks to Alaskan storms) make landfall head on, creating great waves.

Punta Conejo: a rocky point break north of Todos Santos; unique in that's surfable on both north and south swells. Has good right and left breaks. *11 km (7 mi) north of Todos Santos; turn off Hwy. 19 near Km 80.*

Punta Lobos: big point breaks with south swells. *South of Todos Santos; turn off Hwy. 19 at Km 54 onto dirt road, and continue for about 2.5 km (1.5 mi).*

Surfer on the nose of his long-board on a clean wave

Perfect waves in Salsipuedes, Baja California

Playa San Pedrito: a beautiful, broad, curved, sandy beach break, surfable on both west and north swells. *About 5 km (3 mi) south of Todos Santos; turn off Hwy. 19 at CAMPO EXPERIMENTA sign, and continue about 2.5 km (1.5 mi).*

El Pescadero: fast, consistent, right reef and beach breaks; watch out for painful sea urchins in shallow water! *Hwy. 19 at Km 59.*

Playa Los Cerritos: highly versatile beach—in summer, good for beginners, with gentle breaks and a safe, sandy bottom; winter waves are gnarly. Best ones are on northwest swells, though south swells aren't bad. Both left and right beach breaks. Home to Costa Azul Surf Shop; can get crowded. *Less than a km (half a mi) south of Todos Santos; Hwy. 19 at Km 66.*

CABO CORRIDOR

The 20-mile stretch of beautiful beaches and bays between the towns of Cabo San Lucas and San José del Cabo has no less than a dozen surf spots, including some that are hard to find and access. Opportunities range from the expert-only Monuments break just outside of Cabo to the beginner-friendly Old Man's spot. For experts, surfing in the Corridor is generally best in the summer and fall, when storms as far away as New Zealand and Antarctica can send south swells all the way up here.

Playa Monumentos: powerful left point break, offering great gut-wrenching waves on south and west swells. Dangerously shallow at low tide; many sea urchins. Great surf and sunset watching from bluff near parking area. *Far south end of Cabo's El Medano Beach, east of Cabo San Lucas on Hwy 1; pull off at Misiones de Cabo, drive to gate, park at right.*

Playa El Tule: long wide beach with great right reef break in El Tule Arroyo, near highway bridge of same name. One of few places you can still camp; need 4WD to get here. *Midway btw. Cabo San Lucas and San José. East on Hwy. 1, look for EL TULE sign, pull off road and drive toward ocean on soft, sandy road.*

19

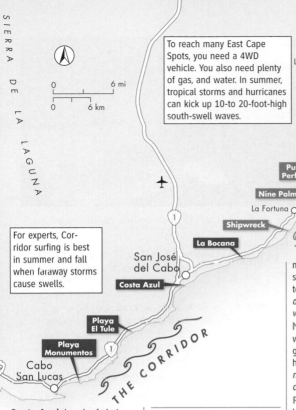

SIERRA DE LA LAGUNA

Cabo Pulmo

Los Frailes

Sea of Cortez

Punta Perfecta

Nine Palms

La Fortuna

EAST CAPE

Shipwreck

La Bocana

San José del Cabo

Costa Azul

Playa El Tule

Playa Monumentos

Cabo San Lucas

THE CORRIDOR

19

0   6 mi
0   6 km

To reach many East Cape Spots, you need a 4WD vehicle. You also need plenty of gas, and water. In summer, tropical storms and hurricanes can kick up 10-to 20-foot-high south-swell waves.

For experts, Corridor surfing is best in summer and fall when faraway storms cause swells.

Costa Azul: beach of choice in summer. World-famous, experts-only Zippers break often tops 12 feet. Has two other popular breaks: Acapulquito (Old Man's)—forgiving with a gentle surf break and good for beginners—and The Rock, a more challenging reef break to the east. The rocks are near the surface; quite shallow at low tide. There's a restaurant and a branch of the Costa Azul Surf Shop here. *Hwy. 1.*

La Bocana: freshwater estuary with a river mouth beach break (i.e., giant tubular waves break upon sand bars created by runoff sand deposited here after powerful summer rains). Both left and right rides. *Hwy. 1, south of Intercontinental hotel.*

EAST CAPE

North and east of San José, up the rough, unpaved East Cape Road, there are many breaks with good waves that are perpetually empty—with good reason. To get here, you need a 4WD vehicle. You also need plenty of gas, sufficient water, an umbrella, and *mucho* sun block. Waves here aren't for beginners, and some of the coast is on private property. Note, too, that locals (both Mexican and gringo) can be protective of their spots. East Cape beaches face south and east, and, in summer, tropical storms and hurricanes can kick up 10-, 15-, and even 20-foot-high south-swell waves—exciting for beginners to watch from the shore.

Shipwreck: fast, right reef break with south swells in summer. Considered the second-best summer surfing spot. Need 4WD to get here. *Off East Cape Rd., about 16 km (10 mi) up a rough, washboard road.*

Nine Palms: right point break with good, long waves and great shape but at least an hour's drive out. *East Cape Rd., near village of Santa Elena and a palm-tree grove.*

Punta Perfecta: right point break; can get big and hollow (i.e., "tubular") during summer's south swells. Out of the way (4WD required) and hard to find; territorial local surfers get testy when asked for directions. *East Cape Rd., near Crossroads Country Club and Vinorama.*

Los Frailes: Waves get big on a south swell. Down a long, dusty, pounding drive (need 4WD). Beautiful white sand beach and tranquil desert surroundings. *East Cape Rd.*

Stand-up paddling: SUPing

LEARNING TO SURF

WHAT TO EXPECT
Expect introductory classes to cover how to lie on the board, paddle properly, pop up into a surf stance, handle wave-riding, and duck incoming waves.

GEARING UP
Both surf shops and schools offer a wide selection of lessons, gear, and boards—sometimes including "skegs," soft, stable beginners's boards with safe rubber fins. Novices will want to use longboards, which offer the most stability. Rash guards (form-fitting polyester vests) protect you from board chafing and sunburn. Booties, rubberized watershoes, protect your feet from rocks, coral and sea urchins.

GETTING OUT THERE
Most agree that the best place for beginners is San José del Cabo's Acapulquito Beach, home to Old Man's surf spot. It has gently breaking, "feathering" (very forgiving) waves and the region's most understanding surfers. Acapulquito Beach is also home to the Cabo Surf Hotel, with a top school. The **Mike Doyle Surf School** (⊕ *http://cabosurfshop.com*) has three full-time teachers, certified by the NSSIA, the National Surf Schools and Instructor's Association (U.S.) and a great selection of more than 60 boards—short, long, "soft" boards for novices, and even a couple of SUP boards. The schools shows informative introductory video in the hotel's air-conditioned viewing room before you hit the beach.

Costa Azul Surf Shop (⊕ *www.costa-azul. com.mx*), with branches in San José del Cabo (near Zipper's Restaurant) and south of Todos Santos, near Los Cerritos Beach, is another option for lessons. Staff here can arrange tours to breaks so far off the path that roads to them aren't always marked on maps, let alone paved. The shop's Web site also has good interactive surfing maps.

Costa Azul's surf excursions—with guides (one guide for every two students) and two-hour lessons—cost US$85 a person.

SURF'S DOWN?

If the surf's flat, *no problema!* The latest craze is SUP-ing, or Stand-Up Paddling. It's done on flat waters using broad, long, lightweight boards that are comfortable to stand on. You paddle along, alternating sides for balance, using what resembles a single-bladed kayak paddle. SUP-ing is easy to master, great exercise, and highly enjoyable.

Accomplished surfers have pushed the SUP-ing envelope, paddling their boards into the surf line (or surf zone) and right into the waves, be they small or large. The paddle is then used to steer, almost like a boat's rudder. One step at a time, though—this type of SUP-ing is *not* as easy as the masters make it look!

Surf's up: you can really ride the waves in Los Cabos.

BOARD SHAPES

Longboard: Lengthier (about 2.5–3 m/9–10.5 feet), wider, thicker, and more buoyant than the often-miniscule shortboards. Offers more flotation and speedier paddling, which makes it easier to get into waves. Great for beginners and those with relaxed surf styles. **Skill level:** Beginner to Intermediate.

Funboard: A little shorter than the longboard with a slightly more acute nose and blunt tail, the funboard combines the best attributes of the longboards with some similar characteristics of the shorter boards. Good for beginners or surfers looking for a board more maneuverable and faster than a longboard. **Skill level:** Beginner to Intermediate.

Fishboard: A stumpy, blunt-nosed, twin-finned board that features a "V" tail (giving it a "fish" like look, hence the name) and is fast and maneuverable. Good for catching small, steep slow waves and pulling tricks. At one point this was the world's best-selling surfboard. **Skill level:** Intermediate to Expert.

Shortboard: Shortboards came on the scene in the late '60s when the average board length dropped from 9'6" to 6'6" (3m to 2m) and changed the wave riding forever. This short, light, high-performance board is designed for carving the wave with a high amount of maneuverability. These boards need a fast steep wave, completely different from the a "longboard" break, which tends to be slower with shallower wave faces. **Skill level:** Expert.

Beginner

Expert

Fish

Funboards

Longboards

Shortboards

Shallow wave faces, easiest surfing

Steeper wave faces, difficult surfing

SURF SLANG

By Leland Baxter-Neal
and Larry Dunmire

Barrel: The area created when a wave breaks onto itself in a curl, creating a tube that's the surfer's nirvana. Also called the green room.

Beach break: The safest, best type for beginners. Waves break over sandy beaches. Found at Acapulquito (Old Man's), San Pedrito, and Los Cerritos.

Drop in: To stand up and drop down in the face of a wave. Also used when one surfer cuts another off: "Hey, don't drop in on that guy!"

Duck dive: Maneuver where the surfer first pushes his or her board underwater and then dives with it, ducking under waves that have broken or are about to break. Difficult with a longboard.

Turtle roll: the surfer rolls over on the surfboard, going underwater and holding the board upside down. Used by longboarders and beginners to keep from being swept back toward shore by breaking waves.

Goofy foot: Having a right-foot-forward stance on the surfboard. The opposite is known as natural.

Close out: When a wave or a section of a wave breaks all at once, rather than steadily

in one direction. A frustrating situation for surfers; there's nowhere to go as the wave crashes down.

Ding: A hole, dent, crack or other damage to a board.

Outside: The area farther out from where waves break most regularly. Surfers line up here, and begin their paddling to catch waves.

Point break: Created as waves hit a point jutting into the ocean. With the right conditions, this can create very consistent waves and very long rides. Punta Lobos, Punta Conejo, and Monuments are examples.

Reef break: Waves break as they pass over reefs and create great (but sometimes dangerous) surf. There's always the chance of being scraped over extremely sharp coral or rocks. Found at El Tule, Shipwreck, and The Rock in Costa Azul.

Right/Left break: Terms for which direction the surfer actually travels on the wave, as seen from his or her perspective. Think of break direction in terms of when you're actually surfing the wave.

Set: waves often come in as sets, or groups of five to seven, sometimes more, in a row.

Stick: A surfboard.

Stoked: really, totally excited—usually about the surf conditions or your fantastic wave ride.

Swells: created by wind currents blowing over the sea's surface. The harder and the longer the winds blow, the larger the waves, and the longer the swell lasts.

Tubed: becoming totally enclosed inside the wave's barrel during a ride. The ultimate "stoke!" Getting "tubed" is also sometimes known as spending time inside the "green room."

Wipeout: a nasty crash off your board, usually having the wave crash down upon you.

(top) A surfer rips it up in Mexico (bottom) Baja California Sur sunset.

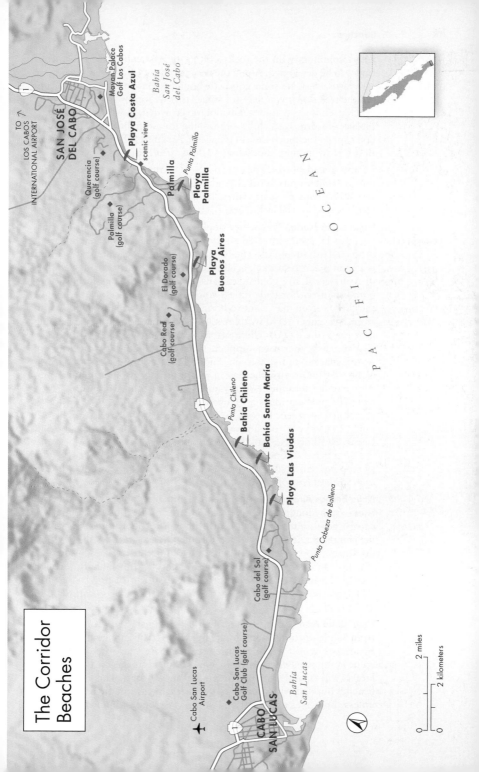

The Corridor Beaches

SAN JOSÉ DEL CABO

TO
LOS CABOS INTERNATIONAL AIRPORT

Mayan Palace Golf Los Cabos

Playa Costa Azul

scenic view

Querencia (golf course)

Palmilla (golf course)

Bahía San José del Cabo

Palmilla

Punta Palmilla

Playa Palmilla

El Dorado (golf course)

Playa Buenos Aires

Cabo Real (golf course)

P A C I F I C   O C E A N

Punta Chileno

Bahía Chileno

Bahía Santa María

Playa Las Viudas

Cabo del Sol (golf course)

Punta Cabeza de Ballena

Cabo San Lucas Airport

Cabo San Lucas Golf Club (golf course)

Bahía San Lucas

CABO SAN LUCAS

2 miles

2 kilometers

0

0

resort community on the rocky cliff at the east end of the beach continues to be developed. Along the western edge of Bahía Chileno, some 200 yards away, are some good-size boulders that you can scramble up. On the trek down you may see some stray wrappers and cans, but the beach itself is clean and usually not too crowded. In winter, this part of the Sea of Cortez gets chilly—refreshing for a dip, but most snorkelers don't spend too much time in the water. **Amenities:** Toilets; parking lot. **Best for:** swimming; snorkeling. ⊠ *Bahía Chileno*

Cabo Acuadeportes. The only business on the beach is Cabo Acuadeportes, which rents snorkel equipment and offers scuba diving and snorkeling trips to nearby sites; hours are erratic and depend on the beach traffic (or the lack thereof). ☎ *624/143–0117*

ⓒ **Bahía Santa María.** This wide, sloping, horseshoe-shape beach is surrounded by cactus-covered rocky cliffs; the placid waters here are a protected fish sanctuary. The bay is part of an underwater reserve and is a great place to snorkel: brightly colored fish swarm through chunks of white coral and golden sea fans. Unfortunately, this little slice of paradise offers no shade unless you sit in the shadows at the base of the cliffs, so you may want to bring a beach umbrella. In high season, from November to May, there's usually someone renting snorkeling gear for $10 a day or selling sarongs, straw hats, and soft drinks. It's best to bring your own supplies, though, including lots of drinking water, snacks, and sunscreen. Snorkel and booze-cruise boats from Cabo San Lucas visit the bay in mid-morning through about 1 pm. Arrive mid-afternoon if you want to get that total Robinson Crusoe feel. The parking lot is a quarter mile or so off the highway and is sometimes guarded; be sure to tip the guard. The bay is roughly 19 km (12 miles) west of San José and 13 km (8 miles) east of Cabo San Lucas. Heading east, look for the sign saying *"Playa Santa María and acceso a playa."* **Amenities:** Toilets; parking lot. **Best for:** snorkeling; swimming; partiers. ⊠ *19 km (12 miles) west of San José del Cabo, 13 km (8 miles) east of Cabo San Lucas.*

Fodor's Choice
★

Playa Buenos Aires. This wide, lengthy, and accessible stretch of beach is one of the longest along the Cabo Corridor. Reef breaks for surfers can be good, but the beach is also known for its riptides, making it unswimmable. It's a great beach for long, quiet runs or walks, and it's not uncommon to find locals with horses to rent for a beachside ride. Whales can easily be spotted from the beach from January through March. **Amenities:** Toilets; parking lot (exit at Km 22 or 24). **Best for:** surfers; walking. ⊠ *Near the Secrets Marquis Hotel Los Cabos/Hilton and stretching down to Meliá Cabo Real.*

Playa Costa Azul. Cabo's best surfing beach runs 3 km (2 miles) south from San José's hotel zone along Highway 1. The Zipper and La Roca breaks are world famous. Surfers gather here year-round, but most come in summer, when hurricanes and tropical storms create the year's largest waves, and when the ocean is at its warmest. This condo-lined beach is popular with joggers and walkers, but swimming isn't advised unless the waves are small and you're a strong swimmer. If you do

Bahía Santa María (Santa Maria Bay) is a popular swimming and snorkeling spot along the Corridor.

decide to take a plunge, be wary of surfers riding into the shore—it's hard to spot a swimmer from on top of a surfboard. The turnoff to this beach is sudden and only available to drivers coming from Cabo San Lucas (not from San José del Cabo). It's on the beach side of the highway, at Zipper's restaurant, which is on the sand by the surf breaks. **Amenities:** Toilets; food concession; picnic tables; parking lot. **Best for:** surfing; walking; partiers. ⊠ *Just over 1 km (½ mile) southwest of San José.*

Playa Las Viudas (*Widow's Beach*). Just west of Santa María Bay, this small public beach is often referred to as Twin Dolphin Beach after the Twin Dolphin Hotel, a longtime landmark that was demolished in mid-2007. It's a great place for snorkeling (bring your own gear), but it is open to the ocean and all the inherent dangers that entails, so swim with extreme caution, or not at all if the water is rough. Low tides reveal great tidal pools filled with anemone, starfish, and other sea creatures (please leave these creatures in the sea). **Amenities:** Toilets; parking lot. **Best for:** snorkeling; swimming. ⊠ *Hwy. 1, Km 12, Santa Maria Bay.*

★ **Playa Palmilla.** Check out the impressive multimillion-dollar villas on the road to Playa Palmilla, the best swimming beach near San José. Turn off the highway as if you're going to the One&OnlyPalmilla and then cross over the highway on an overpass. Continue about half a mile. The entrance is from the side road through the ritzy Palmilla development; take a left before you reach the guardhouse of the One&Only Hotel. There are signs, but they're not exactly large. The beach is protected

Don't Stop the Parade

You've heard the saying "wine, women, and song," right? Well, along the festive Médano Beach it's "*cervezas, chicas, y música*" (beers, babes, and music). A walk along this colorful, pulsating half-mile stretch of beach, on the east side of Cabo San Lucas's harbor, will reveal people checking each other out and local vendors trying to sell something to everyone. Fun-loving crowds sit and sun, and eat and drink, listening to the rock and roll from the beach bars. Teams queue up for impromptu games of soccer and volleyball, Jet Skis roar in the distance, and Cabo's eternally ample sun beats down on it all. El Médano is essentially a daylong parade route, the parade itself fueled by buckets of beer, powerful margaritas, and that carefree feeling of being on vacation. If you don't want to be out on the beach in the thick of it, grab a table at The Office and enjoy it all from the shady haven created by its dozens of blue umbrellas.

by a rocky point, and the water is almost always calm. A few thatched-roof palapas on the sand provide shade; there are trash cans but no restrooms. Panga fishermen have long used this beach as a base, and they're still here, after winning lengthy legal battles to ensure their continued access to the beach that provides their livelihood. Guards patrol the beach fronting the hotel, discouraging nonguests from entering the exclusive resort—although the public legally has access to cross the beach in front of the resort property. **Amenities:** Parking lot. **Best for:** solitude; walking. ⊠ *Entrance on Hwy. 1, at Km 27, 8 km (5 miles) southwest of San José del Cabo.*

CABO SAN LUCAS

Fodor's Choice
★   **Playa del Amor** (*Lover's Beach*). These days, lovers have little chance of finding much romantic solitude here. The azure cove on the Sea of Cortez at the very tip of the Land's End Peninsula may well be the area's most frequently photographed patch of sand. It's a must-see on every first-timer's list. Water taxis, glass-bottom boats, kayaks, and Jet Skis all make the short trip out from Playa Médano to this small beach, which is backed by cliffs. Snorkeling around the base of these rocks is fun when the water is calm; you may spot striped sergeant majors and iridescent green and blue parrot fish. Seals hang out on the rocks a bit farther out, at the base of "El Arco," Cabo's famed arched landmark. Swimming and snorkeling are best on the Sea of Cortez side of Lover's Beach, where the clear, green, almost luminescent water is unquestionably the nicest in Cabo San Lucas. The Pacific side is too turbulent for swimming but ideal for sunbathing. Vendors are usually present, but it's always best to bring your own snacks and plenty of water. The beach is crowded at times, but most people would agree that it's worth seeing, especially if you're a first-timer. To get here, take a five-minute panga water-taxi ride ($7–$10) or the half-hour glass-bottom boat

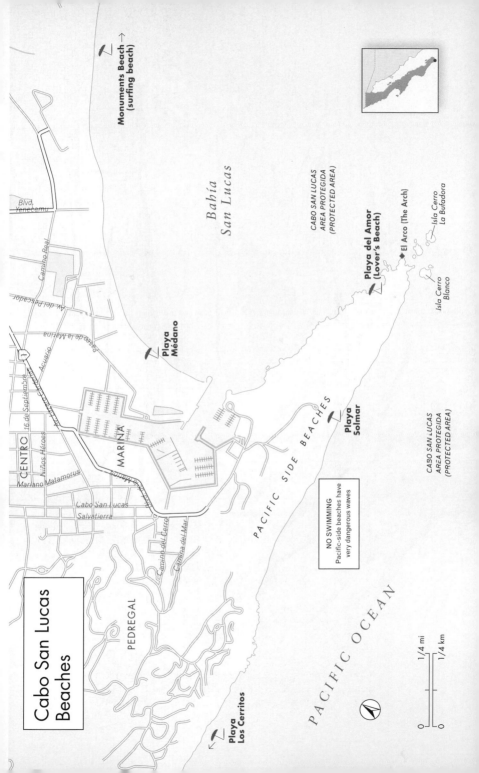

Cabo San Lucas Beaches

Monuments Beach
(surfing beach) →

Blvd. Yenecamu

Bahía San Lucas

Camino Real

Av. del Pescador

Paseo de la Marina

Acuario

Playa
Médano

CABO SAN LUCAS
AREA PROTEGIDA
(PROTECTED AREA)

Playa del Amor
(Lover's Beach)

◆ El Arco (The Arch)

Isla Cerro La Bufadora

Isla Cerro Blanco

1

16 de Septiembre

Niños Héroes

Cárdenas

CENTRO

Mariano Matamoros

MARINA

Cabo San Lucas

Salvatierra

Camino del Cerro

Camino del Mar

PACIFIC SIDE BEACHES

Playa
Solmar

NO SWIMMING
Pacific-side beaches have
very dangerous waves

CABO SAN LUCAS
AREA PROTEGIDA
(PROTECTED AREA)

PEDREGAL

← Playa
Los Cerritos

PACIFIC OCEAN

0 1/4 mi
0 1/4 km

EN ROUTE TO TODOS SANTOS

Playa Los Cerritos. This long, expansive beach on the Pacific Ocean, about 64 km (40 miles) north of Cabo San Lucas and on the way to the town of Todos Santos, is famous among surfers for its wonderful breaking waves in winter. Even if you don't ride the waves, you can watch them crash along the shore. The beach is wide, flat, and ideal for wading and swimming close to shore. Swimming farther out is not recommended because of the strong currents. Most of the surfing crowd camps or stays in RVs near the beach. The developing area covers the basics with a few conveniences—including bustling Los Cerritos Club restaurant and two surf shops. Access to the beach is marked on Highway 19 (which connects Cabo San Lucas and Todos Santos) by a sign for Playa Los Cerritos at Km 64 (13 km [8 miles] south of Todos Santos). The graded dirt road to the beach is 2½ km (1½ miles) from Highway 19. **Amenities:** Toilets; showers (for restaurant patrons); food concession; parking lot; camping. **Best for:** surfing; swimming; snorkeling; walking. ⊠ *64 km (40 miles) north of Cabo San Lucas, 13 km (8 miles) south of Todos Santos.*

tour. Opt for the latter if you wish to have some time to photograph the arch from the Pacific-side view. Both boats leave with relative frequency from the Cabo San Lucas marina or Playa Médano. **Amenities:** None. **Best for:** swimming; snorkeling; sunrise; sunset. ⊠ *Just outside Cabo San Lucas, at El Arco.*

Pisces Water Sports. Contact Pisces Water Sports for Hobie Cats, parasail, Waverunners, ocean kayaks, and sky diving. ⊠ *Playa Médano next to Pueblo Bonito Rosé Hotel*

☯ **Playa Médano.** Foamy plumes of water shoot from Jet Skis and dozens of water taxis buzz through the water off Médano, a 3-km (2-mile) span of grainy tan sand that's always crowded. When cruise ships are in town, it's mobbed. Bars and restaurants line the sand, waiters deliver ice buckets filled with beer to sunbathers in lounge chairs, and vendors offer everything from silver jewelry to hats, T-shirts, and temporary henna tattoos. You can even have your hair braided into tiny cornrows or get a pedicure. Swimming areas are roped off to prevent accidents, and the water is usually calm enough for small children. But be aware: there are quick shoreline drop-offs, so life preservers are a good idea for the little paddlers in your group. Hotels line Médano, which is just north of downtown off Paseo del Pescador. Construction is constant on nearby streets, and parking is virtually impossible. The most popular spot on the beach is around the Baja Cantina Beach Club, where more than half a dozen bar-restaurants have set up beach chairs and tables. This is a hot spot for people-watching (and for singles seeking to be doubles). Be prepared to deal with the many crafts vendors cruising the beach. They're generally not pushy, so a simple head shake and *"no, gracias"* will do. **Amenities:** Food concession. **Best for:** partiers; snorkeling; swimming. ⊠ *Paseo del Pescador.*

Playa Solmar. Huge waves crash onto the sand on the Pacific side of Cabo San Lucas. This wide, beautiful beach stretches from Land's End north to the cliffs of El Pedregal, where mansions perch on steep cliffs. Swimming is impossible here because of the dangerous surf and undertow; stick to sunbathing and strolling. From December to March, you can spot gray whales spouting just offshore; dolphins leap above the waves year-round. The beach is at the end of Avenida Solmar off Boulevard Marina—an easy walk from downtown Cabo San Lucas. Four resorts—Solmar, Terrasol, Playa Grande, and Finisterra—are all on this beach, making it easy to stop for a meal if you get hungry. Crowds are minimal, as guests tend to stick to the hotel pools. **Amenities:** None. **Best for:** walking; solitude. ⊠ *Blvd. Marina to hotel entrances.*

2

Sports and Outdoor Activities

WORD OF MOUTH

"My personal take . . . is that Cabo is better for active people who are doing things like golfing, deep sea fishing (one of the best places in the world, Feb is a good month for striped marlin), SCUBA diving (though La Paz is near some good diving areas too). . . ."
—Bill_H

Updated by
Marie Elena
Martinez and
Bob Fagan

Long stretches of coastline along the Sea of Cortez and the Pacific Ocean make Los Cabos a beautiful spot for a beach vacation. However, you must be careful about where you take a dip, because many of those beautiful beaches border sea waters that are too dangerous for swimming due to strong undercurrents. Nearly 360 warm and sunny days per year make Los Cabos a natural wonderland, where outdoor activities—both land- and water-based—can be enjoyed year-round.

Los Cabos has something for everyone in a relatively small area. Whether you want a people-packed beach or a secluded cove, high-speed Jet Ski rides or leisurely fishing trips, deep-sea scuba expeditions or casual snorkeling, the waters off Cabo and the surrounding area offer endless possibilities.

Waterskiing, jet skiing, parasailing, and sailing are found almost exclusively at Cabo San Lucas's Playa Médano, where you can also go kayaking. At least eight good scuba-diving sites are near Playa del Amor. The East Cape, which includes the town of Cabo Pulmo, is a great area for kayaking, fishing, diving, and snorkeling. In fact, Cabo Pulmo has the only coral reef in the Sea of Cortez and there are numerous spots to dive—even just snorkeling right off the beach is amazing. Both the Sea of Cortez and the Pacific provide great waves for year-round surfing whether you're a longboarder or a hotshot on a short board. Still, in the spot known as the "Marlin Capital of the World," sportfishing remains one of the most famous and popular water sports.

If you'd like to mix up your Los Cabos experience with some land-based adventures, the area's desert terrain lends itself to all sorts of possibilities, whether you're a thrill-seeker or a laid-back bird-watcher. You can explore cactus fields, sand dunes, waterfalls, and mountain forests on foot or horseback. Several tall rock faces make for great climbing and rappelling, and zip-lining (sliding across cables with a pulley) is all the

LOS CABOS GOLF TIPS

■ Make reservations in advance to assure your tee time.

■ The pricing for golf changes frequently and many hotels offer combination promotional packages. Golf here is quite expensive, due, in part, to the cost of the water required to maintain each facility. The fees will typically include range access, the golf cart, and bottled water.

■ Twilight rates can offer significant savings; check ahead if that interests you.

■ Though Cabo is a casual, laid-back area, appropriate golf attire is required at all facilities: no T-shirts, tank tops, halter tops, cutoffs, swimwear, blue jeans, or denim.

■ During the warm season, be sure to drink plenty of water.

■ Mexican banks have made it increasingly difficult for all businesses, including golf courses, to accept U.S. currency, but all golf courses accept major credit cards.

■ Consider using a reputable golf-tour operator. An experienced operator can be of immense assistance and can provide direct transport to the course that fits your desires and logistics. Refer to **Cabo Golf Tours** (☎ *877/718–4617* ⊕ *www.cabogolttours.net*).

rage around Arroyo Azul. Back in town, you can play beach volleyball on Playa Médano, tennis at one of hotels or at the Fonatur complex, get in a workout at your hotel or one of several gyms, or play a round of golf at one of the many courses available. If you are fortunate enough to be in Los Cabos during the whale migration (December through April)—when the weather is absolutely fantastic—a whale-watching trip with one of the many tour-boat operators is a must.

SAN JOSÉ DEL CABO AND THE CORRIDOR

GO-CARTS

Cabo Karting Center. High-performance outdoor go-carting has come to Cabo Karting Center. Here you can race high-speed go-carts on a professionally designed formula racecourse for $29 for a 14-lap race, with discounted prices for members and various combo packages available. ✉ *Hwy. 1 across from Los Patios Hotel, next to Cabo Cielo, Corridor, Cabo San Lucas* ☎ *624/144–7073.*

GOLF

Greens fee prices quoted include off- and high-season rates and are subject to frequent change.

Los Cabos has become one of the world's top golf destinations, thanks to two factors. First came the support of Fonatur, Mexico's government tourism-development agency. In 1988 it expanded Los Cabos' appeal beyond sportfishing by opening a 9-hole course in San José. The second reason is that the Cabo area features some of the best winter weather in North America—Los Cabos doesn't experience even the occasional frigid winter possible in the southern United States. Green fairways dot the arid landscape like multiple oases in the desert. You will encounter many sublime views of the Sea of Cortez, and, on a few courses, play alongside it. Otherwise the motif is desert golf. The other strength of the area is that the overall quality of golf is quite high, with the likes of Tom Nicklaus, Robert Trent Jones II, Tom Weiskopf, Roy Dye, and Greg Norman applying their design talents here.

Cabo Real Golf Course. This visually attractive layout features spectacular views of the mountains and sea, as well as a challenging test. Designed by Robert Trent Jones Jr., Cabo Real has straight and narrow fairways, difficult slopes, and strategically placed bunkers. The first six holes are in mountainous terrain, working their way up to 500 feet above sea level. The course then heads back to the water and eventually descends down to the Sea of Cortez by the 14th hole. Recovering from mistakes here can be quite difficult. In 2012, the back nine was redesigned by Jones with a new green on the 14th repositioned closer to the sea and the old 15th removed. Par changed from 72 to 71 and as of this writing a course rating and final yardage is yet to be determined. The course played host to the PGA Senior Slam in 1996 and 1999. ⊠ *Hwy. 1, Km 19.5, San José del Cabo* ☏ *624/173–9400 or 877/795–8727* ⊕ *www.questrogolf.com* ⅄. *18 holes. 6,848 yards. Par 71. Slope/rating 141/72.9. Greens fee: $225—includes cart, water, practice balls, and towel; $150 after 1:30 pm. Walking is not permitted. Lessons available.* ⌒ *Facilities: Practice range, putting green, snack bar, restaurant, golf carts, Taylormade rental clubs, $55.*

Camp Campestre San Jose Golf Course. Here you are greeted by panoramic views stretching to the Sea of Cortez, canyons, and mountains on a Jack Nicklaus design. This semiprivate course also features dramatic elevation changes and undulating tricky multilevel putting surfaces. Attractive bunkering requires well-placed tee shots and very accurate iron play. They have used paspalum grass throughout the course that sets Camp Campestre among the best manicured in the region. ⊠ *Km. 119, Libramiento Aeropuerto, San José del Cabo* ☏ *877/795–8727* ⊕ *www.questrogolf.com* ⅄. *18 holes. 7,045 yards. Par 71. Slope/rating 142/74.4. Greens fee: $160–$220.* ⌒ *Facilities: Carts, practice range, putting green, short-game area, restaurant, snack bar, rental clubs.*

One&Only Palmilla Golf Course. Here you will encounter 27 holes of some of the best resort golf that Mexico has to offer. Crafted by Jack Nicklaus, it was his first work here. The Mountain and Arroyo Nines came first, with the Ocean Nine finished later. Generous target-style fairways wind their way through rugged mountainous desert terrain that is beautifully landscaped. The Ocean Nine drops 600 feet in elevation as you visit the edge of the Sea of Cortez, while the Mountain and Arroyo Nines are positioned higher and farther back from the water. Many will remark that the stretch of 6 to 8 holes on the Arroyo Course is one of the best anywhere, while the 3rd through 5th holes really get your attention on the Mountain Course. No matter the combination of Nines, you won't feel cheated and the conditioning is usually excellent though expensive. ✉ *Hwy. 1, Km 7.5, San José del Cabo* ☎ *624/144–5250* ⊕ *www.palmillagc.com* ⚑ *27 holes. Mountain Nine, 3,602 yards; Ocean Nine, 3,527 yards; Arroyo Nine, 3,337 yards. All nines are par 36. Slope/ratings vary between 140/74.2 and 137/72.9. Greens fee: $160–$220.* ☞ *Facilities: Practice range, putting green, lessons, beverage cart, limited restaurant, Callaway rental clubs.*

Puerto Los Cabos Golf Course. This 18-hole golf course features an unusual combination of one Nine designed by Jack Nicklaus and the other by Greg Norman. Eventually each will build a second line to make this into two separate courses. This does not detract from its appeal as this is one of the area's most popular courses for visitors. Nicklaus's Nine features more expansive driving areas whereas the Norman Nine puts more of a premium on driving accuracy. Both Nines feature attractive bunkering and paspalum putting surfaces. ✉ *Paseo de los Pescadores, San José del Cabo* ☎ *624/173–9400 or 877/795–8727* ⊕ *www.questrogolf.com* ⚑ *18 holes. Par 73. 7,461 yards. Slope rating 145/75.9 Greens fee: $150–$195.* ☞ *Facilities: Practice range, putting green, short-game area, carts, restaurant, rental clubs.*

Punta Sur Golf Course. Los Cabos' original course opened in 1987. Of all the golf courses in the area, this one would be the "starter" golf course. Formerly known as San Jose Municipal Golf Course, the layout has wide fairways and few obstacles or slopes. It's fairly flat and good for beginners or as a warm-up. The 9-hole course is lined with residential properties (broken windows are not unusual). Some holes (particularly the 7th) have nice ocean views. Beware, you will find the three par-3's to be long and testing. The conditioning is average and this heavily played course does not take reservations as it is played on a first-come, first-served basis. It was designed by Mario Schjtanan and Joe Finger. ✉ *Paseao Finisterra, No.1, San José del Cabo* ☎ *624/142–0905* ⊕ *www.vidantagolf.com* ⚑ *9 holes. 3,153 yards. Par 35, 32 bunkers, rated at 68.2 (18-hole equivalent). Greens fee: $100, cart included* ⊙ *7 am–6:30 pm* ☞ *Facilities: Putting green, short game area, hitting nets, carts, pull carts, men's and women's rental clubs ($30), shoe rentals, pro shop, golf lessons, bag storage, restaurant, bar, snack bar, swimming pool, tennis, gym.*

THE WORLD OF CACTUS

It's easy to drive right by Cacti Mundo (Cactus World) botanical gardens in San José—but you should make a point of stopping. There are thousands of species of the prickly plants from all over the world, including many rare cacti unique to Baja. The displays are beautifully landscaped in pleasing patterns and the staff is happy to answer questions. You'll come away with a different perspective on the environment off the beach in this desert clime. Cacti Mundo is open every day from 8 am to 6 pm, and admission costs $3. ✉ *Blvd. Mijares 3* ☎ *624/143–8262* ⊕ *www.cactimundo.com.*

GUIDED ADVENTURE TOURS

★ **Baja Outback.** Baja Outback offers a variety of drive-yourself trips (with a guide in the passenger seat) that range from four hours to several days long. The routes run through Baja backcountry, where you have the opportunity to explore the Cape's rarely seen back roads while learning desert lore from a knowledgeable guide-cum-biologist. One option takes you to a remote mountain ranch before lunching and snorkeling at Cabo Pulmo. Day trips begin at $160 per person, and can include anything from hiking to diving. Baja Outback also offers multiday tour packages for adventure-driven vacationers. ⊠ *San José del Cabo* ☎ *624/142–9215* ⊕ *www.bajaoutback.com.*

★ **Baja Wild.** Baja Wild has a number of adventure packages including the "Six Day Inn-to-Inn Hiking, Biking, Kayaking, Snorkeling, Surfing, and Whale-Watching Adventure" that cost about $1,645 per person. You'll see the natural side of Cabo, with hikes to canyons, hot springs, fossil beds, and caves with rock paintings. Backcountry jeep tours start at $420 per vehicle. Full-day kayak tours at Cabo Pulmo run $140. Half-day ATV tours in the desert cost $80. ⊠ *Plaza Costa Azul, Hwy. 1, Km 28, San José del Cabo* ☎ *624/172–6300* ⊕ *www.bajawild.com.*

HIKING

Baja Wild. Trips with Baja Wild include hikes to canyons, small waterfalls, hot springs, a fossil-rich area, and caves with rock paintings. You can also take customized jeep expedition trips to La Sierra de la Laguna, a series of mountain peaks submerged in water millions of years ago. The highest peak, at 7,000 feet above sea level, is ringed by pure pine forests. Rock-climbing and rappelling trips are also available. An all-day group hiking trip includes lunch, guide, equipment, and transfer. ⊠ *Plaza Costa Azul, Hwy. 1, Km 28* ☎ *624/172–6300* ⊕ *www.bajawild. com* ⊠ *$125 per person; private (2 person) trips are $350.*

☾ **Cuadra San Francisco Equestrian Center.** The Cuadra San Francisco Eques-
★ trian Center offers trail rides and lessons on 50 beautiful and extremely well-trained horses. Trail rides go into the hills overlooking the Cabo Real property or to the San Carlos arroyo; both focus on the flora as much as the riding. Trips are limited to 20 people, with one guide for every 6 or 7 people. Cuadra also specializes in private trail rides. Reserve at least a day in advance and request an English-speaking guide. Note that you must query them for rates. ⊠ *Hwy. 1, Km 19.5, across from Casa del Mar and Las Ventanas al Paraíso hotels* ☎ *624/144–0160* ⊕ *www.loscaboshorses.com.*

KAYAKING

One of the most popular, practical, and eco-friendly ways to explore the pristine coves that dot Los Cabos' western shoreline is by kayak. Daylong package tours that combine kayaking with snorkeling cost anywhere from $70 to $125. Single or double kayaks can be rented by the hour for $15 to $20.

Baja Wild. For a combined kayak and snorkeling trip, try Baja Wild. Daylong outdoor trips include surfing; hiking; ATV; and whale-watching trips, as well as baby sea turtle release excursions (turtle release only happens from late September through November). All trips include transportation, equipment, and lunch; you can substitute scuba diving for snorkeling. A full-day tour costs $140. ✉ *Hwy. 1, Km 28, s/n Local 5, Plaza Costa Azul* ☎ *624/172-6300* ⊕ *www.bajawild.com.*

Los Lobos del Mar. Los Lobos del Mar rents kayaks and offers tours along the Corridor's peaceful bays. These outings are especially fun in winter when gray whales pass by offshore. ✉ *Off Hwy. 19 and Hwy. 1, near Villa del Palmar* ☎ *624/143-3348* ⊕ *www.cabobandb.com/sea_kayaks.htm* 🔖 *Prices start at $55.*

> **FLUTTER BY**
>
> Walk amid hundreds of butterflies at Sia Tikuva, a butterfly farm. Learn about the life of the flitting mariposas, and the magnificent flight of the monarchs here in the Baja Peninsula and Mexico. Move slowly and relax and you'll have dozens of these magical creatures landing on you in no time. ✉ *Ocotillo 1701, near the San José hotel beaches* ☎ *624/120-6233 or 624/114-3299* ⊕ *www.siatikuva.com.*

SCUBA DIVING

Expert divers head to the **Gordo Banks** (100–130 feet; also known as the Wahoo Banks), which arc 13 km (8 miles) off the coast of San José. The currents here are too strong for less experienced divers. This is the spot for hammerhead sharks—which are not generally aggressive with divers—plus many species of tropical fish and rays, and, if you're lucky, dolphins. Fall is the best time to go.

The Corridor has several popular diving sites. **Bahía Santa Maria** (20–60 feet) has water clear enough to see hard and soft corals, octopuses, eels, and many tropical fish. **Chileno Reef** (10–80 feet) is a protected finger reef 1 km (½ mile) from Chileno Bay, with many invertebrates, including starfish, flower urchins, and hydroids. The **Blowhole** (60–100 feet) is known for diverse terrain—massive boulders, rugged tunnels, shallow caverns, and deep rock cuts—which house manta rays, sea turtles, and large schools of amberjacks and grouper.

SPORTFISHING

The waters off Los Cabos are home to more than 800 species of fish—a good number of which bite all year round. It's easy to arrange charters online, through hotels, and directly with sportfishing companies along El Médano Beach and along the docks at Marina Cabo San Lucas. Indeed, to select a company yourself, consider hanging out at the marina between 1 pm and 4 pm when the boats come in, and asking the passengers about their experiences.

Prices range from $200 or $250 a day for a panga to $500 to $1,700 a day for a larger cruiser with a bathroom, a sunbathing deck, and possibly a few other amenities. The sky's the limit with the larger private yachts (think 80 feet); it's not unheard of for such vessels to cost $5,000 or $7,000 a day. All rates include a captain and crew, tackle, bait, fishing licenses, drinks, and—sometimes—lunch. Most hotels in San José will arrange fishing trips.

All of the Corridor hotels work with fishing fleets anchored at the Cabo San Lucas marina and a few with boats in Puerto Los Cabos, so any one of them can help you set up your fishing trips. The major drawback of arranging a fishing trip from one of the Corridor hotels is the travel time involved in getting down to the water. It takes up to half an hour or more to reach the docks from Corridor hotels, and most boats depart at 6:30 am.

Deportiva Piscis Fishing Tackle Shop. Fishing gear and line are available at Deportiva Piscis Fishing Tackle Shop. ⊠ *Calle Mauricio Castro, near Mercado Municipal* ☎ *624/142–0332.*

Francisco's Fleet. Long a favorite for its great selection of pangas and superpangas, Francisco's Fleet has boats available at both Playa Palmilla in the Corridor and La Playita in the San José del Cabo area. It has seven comfortable and speedy little rides that rent for $195 per day, not including fishing licenses, food, or drinks; it's solely represented by the Jig Stop in Dana Point, California, who also represents the Abaroa, Gaviota, and Ana Mar fleets and a total of about 30 boats. Cruisers range up to $560 per day. ☎ *624/142–1152 or 800/521–2281* ⊕ *www.jigstop.com.*

Gordo Banks Pangas. The pangas of Gordo Banks Pangas are near some of the hottest fishing spots in the Sea of Cortez: the Outer and Inner Gordo banks. The price for three anglers in a small panga runs from $210 to $400. Cruisers, which can accommodate four to six people, are available for $380 to $470 per day. ⊠ *La Playa near San José del Cabo, San José del Cabo* ☎ *624/142–1147, 619/488–1859 in U.S.* ⊕ *www.gordobanks.com.*

SURFING

You can rent a board right at the beach at Costa Azul in San José del Cabo, or at the Cabo Surf Hotel, and paddle right into the gentle, feathering waves at the Old Man's surf spot. If you're at the intermediate level or above, walk a short distance eastward to La Roca (The Rock) break. Big waves are best left to the experts up north, in Todos Santos.

Baja Wild. Baja Wild offers daylong trips to surfing hot spots throughout the Cape region for beginners and experts. A fee of $90 per person includes transportation, equipment, and instruction for a half day at Costa Azul. Full-day surf tours on the Pacific cost $110 per person. ⊠ *Hwy. 1, Km 28, s/n Local 5, Plaza Costa Azul* ☎ *624/172–6300* ⊕ *www.bajawild.com.*

Costa Azul Surf Shop. For good surfing tips, rentals, and lessons, head to Costa Azul Surf Shop. Surfboard rentals are $20 a day and lessons are $55 and include the surfboard rental. ⊠ *Hwy. 1, Km 27.5* ☎ *624/142–2771 or 624/142–4454* ⊕ *www.costa-azul.com.mx.*

Fodor's Choice **Mike Doyle Surf School.** The Mike Doyle Surf School is the top "surfer-
★ friendly" location in all of Los Cabos. If you stay at the Cabo Surf
Hotel where Mike Doyle's is located, you can check the surf conditions
from the restaurant, bar, pool, or even from your balcony. The school
has 60 rental boards, from soft foam boards (great for beginners and
kids), to short boards, long boards, and paddleboards. There are two
surf instructors available at the shop for lessons. ⊠ *Cabo Surf Hotel, on
the beach at the bottom of the steps, just below the 7 Seas restaurant,
San José del Cabo* ☎ *624/172–6188, 858/964-5117 in U.S.* ⊕ *www.
cabosurfshop.com* ⊠ *$75 group rate; $95 for private instruction.*

CABO SAN LUCAS

BOATING

The themes of Los Cabos boat tours vary, but all tours follow essentially the same route: through Bahía Cabo San Lucas, past El Arco and
the sea-lion colony, around Land's End into the Pacific Ocean, and
then eastward through the Sea of Cortez along the Corridor. Costs run
about $40–$50 per person; all tours include an open bar and some
offer lunch and snorkel tours. Many of these operators offer whale-
watching trips as well.

☺ **Cabo Expeditions.** Winter-season whale-watching (December–April) in
the Sea of Cortez with Cabo Expeditions is done from small, customized, inflatable Zodiac boats that allow passengers to get close to gray
and humpback whales. Oftentimes during the 2½-hour trip, the whales
even approach the boats with their babies. Fourteen passengers are
allowed per tour; ages five and up. ⊠ *Cabo Marina, near Wyndham
Hotel* ☎ *624/143–2700* ⊕ *www.caboexpeditions.com.mx* ⊠ *$85.*

Cabo Rey. Enjoy panoramic views of Los Cabos including the famous
Arch, Lover's Beach, Santa María Bay, Chileno Bay, the Old Lighthouse
from the high-speed perch of a Rolls Royce Jet boat! For one-hour rides
prices begin at $29; includes whale-watching during winter months for
$39. ⊠ *Blvd Marina, Cabo Marina* ☎ *624/105–1976, 866/460–4105 in
U.S.* ⊕ *www.caborey.com.*

☺ **Encore.** The 60-foot sailboat *Encore* carries 25 passengers. Whale-
watching tours are offered in the morning from January to March, and
sunset cruises are offered throughout the year. *Encore* tours are more
sedate than those on the party boats, and you inquire through Cabo
Yacht Center. ⊠ *Cabo Yacht Center, Cabo Marina* ☎ *624/143–3020*
⊕ *www.caboyachtcenter.net.*

Jungle Cruise. The *Jungle Cruise* is both a snorkeling tour boat as well
as your typical afternoon booze cruise, complete with loud reggae and
other party music. It attracts a twenty- to thirty-something crowd and
heads out at 10:30 am to 2:30 pm Tuesday through Sunday, from April
through November only. ⊠ *Cabo Marina, Main Dock* ☎ *866/348–6286
or 624/143–8150* ⊠ *$45, open bar.*

Continued on page 64

SPORTFISHING

By Larry Dunmire

Cabo San Lucas is called both the Marlin Mecca and Marlin Capital of the World for good reason. Thanks to the warm waters of the Sea of Cortez, the tip of the Baja Peninsula has one of the world's largest concentrations of billfish. And, no matter what time of year you visit, there's a great chance—some locals say a 90% one—you'll make a catch, too.

More than 800 species of fish swim off Los Cabos, but anglers pursue only about half a dozen types. The most sought-after are the huge blue or black marlin, which have been known to fight for hours. The largest of these fish—the so-called granders—weigh in at 1,000 pounds or more. The more numerous, though smaller (up to 200 pounds), striped marlin are also popular catches.

Those interested in putting the catch-of-the-day on their table aim for the iridescent green and yellow dorado (also called mahi-mahi), tuna, yellowtail, and wahoo (also known as ono)—the latter a relative of the barracuda that can speed along at up to 50 mph. Also gaining popularity is light-tackle fly-fishing for roosterfish, jack crevalle, and pargo from small boats near the shore.

Something's always biting, but the greatest diversity of species inhabit Cabo's waters from June through November, when sea temperatures climb into the high 80s.

A billfish catch in progress (above).

WHAT TO EXPECT

You don't need to be experienced or physically strong to sportfish. Your boat's captain and crew will happily help you along, guiding you on how to properly handle the equipment.

Some of the larger boats have the so-called fighting chairs, which resemble a dentist's chair, firmly mounted to the deck. These rotate smoothly allowing you to follow the movement of a hooked fish and giving you the support you need to fight with a large black or blue marlin for an extended period of time.

Experienced fishermen sometimes forego chairs for the stand-up technique using a padded harness/fighting belt that has a heavy-duty plastic-and-metal rod holder connected to it. Though physically demanding—especially on the arms and lower back—this technique often speeds up the fight and is impressive to watch.

FISHING TWO WAYS

Most of Cabo's boats are equipped for the more traditional heavy-duty sportfishing using large, often cumbersome rods and reels and beautiful, colorful plastic lures with hooks. A modified form of fly-fishing is gaining popularity. This requires a finessed fly-casting technique and spot-on timing between crew and the fisherman. It utilizes ultra-lightweight rods and reels, relatively miniscule line, and a technique known as bait and switch.

You attract fish as near to the back of a boat as possible with hook-less lures. As the crew pulls in the lures, you cast your fly (with hooks) to the marlin. Fights with the lighter equipment—and with circle hooks rather than regular ones—are usually less harmful, enabling more fish to be released.

Sportfishing in Los Cabos; one man's catch (top)

CONSERVATION IN CABO

You're strongly encouraged to use the less-harmful circle hooks (shaped like an "O"), as opposed to straight hooks (resemble an L), which do terrible internal damage. It's now common to release all billfish, as well as any dorado, wahoo, or tuna that you don't plan to eat. Folks here frown on trophy fishing unless it takes place during an official tournament. Instead, quickly take your photos with the fish, then release it.

The Cabo Sportfishing Association has a fleet-wide agreement that no more than one marlin per boat be taken per day. Usually all are released, denoted by the "T" flags flown from a boat's bridge as it enters the marina.

The few marlin that are brought in are hoisted and weighed, photographed, and then put to good use—taken to be smoked or given to needy locals. You can ask the crew to fillet the tastier species right on your boat, and you can usually arrange for the fish to be smoked or vacuum-packed and frozen to take home. Many restaurants, especially those found marina-side in Cabo San Lucas, will gladly prepare your catch any way you like. You hook it, they cook it.

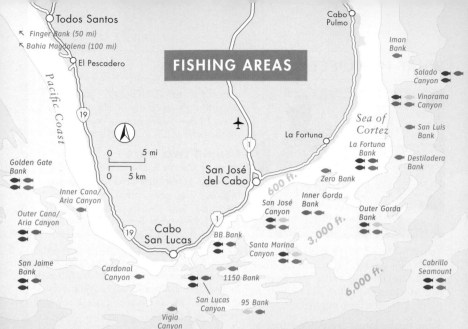

FISHING AREAS

Todos Santos
- Finger Bank (50 mi)
- Bahia Magdalena (100 mi)

El Pescadero

Cabo Pulmo

Iman Bank

Salado Canyon

Vinorama Canyon

Pacific Coast

San Luis Bank

Sea of Cortez

La Fortuna

La Fortuna Bank

Destiladera Bank

Golden Gate Bank

San José del Cabo

Zero Bank

Inner Cana/ Aria Canyon

Inner Gorda Bank

Outer Gorda Bank

Outer Cana/ Aria Canyon

San José Canyon

Cabo San Lucas

BB Bank

Santa Marina Canyon

San Jaime Bank

Cardonal Canyon

1150 Bank

San Lucas Canyon

95 Bank

Cabrillo Seamount

Vigia Canyon

0   5 mi
0   5 km

600 ft.

3,000 ft.

6,000 ft.

	FISH	AVAILABILITY
	Billfish*	Year around
	Yellowfin Tuna	Year around
	Dorado	July–December
	Wahoo	Year around
	Yellowtail	January–May
	Reef fish**	March–December

*Billfish include marlin, sailfish, and swordfish

**Reef fish include roosterfish, cabrilla, sierra, pargo, and dog snapper.

For more information on fishing locations, check out BajaDirections.com.

Although there are many great fishing areas amid the underwater canyons and seamounts off the Baja coast, there are four major spots within 40 to 50 km (25 to 30 mi) of Cabo. From north to south these banks are the Golden Gate, San Jaime, the Gordo Banks (outer and inner), and the San José Canyon. All are within an hour or so of the Marina Cabo San Lucas, if you've chartered one of the faster boats. Farther north, about 80 km (50 mi) on the Pacific side above Todos Santos, is the Finger Bank. Also on the Pacific side, more 160 km (100 mi) north of Cabo,

is Bahia Magdalena (Mag Bay), where the waters teem with marlin and game fish, and experienced anglers have been known to catch and release as many as 67 billfish in one day.

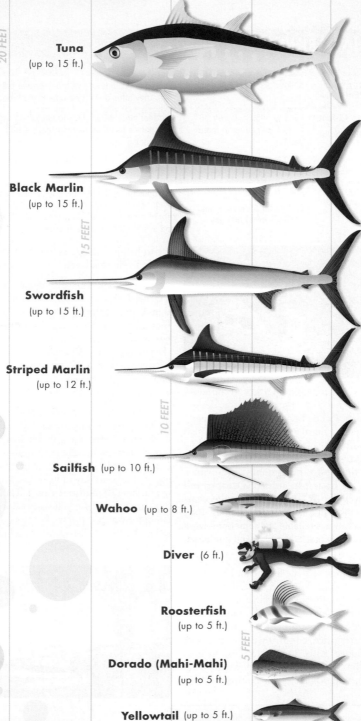

Tuna (up to 15 ft.)

Black Marlin (up to 15 ft.)

Swordfish (up to 15 ft.)

Striped Marlin (up to 12 ft.)

Sailfish (up to 10 ft.)

Wahoo (up to 8 ft.)

Diver (6 ft.)

Roosterfish (up to 5 ft.)

Dorado (Mahi-Mahi) (up to 5 ft.)

Yellowtail (up to 5 ft.)

20 FEET

15 FEET

10 FEET

5 FEET

CHARTERING A BOAT

TYPE OF BOAT	COST	CHARACTERISTICS
PANGAS or SUPERPANGAS	$200 to $350 for 6 hours.	Best for short trips and with one or two passengers. They often don't have a head (bathroom).
28- to 42-foot CRUISERS	$375 to $850 a day for 28 to 35 footers (two to three people). $900 to $1,700 a day for 35 to 42 footers.	Good for more-distant (30–40 mi) fishing trips. They have a head, sunbathing space, and air-conditioning.
LARGE, LUXURY CRUISERS	Start at $2,000. 80-foot for $5,000 day and 111-foot for $7,000 day.	Air-conditioning through the yacht's interior, heads with hot-water showers, elegant state-rooms, state-of-the-art electronics, full kitchens, and luxuries like on-deck Jacuzzis.

You can arrange charters at hotels—through a concierge or a charter desk—at Los Cabos tackle shops, or directly through charter companies. It's also possible to make arrangements online before you arrive. Indeed, it's good to do this up to three months in advance for the busiest months of October and November. ■**TIP➔** Don't arrange charters through time-share companies. They aren't always reliable and sometimes work with boats that aren't that well equipped.

Rates usually include a captain and crew, tackle, bait, fishing licenses, and soft drinks. You often need to bring your own lunch; if it is included, it usually costs extra, as do alcoholic drinks. Unless you're quoted an all-inclusive charter price, confirm what is and isn't included. Also, a tip of 15% of the cost of the charter will be appreciated. Note, too, that some charter companies will

try to help solo anglers hook up with a group to share a boat.

A walk along the perimeter of the Marina Cabo San Lucas demonstrates that Cabo really is all about fishing. Indeed, this is where most vendors are based and where most yachts set sail. (Departures are generally predawn—between 6 and 6:30 AM—so it's not a bad idea to locate your dock and boat ahead of time, in the light of day.)

It seems as if every yacht tied to the docks is a sport fisher, and you'll see different colored flags flying from the boats' outriggers. These designate the numbers and types of fish caught during the previous day of fishing as well as the number of marlin released. The blue flags are for marlin, yellow for dorado, white for wahoo, and red for tuna. Each red and white "T"-flag means a billfish was tagged and released.

A cruiser out to sea (top). Back to the marina (bottom).

SPORTFISHING TOURNAMENTS

In May, the International Game Fishing Association Offshore Championship attracts anglers from 60 countries who fish with lightweight 40-pound test line and circle hooks. Fish are caught and released, and catches are verified with cameras.

October and November are the top tournament months, with events like the fun, anything-goes Western Outdoors Tuna Tournament ($700 entry fee) and the three-day, 175-boat Bisbee Black & Blue Jackpot, whose entry fees can set a team back more than $70,000 (to enter all categories) and whose winners have taken home a pot of as much as $3,838,620 (Team Bad Company in 2007). Other events include the Los Cabos Billfish Tournament, which takes place in Cabo San Lucas, and San José del Cabo's IGT Billfish Tournament.

Money tournaments such as the Bisbee are "kill" tournaments, as fish must be brought in and weighed to win the big cash prizes. To qualify, a fish must be over 300 pounds; teams are penalized for underweight fish. In catch-and-release tournaments crews are adept at determining the weight of a fish, and the release rate is often as high as 98%.

Sailfish on deck—almost (above).

DID YOU KNOW?

Visiting El Arco, a gorgeous rock formation at the southernmost tip of the Baja Peninsula, makes for a thrilling day trip from Cabo San Lucas.

Kaleidoscope. *Kaleidoscope* is a luxurious, 100-foot power catamaran with comfortable seating inside and out. The whale-watching tour (10 am to 12:30 pm) and the sunset cruise (5 to 7) are geared toward couples and families. ⊠ *Marina, at Madero* ☎ *624/148–7318* ⊕ *www. kaleidoscopetravel.ca.*

Oceanus. The double-decker party boat *Oceanus* has snorkel cruises ($45) from 11 am to 3 pm and a sunset cruise with a live band ($45) that leaves at 5 pm (6 pm in summer) from the main dock in Cabo San Lucas. They also have individual subs for rent ($85). You can rent the *Oceanus* for birthdays, weddings, and other special occasions. Deep discounts can be found when booking online. ⊠ *Blvd. Marina* ☎ *624/143–1059 or 624/143–3929* ⊕ *www.oceanusloscabos.com.mx.*

Pez Gato. Pez Gato has two 42-foot catamarans, *Pez Gato I* and *Pez Gato II*. It has snorkeling cruises, a romantic sunset cruise, the rowdier booze cruise, and in-season whale watching. Rates begin at $39; 10% off for booking online. ⊠ *Camino del Cerro 215* ☎ *624/143–3797* ⊕ *www.pezgatocabo.com.*

Sunderland Pirate Ship. Cruises on the remarkable *Sunderland Pirate Ship*, built in 1885, are ideal for families with children. Deckhands dressed in pirate garb let kids help hoist the sail and tie knots while they learn about the rich history of pirates in Cabo San Lucas. There's even a working cannon on board. The whale-watching trip uses hydrophones to listen to the whales' song ($59). The 105-foot ship can hold 150 people and is available to rent for private events. It sails from 10:30 to 1 and includes hot dogs and hamburgers. The two-hour sunset cruise departs at 5 pm from Monday through Saturday ($69). Kids under age 12 ride free; discounts online. ⊠ *East end of Marina* ☎ *624/105–0955, 866/885–6555 from U.S.* ⊕ *www. thecabopirateship.com.*

FLIGHTSEEING

Aereo Calafia. One of the most spectacular ways to view Baja is from the air. Aereo Calafia is a private charter company that offers one very special small-plane flight to Magdalena Bay where gray whales calve during winter months. The tours include the flight, a boat tour among the whales, and lunch, for $425 per person. ⊠ *Calle Adolfo Lopez Mateos Manzana 02* ☎ *624/143–4302 or 624/143–5280* ⊕ *www. aereocalafia.com.mx.*

Cabo Sky Tours. Cabo Sky Tours offers exciting aerial tours over Los Cabos in gas-powered hang gliders. A 20-minute flight costs $75 for an adult under 200 pounds, $105 for one adult with child. ☎ *624/144–1294 office, 624/150–1000 cell* ⊕ *www.skytourscabo.com.*

FOUR-WHEELING

Riding an ATV across the desert is a thrill, but it is one of the more dangerous things you can do in this area. As fun as these tours may be, it is worth thinking about the destruction these vehicles cause to the fragile desert terrain. Additionally, many of the companies do not have insurance, and will make you sign explicit release-of-liability forms before going. They do issue helmets, goggles, and handkerchiefs to protect you from the sand and dust. When ATV trips are properly conducted, they can be safe and fun. The most popular trip passes first through Cabo San Lucas, continues through desert cactus fields, and arrives at a big play area of large sand dunes with open expanses and specially carved trails, at the foot of **El Faro Viejo**, the old lighthouse. You can reach frighteningly high speeds as you descend the tall dunes. Navigating the narrow trails in the cactus fields is exciting but not for the fainthearted or steering-impaired. Another favorite trek travels past interesting rock formations, little creeks, and the beach on the way to a small mountain village called **La Candelaria**.

A three-hour trip costs about $80 for a single or $100 for a double (two people sharing an ATV) and includes boxed lunches and drinks. Six-hour trips to La Candelaria include lunch and cost about $105 for a single and $130 for a double. Wear tennis shoes, clothes you don't mind getting dirty, and a long-sleeve shirt or sweatshirt for afternoon tours in winter.

Baja Buggy's. These eco-friendly, extreme buggy tours are a bit pricey, but nontheless a phenomenal thrill ride. Travel from desert to ocean through mountains and across canyons at Migrino Sandy River bed and then onto La Candelaria, a 300-year old aboriginal village. ⊠ *Aquiles Serdán #4, Centro, Cabo San Lucas* ☎ *624/105–9331 or 624/105–9318* ⊕ *www.bajabuggys.com* ▱ *$160; transportation included.*

Cactus ATV's. Tours are almost always full at Cactus ATVs, so reserve a day in advance. A Candelaria trip leaves at 9 am, noon, and 3 pm daily, as well as a host of desert and beach tours. Boxed lunch and drinks included. Rates from $80 per rider. ⊠ *Hwy. 19, Cabo San Lucas* ☎ *624/130–6864 or 915/288–8687* ⊕ *cactusatvtours.com.*

GOLF

Greens fee prices quoted include off- and high-season rates and are subject to frequent change.

Cabo del Sol Desert Course. The sister to the Ocean Course, the Desert Course designed by Tom Weiskopf sits on the other side of the Corridor away from the water and features an inland desert motif complete with artistic bunkering. Don't be fooled; the layout here is still very good. In fact, *Golf Digest* has rated it the #6 Best Resort Course in Mexico, placing it only behind the Ocean Course among its Cabo rivals. The Desert Course is very playable, yet from the back tees it may be even harder than the Ocean Course. The attractive layout includes one of the area's longest par-5 holes at 625 yards. Special rates are available if you play both this and the Cabo del Sol Ocean Course. ⊠ *Hwy. 1, Km 10.3, Cabo San Lucas* ☎ *624/145–8200* ⊕ *www.cabodelsol.com* ⌡ *18 holes. Par 72. 7,049 yards. Slope/rating 144/74.3. Greens fee: $190–$230.* ⌔ *Facilities: Practice range, putting green, short game area, golf carts, men's and women's lounge* *with showers, golf shop, beverage cart, snack bar, restaurant, lessons, club storage, rental clubs Taylormade $65.*

Cabo del Sol Ocean Course. The Ocean Course has been included in *Golf Digest*'s "Top 100 Courses in the World" as it combines the best of ocean and desert golf. Designer Jack Nicklaus brags that it has the best three finishing holes in the world. On the par-3 17th hole, you drive over an ocean inlet with waves crashing below. The par-4 18th hole is a mirror image of the 18th at Pebble Beach, California. Five holes are seaside, with the 5th and 17th named as one of the "Top 500 Holes in the World" by *Golf World*. The Ocean Course is easily the priciest public-access course in the region, but is generally considered to be the best. ⌧ *Hwy 1, Km 10.3, Cabo San Lucas* ☎ *624/145–8200* ⊕ *www.cabodelsol.com.* **⅃** *18 holes. Par 72. 7,091 yards. Slope/rating 137/74.1. Greens fee: $255–$355* ☞ *Facilities: Practice range, putting green, short game area, golf carts, men's and women's lounge with showers, golf shop, beverage cart, snack bar, restaurant, lessons, club storage, rental clubs Taylormade $65.*

Cabo San Lucas Country Club. This 18-hole course, designed by Pete Dye's late brother Roy, has lots of length along with seven lakes. It has small-ish greens for the approaches, which makes for a real challenge. Routed through avenues of blanco trees, cardon cacti, and bougainvillea, its primary attraction may be the views, which include the famed landmark "the Arch at Land's End." It's the golf course that's most convenient to downtown. Unfortunately it's also adjacent to a sewage treatment plant so the smell can be very unpleasant at times. The conditioning is also spotty at best. ⌧ *Hwy. 1, Km 3.7, Cabo San Lucas* ☎ *624/143–4653 or 888/239–7951* ⊕ *www.cabosanlucascountryclub.com* **⅃** *18 holes. Par 72. 7,220 yards. Slope rating 75.4/138. Greens fee: $99–$150. U.S. currency not accepted, but credit cards are.* ☞ *Facilities: Pro shop, practice range, putting green, golf carts, rental clubs, bar, snack bar.*

GUIDED TOURS

ADVENTURE

Cabo Adventures. Another sports-and-adventures operator with a wide variety of unusual activities is Cabo Adventures. Along with its popular Dolphin Encounters program are the Desert Safaris, which take you into the Sierra Mountains by Swiss-made Unimog to commune with camels, of all things! Four-hour Desert Safaris cost $99 per person. ⌧ *Marina Cabo San Lucas, Blvd. Paseo de la Marina, Cabo San Lucas* ☎ *624/173–9500 or 866/526–2238* ⊕ *www.cabo-adventures.com.*

HORSEBACK RIDING

Cantering down an isolated beach or up a desert trail is one of the great pleasures of Los Cabos (as long as the sun isn't beating down too heavily). The following company has well-fed and well-trained horses. One-hour trips generally cost about $35 per person, two-hour trips about $65.

Horseback riding along stretches of desolate Los Cabos beaches is a treat not to be missed.

Red Rose Riding Stables. The popular Red Rose Riding Stables has healthy horses for all levels of riders. The outfitter leads trips to the beach and the desert. Groups are sometimes too large to suit all riders' levels of expertise; consider this if you're an expert rider, or a newbie riding with a bunch of experts. ⊠ *Hwy. 1, Km 4* ☎ *624/143–4826.*

JET SKIING AND WATERSKIING

Competition among operators in Cabo San Lucas is pretty fair, so most offer comparable, if not identical, prices. Both jet skiing and waterskiing cost about $45 for a half hour and $70 for a full hour.

Omega Sports. Omega Sports offers jet skiing. ⊠ *3 locations on Playa Médano, near ME Cabo resort, Cabo San Lucas* ☎ *624/143–5519.*

Pisces Watersports. You might want to try a ride on the wild and crazy banana boat—a long, yellow, inflatable raft towed by high-speed motorboats. Pisces Watersports is a large jet-skiing and waterskiing operation that also gives 12-minute banana boat rides. This is also a good place to rent Hobie Cats by the hour and miscellaneous water-sports equipment. ⊠ *Far side of Playa Médano, Cabo San Lucas* ☎ *624/148–7530 cell phone.*

Tio Sports. Tio Sports was one of the original water-sports companies on El Médano Beach about 20 years ago and it's still a major operator with a sports palapa located on the beach at the ME Cabo Resort, plus stands and offices throughout Los Cabos. It provides aquatic tours, horseback rides, kayak rentals, and packages that include scuba and snorkeling. ⊠ *Playa Médano, Near ME Cabo, Cabo San Lucas* ☎ *624/143–3399* ⊕ *www.tiosports.com.*

KAYAKING

In Cabo San Lucas, Playa Médano is the beach for kayaking. A number of companies located along El Médano near the Baja Cantina Beachside, at the bottom of Cabo Villas, offer kayak rentals, and there are guided tours that go out to Lover's Beach to view El Arco, and around the Land's End Rocks. Rates are pretty uniform from one operator to the other; you don't need to waste precious time by trying to comparison shop.

Cabo Acuadeportes. The palapa for Cabo Acuadeportes is one of the largest on Playa Medano. It offers snorkeling and waterskiing, as well as good prices on kayak rentals. ⊠ *Playa Médano* ☎ *624/143–0117.*

Tio Sports. Tio Sports, located right on Medano Beach, has aquatic tours, horseback riding, kayak rentals, and packages that include snorkeling. ⊠ *Playa Médano* ☎ *624/143–3399* ⊕ *www.tiosports.com.*

MOTORCYCLING

Hop on a hog and live your own *Easy Rider* fantasy, Baja style. Do yourself and the bike a big favor and avoid the dirt roads, though.

Harley-Davidson Los Cabos. The Harley-Davidson Los Cabos, in the Puerto Paraíso Entertainment Plaza, rents Fatboys, Electric Glides, Road Kings, and Heritage Classics. Ask the shop employees for suggestions on scenic tour routes. Rentals begin at $200 a day; additional days are $180. ⊠ *Puerto Paraiso Mall, Blvd. Lázaro Cárdenas* ☎ *624/143–3337* ⊕ *www.harleybmc.com.*

PARASAILING AND SAILING

Parasailing costs about $40 for an eight minute flight. This is a high-risk sport, so proceed at your own risk. Sailboats and Windsurfers average about $30 per hour.

Cabo Acuadeportes. Cabo Acuadeportes, one of the oldest operators in the area, rents Windsurfers and Sunfish sailboats. Both can be rented by the hour. This is the first shop on Playa Médano when coming from the Cabo San Lucas marina. ⊠ *Playa Médano* ☎ *624/143–0117* ⊠ *Bahía Chileno 16 km [9 miles] west of San José del Cabo, 16 km [9 miles] east of Cabo San Lucas.*

SCUBA DIVING

Generally, diving costs about $60 for one tank and $85 for two, including transportation. Equipment rental, dives in the Corridor, and night dives typically cost extra. Full-day trips to Gordo Banks and Cabo Pulmo cost about $200, including transportation, food, equipment, and two tanks. Most operators offer two- to four-day package deals.

Most dive shops have courses for noncertified divers; some may be offered through your hotel. Newly certified divers may go on local dives no more than 30 to 40 feet deep. Divers must show their C-card (diver certification card) before going on dives with reputable shops. Many operators offer widely recognized Professional Association of Diving Instructors (PADI) certification courses, which usually take place in hotel pools for the first couple of lessons.

At sites in **Bahía San Lucas** near El Arco you're likely to see colorful tropical fish traveling confidently in large schools. Yellow angelfish, green and blue parrot fish, red snappers, perfectly camouflaged stonefish, and long, slender needlefish share these waters. Divers regularly see stingrays, manta rays, and moray eels. The only problem with this location is the amount of boat traffic. The sound of motors penetrates deep into the water and can slightly mar the experience. **Neptune's Fingers** (60–120 feet) is a long rock formation with abundant fish. About 150 feet off Playa del Amor, **Pelican Rock** (25–100 feet) is a calm, protected spot where you can look down on Sand Falls (discovered by none other than Jacques Cousteau). **The Point** (15–80 feet) is a good spot for beginners who aren't ready to get too deep. The Shipwreck (40–60 feet), an old Japanese fishing boat, is close to Cabo San Lucas, near the Misiones del Cabo Hotel.

> ## MATANCITAS MAN
>
> The remains of pre-Hispanic Indians, found in the giant sand dune region near the current Cabo San Lucas Lighthouse, were given the name of Matancitas Man by archaeologists. These people were precursors to the Pericú Indians that lived in the Cape when explorer Hernán Cortés arrived in 1535.

OPERATORS

★ **Amigos del Mar.** The oldest and most complete dive shop in Los Cabos area is Amigos del Mar. Its dive boats range from a 22-foot *panga* (a small, open-air unmotorized skiff) to a 25-foot runabout and 33- and 36-foot dive catamarans. The staff is courteous and knowledgeable, and all the guides speak English. ⊠ *Blvd. Marina, Plaza Galicota, across from Finisterra Hotel, Cabo San Lucas* ☎ *624/143–0505, 513/898–0547 in U.S.* ⊕ *www.amigosdelmar.com* ✉ *Two-tank dives start at $85; equipment rental, $30.*

Cabo Acuadeportes. A straw-covered palapa on Playa Médano in Cabo San Lucas, Cabo Acuadeportes is the largest water-sports outfitter offering snorkeling rentals and arranged boat dives for those with experience. Boat and shore dives can also be arranged at the sister shop at Chileno Bay in the Corridor. ⊠ *Playa Médano, Cabo San Lucas* ☎ *624/143–0117* ⊠ *Bahía Chileno, 16 km [9 miles] west of San José del Cabo, 16 km [9 miles] east of Cabo San Lucas.*

Manta Scuba. This centrally located PADI 5-star outfit makes trips locally in the Corridor, as well as to Cabo Pulmo, Gordo Banks, and East Cape. Two-tank dives start at $90, depending on location, and equipment rental is $27. ⊠ *Plaza Gali, Cabo Marina, Cabo San Lucas* ☎ *877/287–1120 or 624/144–3871* ⊕ *www.caboscuba.com.*

Solmar V. Find luxury on the über-comfortable dive boat *Solmar V*, which takes nine-day remote adventure diving trips to the islands of Socorro, San Benedicto, and Clarion, as well as to the coral reefs at

Cabo Pulmo. There are also five-day trips out of Ensenada, northern Baja. Twelve cabins with private baths serve a maximum of 24 passengers. This is one of Cabo's top diving experiences, so book well in advance. ⊠ *Cabo San Lucas* ☎ *866/591–4906 toll free, 310/455–3600 in U.S.* ⊕ *www.solmar5.com* ✉ *from $1,795 to $3,299.*

SNORKELING

Many of the best dive spots are also good for snorkeling. Prime areas include the waters surrounding **Playa del Amor, Bahía Santa María, Bahía Chileno,** and **Cabo Pulmo.** Nearly all scuba operators also offer snorkel rentals and trips. Equipment rentals generally cost $10 per hour ($20 for the day). Two-hour guided trips to Playa del Amor are about $40; day trips to Cabo Pulmo cost about $150. Most of the snorkeling and excursion boats are based in the Cabo San Lucas harbor and the best place to make reservations is along the marina walkway, near the Wyndham Hotel or at the beach palapas along El Médano Beach.

SNORKELING TOURS BY BOAT

If you're willing to plan ahead, booking online will often bring you significant discounts on these tours.

Buccaneer Queen. A tall ship, once used in TV commercials, the *Buccaneer Queen* Pirate Ship now carries passengers on snorkeling and sunset cruises as well as private charters. Snorkeling tours start at $55 for adults and $25 for kids (8 to 13) and includes lunch, open bar, and equipment rental. ⊠ *Cabo Marina, Dock 1, Cabo San Lucas* ☎ *624/144–4217* ⊕ *www.buccaneerloscabos.com.*

Cabo Snorkeling. Cabo Snorkeling runs a bunch of snorkeling adventures throughout Los Cabos. For a younger, party-oriented crowd, try the Jungle Party Snorkeling Tour or Cabo Fun Tour. Offering a slightly smaller, less luxurious boat than some of the others docked in Marina, these trips are less about luxury and more about fun. Four-hour trips cost $45 to $49 and include a light lunch, equipment, and, of course, booze. ⊠ *Cabo San Lucas* ☎ *888/557–3330 in U.S., 800/681–1858 in Mexico* ⊕ *cabosnorkeling.com.*

La Princesa. The most upscale boat in Los Cabos is a beautiful 48-foot catamaran called *La Princesa.* Daily trips to Bahía Santa María or Bahía Chileno depart between noon and 3 pm. For $49 per person, you get a mini-Cabo adventure, drinks, a light lunch, and equipment. If *La Princesa* isn't available, there are other yachts you can choose from for similar adventures. ⊠ *Cabo San Lucas Marina, Cabo San Lucas* ☎ *624/143–7676* ⊕ *www.laprincesacharters.com.*

Oceanus. Oceanus leaves at 11 am for four-hour snorkeling cruises that cost $45. It also departs at 4 pm for a $45 sunset dinner cruise. Discounts of up to 40% can be found online. ⊠ *Blvd. Marina, near Wyndham Hotel, Cabo San Lucas* ☎ *624/143–1059 or 624/143–3929* ⊕ *www.oceanusloscabos.com.mx.*

Pez Gato. Pez Gato has several cruising options including a $49-per-person snorkeling trip to Bahía Santa María and includes all snorkel gear, beverages, lunch of deli sandwiches, chips, and fresh fruit basket. Children 5 to 11 are half price and under 5 are free. ⊠ *Cabo Marina, near Wyndham Hotel, Cabo San Lucas* ☏ *624/143–3797* ⊕ *www. pezgatocabo.com.*

SPORTFISHING

Most vendors are at the Marina Cabo San Lucas. Ships tend to depart from sportfishing docks at the south end of the marina, near the Puerto Paraíso Mall, or from the docks at the Wyndham Hotel. It's very important to get specific directions and departure times, since it's hard to find your spot at 6:30 in the morning.

Gaviota Fleet. The Gaviota Fleet currently holds the record for the largest marlin caught in Cabo San Lucas's waters. The company has charter cruisers and superpangas from 23 feet to 36 feet. Egg Harbor yachts and rates range from $200 to $785, all-inclusive for the larger boats. ⊠ *Docked between Gates 2 and 3 across from the Marina Fiesta Hotel, office at Villa Serena RV Park, Cabo San Lucas* ☏ *888/522–2442* ⊕ *www.gaviotasportfishing.com.*

Jig Stop Tours. Jig Stop Tours is located in Southern California and books fishing trips for a number of Los Cabos fleets like Gaviota, Pisces, and Francisco's Fleets. It is one of the best, and easiest, one-stop fishing shops in the United States. ⊠ *34186 Coast Hwy., Dana Point, California, USA* ☏ *800/521–2281* ⊕ *www.jigstop.com.*

Minerva's. Renowned tackle store Minerva's has been around for more than 30 years and has its own fleet with three Bertram charter-fishing boats from 33 feet to 40 feet, and prices ranging from $690 to $900, all-inclusive. ⊠ *Madero between Blvd. Marina and Guerrero, Cabo San Lucas* ☏ *624/143–1282* ⊕ *www.minervas.com.*

Fodor'sChoice **★** **Picante Fleet.** One of the top sportfishing fleets, Picante Fleet, offers a wide selection of 20 well-equipped, top-of-the-line, 31-foot to 68-foot Cabo sport fishers. If you prefer smaller boats, there's the Picantito fleet, with a trio of 24-foot Shamrock walk-around boats. These are primarily used for fishing close to shore. Picante offers trips and boats that vary in size and price, beginning at $325 and rocketing up to $3,850. ⊠ *Puerto Paraíso Mall Local 39-A, near Harley-Davidson Store, Cabo San Lucas* ☏ *624/143–2474, 714/442–0644 in U.S.* ⊕ *www.picantesportfishing.com.*

Fodor'sChoice **★** **Pisces Sportfishing Fleet.** Some of Cabo's top hotels use the extensive range of yachts from Pisces Sportfishing Fleet. The fleet includes the usual 31-foot Bertrams, but also has a sizable fleet of 50- to 70-foot Viking, Mikelson, Hatteras, and Ocean Alexander yachts with tuna towers, air-conditioning, and multiple staterooms. Pisces also has luxury yachts up to 110 feet in length. Chartering a 31-foot Bertram goes for $1,195, all-inclusive, for up to six people, and trips last for around seven or eight hours. Prices range from $445 to $2,700. ⊠ *Cabo Maritime Center, Blvd. Marina, Cabo San Lucas* ☏ *624/143–1288, 877/286–7938 toll free in U.S.* ⊕ *www.piscessportfishing.com.*

Continued on page 76

A WHALE'S TALE
by Kelly Lack and Larry Dunmire

Seeing the gray whales off Baja's western coast needs to be on your list of things to do before you die. "But I've *gone* whale watching," you say. Chances are, though, that you were in a big boat and might have spotted the flip of a tail 100 yards out. In Baja your vessel will be a tiny panga, smaller than the whales themselves; they'll swim up, mamas with their babies, coming so close that you can smell the fishiness of their spouts.

Grey Whales Guerrero Negro

WHEN TO GO

Gray whales and tourists both head south to Baja around December—the whales in pods, the snowbirds in RV caravans—staying put through to April to shake off the chill of winter. So the beaches, hotels, restaurants, and bars during whale-watching season will be bustling. Book your room five to six months ahead to ensure a place to stay. The intense experience that awaits you at Magdalena Bay, San Ignacio, or Scammion's Lagoon is worth traveling in high season.

Though the average life span of a gray whale is 50 years, one individual was reported to reach 77 years of age—a real old-timer.

THE GRAY WHALE:
Migrating Leviathan

Yearly, gray whales endure the longest migration of any mammal on earth—some travel 5,000 miles one way between their feeding grounds in Alaska's frigid Bering Sea and their mating/birthing lagoons in sunny Baja California. The whales are bottom-feeders, unique among cetaceans, and stir up sediment on the sea floor, then use their baleen—long, stiff plates covered with hair-like fibers inside their mouths—to filter out the sediment and trap small marine creatures such as crustaceanlike Gammarid amphipods.

DID YOU KNOW?

Gray whales' easygoing demeanor and predilection for near-shore regions makes for frequent, friendly human/whale interactions. Whalers, however, would disagree. They dubbed mother grays "devilfish" for the fierce manner in which they protect their young.

WHALE ADVENTURES

Cabo Expeditions (*www.caboexpeditions. com.mx*) was the first with whale watching tours more than a dozen years ago. The staff is well-trained, and owner Oscar Ortiz believes not only in seeing the whales, but also saving them. Last year his Zodiacs rescued two grays from entanglement in giant fishing nets. Boats depart from the Cabo San Lucas Marina, near Dock M.

You've seen whales, but how about swimming with them? **Baja AirVentures** (*www. bajaairventures.com*) arranges weeklong trips to Bahia de los Angeles where you can swim with whale sharks daily. (Don't worry—the toothless plankton eaters are much more like whales than sharks.)

You fly from San Diego to the secluded Sea of Cortez fishing village, then take pangas out to Las Animas Wilderness Lodge, where you stay in spacious, comfortable yurts.

WHALE NURSERIES: THE BEST SPOTS FOR VIEWING

If you want an up-close encounter, head to one of these three protected spots where the whales gather to mate or give birth; the lagoons are like training wheels to prep the youngsters for the open ocean.

Laguna Ojo de Liebre (Scammon's Lagoon). Near Guerrero Negro, this lagoon is an L-shaped cut out of Baja's landmass, protected to the west by the jut of a peninsula.

Laguna San Ignacio. To reach the San Ignacio Lagoon, farther south than Scammon's, base yourself in the charming town of San Ignacio, 35 miles away. This lagoon is the smallest of the three, and along with Scammon's, has been designated a U.N. World Heritage site.

Bahía de Magdalena. This stretch of ocean, the farthest south, is kept calm by small, low-lying islands (really just humps of sand) that take the brunt of the ocean's waves. Very few people overnight in nearby San Carlos; most day-trip in from La Paz or Loreto.

WHAT TO EXPECT

The experience at the three lagoons is pretty standard: tours push off in the mornings, in *pangas* (tiny, low-lying skiffs) that seat about eight. Wear a water-resistant windbreaker—it will be a little chilly, and you're bound to be splashed once or twice.

The captain will drive around slowly, cutting the motor if he nears a whale (they'll never chase whales). Often the whales will approach you, sometimes showing off their babies. They'll gently nudge the boat, at times sinking completely under it and then raising it up a bit to get a good, long scratch.

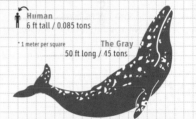

Human
6 ft tall / 0.085 tons

* 1 meter per square

The Gray
50 ft long / 45 tons

3

IN FOCUS A WHALE'S TALE

Baja whale watching, gray whale

Solmar Fleet. Once the largest fleet in Cabo San Lucas, the long-established Solmar Fleet has been subdivided into several parts and its fleet representatives are now located in both the Solmar Hotel and Playa Grande Hotel. Solmar offers 13 sportfishing yachts, from superpangas to 26- and 36-footers. Solmar boats and tackle are always in good shape, and its longtime regulars wouldn't fish with anyone else. Prices range from $400 to $750 for a day's trip. ⊠ *Blvd. Marina, Solmar Resort, Cabo San Lucas* ☎ *624/145–7575 or 800/344–3349* ⊕ *www.solmar.com.*

WHALE-WATCHING

The gray-whale migration doesn't end at Baja's Pacific lagoons. Plenty of whales of all sizes make it down to the warmer waters off Los Cabos and into the Mar de Cortés. To watch whales from shore, go to the beach at the Solmar Suites, the Finisterra, or any Corridor hotel, or the lookout points along the Corridor highway. *Virtually all of the companies listed in "Boating" offer whale-watching tours (about $30–$50 depending on size of boat and length of tour) from Cabo San Lucas. One of the biggest is*

Cabo Expeditions. Like many tour operators, Cabo Expeditions offers snorkeling and in-season whale-watching tours in hard-bottom inflatable boats. ⊠ *Cabo Marina, Cabo San Lucas* ☎ *624/143–2700* ⊕ *www.caboexpeditions.com.mx* ⚑ *$85 adults; $55 children.*

EAST CAPE

KAYAKING

If you have your own transportation, it is well worth driving out to Cabo Pulmo, where you can rent snorkel gear and a kayak or arrange a dive or fishing trip with one of the operators in this tiny, super-*tranquilo* village. In these incredible waters, you'll be able to check out everything from the smallest sea horse to a giant black sea bass.

Cabo Pulmo Dive Center. This 5-star PADI certified outfit offers a six-hour guided tour to the sea-lion colony and environs includes lunch and snorkeling gear. Tours depart at 9 am. Cap off the tour by spending the night at the tranquil, reasonably priced resort, where rooms start at just $49 per night. ⊠ *Hwy. 1 at La Ribera turnoff* ☎ *624/141–0726* ⊕ *www.cabopulmo.com.*

Cabo Pulmo Sport Center. Cabo Pulmo Sport Center has the gregarious César at the ready. He is a wellspring of knowledge and will happily advise you on the best spot to paddle, depending on the conditions of the day. He's also an expert birder. The center has a couple of very clean, simple casitas for rent ($90 per night) should you decide to extend your stay. ⊠ *Hwy. 1 at La Ribera turnoff, at the end of the road in the waterside palapa* ☎ *624/130–0235* ⊕ *www.cabopulmosportcenter.com.*

CLOSE UP

An Underwater Paradise

One of Baja's true gems is Cabo Pulmo, the raw, unspoiled national marine preserve along the Sea of Cortez. More than 8 km (5 miles) of nearly deserted rocky beach border the only living coral-reef system on the Sea of Cortez. Several dive sites reveal hundreds of species of tropical fish, large schools of manta rays, and a sea-lion colony. This is a nearly perfect place for scuba diving and snorkeling.

The village of Cabo Pulmo has 100 or so residents, depending on the season. Power comes from solar panels, and drinking water is trucked in over dirt roads.

The town has two small general stores and three restaurants. Cabo Pulmo is a magnet for serious divers, kayakers, and windsurfers and remains one of southern Baja's natural treasures.

3

SCUBA DIVING

Cabo Pulmo/Parque Marino Nacional Cabo Pulmo, a 25,000-year-old coral reef, has been legally protected since 1995 and is home to more than 2,000 different kinds of marine organisms—including more than 230 species of tropical fish and a dozen kinds of petrified coral. The area is renowned among diving aficionados, whose favorite months to visit are June and July, when visibility is highest. The park isn't difficult to access. Head southwest from La Ribera and it's just 8 km (5 miles) from the end of the paved road; it's bordered by Playa Las Barracas in the north and Bahía Los Frailes to the south. It can also be reached by the well-maintained dirt road running along the coast from San José del Cabo. It'll take you three hours or more this way, but the coast along this route is unmatched. (Though, if it's raining, stick to the paved route.) There are two main dive centers offering full gear rentals, kayaks, snorkel gear, and sportfishing tours.

Fodor's Choice ★ **Parque Nacional Marino Cabo Pulmo.** This 25,000-year-old coral reef has been legally protected since 1995 and is home to more than 2,000 different kinds of marine organisms—including more than 230 species of tropical fish and a dozen kinds of petrified coral. The area is renowned among diving aficionados, whose favorite months to visit are June and July, when visibility is highest. The park isn't difficult to access. Head southwest from La Ribera and it's just 8 km (5 miles) from the end of the paved road; it's bordered by Playa Las Barracas in the north and Bahía Los Frailes to the south. It can also be reached by the well-maintained dirt road running along the coast from San José del Cabo. It'll take you three hours or more this way, but the coast along this route is unmatched. (Though, if it's raining, stick to the paved route.) There are two main dive centers, **Cabo Pulmo Dive Center** and **Cabo Pulmo Divers,** offering full gear rentals, kayaks, snorkel gear, and sportfishing tours. ⊠ *Hwy. 1, Km. 31, San José del Cabo* ⊕ *www.cabopulmopark.com.*

Mutual curiosity between a scuba diver and a gentle whale shark (*Rhincodon typus*).

OPERATORS

Cabo Pulmo Dive Center. Cabo Pulmo Dive Center is a full-service PADI dive shop offering a variety of trips and dive lengths. It also has the best accommodations in the village, starting at just $49 per night for the econo-option. ✉ *Hwy. 1 at La Ribera turnoff* ☎ *624/141–0726 or 562/366–0722* ⊕ *www.cabopulmo.com.*

Cabo Pulmo Divers. Cabo Pulmo provides some of the more exceptional dives in the area, and Cabo Pulmo Divers has everything you need, including certification classes (multiday). This local family-run shop is right on the beach and offers full diving services, as well as cheap rooms from $49 to $99 dollars per night. ✉ *Hwy. 1 at La Ribera turnoff, at the end of the road, in the palapa right by the water on the beach, Cabo Pulmo* ☎ *624/141–0726* ⊕ *www.cabopulmo.com.*

SPORTFISHING

Outside Parque Marino Nacional Cabo Pulmo (where you aren't allowed to fish), just north of Cabo Pulmo, there are a number of excellent spots to try your luck at hooking a marlin, tuna, giant sea bass, or snapper. It's best to stop by some of the local dive shops and make arrangements for them to take you out.

Where to Eat

WORD OF MOUTH

"we loved taking our freshly caught Dorado/Mahi Mahi to Alexander's, where they cooked it a couple of ways (with a very nice plate presentation/rice/vegetables, etc for only $10)."

—Tomsd

THE SCENE

Updated by
Marie Elena
Martinez

Prepare yourself for a gourmand's delight. The competition, creativity, selection, and, yes, even the prices are utterly beyond comprehension. From elegant dining rooms to casual seafood cafés to simple *taquerías,* Los Cabos serves up anything from standard to thrilling fare.

Seafood is the true highlight here. Fresh catches that land on the menus include dorado (mahimahi), *lenguado* (halibut), *cabrilla* (sea bass), *jurel* (yellowtail), wahoo, and marlin. Local lobster, shrimp, and octopus are particularly good. Fish grilled over a mesquite wood fire is perhaps the most indigenous and tasty seafood dish, while the most popular may be the tacos *de pescado* (fish tacos): traditionally a deep-fried fillet wrapped in a handmade corn tortilla, served with shredded cabbage, cilantro, and salsas. Beef and pork—commonly served marinated and grilled—are also delicious. Many restaurants import their steak, lamb, duck, and quail from the state of Sonora, Mexico's prime pastureland, and also from the United States, though many of the high-end spots are only using local ingredients.

In San José, international chefs prepare excellent Continental, French, Asian, and Mexican dishes in lovely, intimate restaurants, and it's where the major portion of the area's explosion in new eateries has occurred. The Corridor is the place to go for exceptional (and expensive) hotel restaurants, while intense competition for business in Los Cabos means many restaurants go through periodic remodels and reinvention, the Corridor restaurants included. With San José emerging as the hotbed of culinary activity, it's fair to say that Cabos San Lucas lags somewhat behind. But Cabo has comfort food covered, with franchise eateries from McDonald's, Subway, Johnny Rocket's, Domino's, and Ruth's Chris Steak House.

PLANNING

EATING OUT STRATEGY

Although Mexicans often prefer dining late into the evening, be warned that if you arrive at restaurants in Los Cabos after 10 pm, you're taking your chances. Most places are open year-round, sometimes closing for a month in the middle of the hot Baja summer, and many Los Cabos restaurants close one night a week, typically Sunday or Monday.

PRICES

Restaurants in Los Cabos tend to be pricey, even by U.S. standards. Some add a fee for credit card usage. If you wander off the beaten path—often only a few blocks from the touristy areas—you can find inexpensive, authentic Mexican fare (though still more expensive than elsewhere in Mexico), although many of these spots may not accept credit cards.

Prices in the reviews are per person for a main course at dinner excluding service charges or taxes.

RESERVATIONS

Reservations are mentioned when essential, but are a good idea during high season (mid-November to May). Restaurant websites are common, and many let you make online reservations.

SMOKING AND DRINKING

Mexican law prohibits smoking in all enclosed businesses, including restaurants. The drinking age here is 18. Establishments do ask for IDs.

TIPPING

You won't find much consistency in tipping expectations among Los Cabos restaurants. Some upscale places automatically add a 15% service charge (or even up to 18%) to the bill—look for the word *"servicio"*—but no one will object if you leave a few pesos more for good service. If a service charge is not included in your bill, a tip of 15% is common.

WHAT TO WEAR

Dress is often casual. Collared shirts and nice slacks are fine at even the most upscale places; shirts and shoes (or sandals) should be worn any time you're away from the beach.

SAN JOSÉ DEL CABO

San José's downtown is lovely, with adobe houses fronted by jacaranda trees. Entrepreneurs have converted many of the old homes into stylish restaurants, and new and inventive cuisine abounds—fitting for a town with an art district that is burgeoning as well. Boulevard Mijares is San José's Restaurant Row, so simply meander down the main boulevard to find one that will thrill your taste buds and delight your senses.

$$ ✕ **Baan Thai.** The aromas alone are enough to bring you through the
THAI door, where you'll be greeted with visual and culinary delights. The small, comfortable, formal dining room has Asian antiques, and a fountain murmurs on a patio in the back. The chef blends Asian spices with aplomb, creating sublime pad thai, chicken curry, Thai lamb shank,

BEST BETS FOR LOS CABOS DINING

With hundreds of restaurants to choose from, how will you decide where to eat? Fodor's writers and editors have selected their favorite restaurants by price, cuisine, and experience in the Best Bets lists below. In the first column, Fodor's Choice properties represent the "best of the best" in every price category. You can also search by neighborhood for excellent eats—just peruse our reviews on the following pages.

Fodor's Choice ★

Casiano's, $$$$ p. 83
Deckman's, $$ p. 85
El Farallon, $$$$ p. 98
Flora's Field Kitchen, $$ p. 85
Market, $$$$ p. 93
Mi Cocina, $$ p. 88
Nick-San–Cabo, $$ p. 102
Nick-San–Palmilla, $$ p. 93
Sunset Da Mona Lisa, $$$ p. 94

Best By Price

$

7 Seas Restaurant, p. 91
Crazy Lobster's Bar and Grill, p. 98
Las Guacamayas, p. 87
Marisquería Mazatlán, p. 101
Taqueria Rossy, p. 89

$$

Bar Esquina, p. 97
Deckman's, p. 85
Flora's Field Kitchen, p. 85
Mi Cocina, p. 88
Nick-San–Cabo, p. 102
Nick-San–Palmilla, p. 93

$$$

Sunset Da Mona Lisa, p. 94

$$$$

Casiano's, p. 83
El Farallon, p. 98
Market, p. 93
The Restaurant at Las Ventanas, p. 94

Best By Cuisine

BEST ASIAN

Baan Thai, $$ p. 81
Market, $$$$ p. 93
Nick-San (both locations), $$

BEST ITALIAN

Capo San Giovanni's Mari e Monti, $$ p. 98
La Dolce, $$ p. 87
Sunset Da Mona Lisa, $$$ p. 94

BEST MEXICAN

Edith's, $$$ p. 98
El Comal, $$ p. 85
La Fonda, $$ p. 99
Mi Casa, $$ p. 102
Tequila Restaurante, $$ p. 89

BEST SEAFOOD

Crazy Lobster Bar & Grill, $ p. 98
El Farallon, $$$$ p. 98
Lorenzillo's, $$$ p. 100
Mariscos Mocambo, $$ p. 100
Marisquería Mazatlán, $ p. 101
Nick-San (both locations), $$

BEST ECLECTIC

Casiano's, $$$$ p. 83
Deckman's, $$ p. 85
Flora's Field Kitchen, $$ p. 85

Best By Experience

BEST FOR ROMANCE

Casiano's, $$$$ p. 83
El Farallon, $$$$ p. 98
Flora's Field Kitchen, $$ p. 85
Mi Cocina, $$ p. 88
Sunset de Mona Lisa, $$$ p. 94
Voilá Bistro, $$ p. 91

BEST FOR MAKING THE SCENE

Bar Esquina, $$ p. 97
Nick-San (Both Locations), $$
Nikki Beach, $$ p. 102

BEST LOCAL FLAVOR

El Ahorcado, $ p. 85
Gordo Lele's Tacos & Tortas, $ p. 99
Las Guacamayas, $ p. 87
Taqueria Rossy, $ p. 89

BEST BEACHY VIBE

Baja Cantina Beach, $ p. 97
The Office, $$ p. 103
Zippers, $$ p. 95

and the catch of the day with lemon–black bean sauce. New favorites are mussels in a coconut broth, and shrimp with chilies and peanuts. To wash it all down? Try the Ginger Martini. Prices are reasonable for such memorable food. ⑤ *Average main: $15* ✉ *Morelos and Obregon, next to Baja Brewing Company, Centro* ☎ *624/142–3344* ⊕ *www.bajabaanthai.com* ◔ *No lunch Sun.* ✛ *1:C2*

$$ ✗ **Baja Brewing Company.** Baja's popular brewery is right in the middle
AMERICAN   of San José del Cabo. Fun and upbeat, this brewpub has great music and serves up filling pub meals. Burgers, shepherd's pie, soups, salads, and pizza—and more elegant entrées such as filet mignon—should be accompanied with a pint of any of seven special San José cervezas, along with seasonal offerings, all brewed within sight of the bar and restaurant. Two other branches can be found in Cabo San Lucas. ⑤ *Average main: $13* ✉ *Morelos 1277, Comonfort and Obregón, Centro* ☎ *624/146–9995* ⊕ *www.bajabrewingcompany.com* ✛ *1:C2.*

$ ✗ **Buzzard's Bar & Grill.** Fronted by miles of secluded beach, this casual
AMERICAN   seaside cantina (with cheap cervezas) gets rave reviews from locals who make the slightly involved drive out of San José del Cabo. Former Southern California restaurant owners Denny and Judie Jones serve up hefty, reasonably priced New York steaks; seafood entrées, such as coconut shrimp; "burritos like bombs"; hefty burgers; and, without a doubt, *lo mas grande* (the biggest in the world) flan. Indeed, this custardlike dessert could easily be enough for two or three—try it with a shot of Kahlúa poured over the top. Also, Sunday breakfast is a big hit. To get here, turn off Boulevard Mijares at the signs for Puerto Los Cabos and follow the road up the hill, around the small traffic circle, and continue out into the desert, toward the sea. You'll find the restaurant about 5 km (3 miles), about a 10-minute drive, from San José in the Laguna Hills neighborhood. Check out the website for more detailed directions before you head out. ⑤ *Average main: $9* ✉ *Old East Cape Rd., Laguna Hills* ☎ *624/113–6368* ⊕ *www.buzzardsbar.com* ▭ *No credit cards* ◔ *Closed Aug. and Sept. No dinner Sun.* ✛ *1:D5*

$$$$ ✗ **Casiano's.** "No menu, no rules" is the way chef Casiano Reyes
ECLECTIC   describes the "spontaneous cuisine" dining experience at this gem
Fodor's Choice located in a tranquil and elegant new location. If you're open-minded
★   and adventurous, you'll relish this creative spot where a changing palette of local ingredients inform a free-form menu. Once you're seated in the bi-level, indoor-outdoor space, your waiter will offer a list of the day's ingredients, which can include anything from goat cheese, heirloom tomatoes, and lobster, to scallops, fillet of beef, and foie gras. Inform the kitchen of your preferences, and the talented, Oaxacan-born Reyes will whip up a tasting menu to delight your senses. Standouts include the seasonal Mexican specialty *chiles en nogada*, scallops with cauliflower and capers, and sea bass with lentils over sweet corn puree. Tasting menus and food–wine pairings are pricier, but worth it. ⑤ *Average main: $60* ✉ *Paseo de Las Misiones 927, Col. Club de Golf Fonatur, Fonatur* ☎ *624/142–5928* ⊕ *www.casianos.com* ⌂ *Reservations essential* ✛ *1:A6.*

4

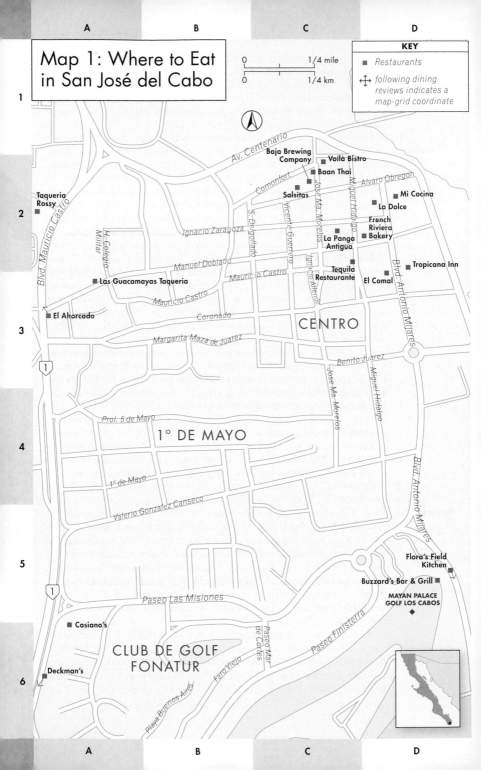

$$ ✕ **Deckman's.** Open for two seasons, Deckman's is doing something
ECLECTIC very different than its counterparts. With a daily changing menu that
Fodor's Choice showcases all-Mexican ingredients used in elevated ways, this indoor-
★ outdoor restaurant is a revelation for food lovers. Chef Drew Deck-
man spent 10 years in France, Switzerland, and Germany cooking with
masters such as Paul Bocuse and Jacques Maximin, earning a coveted
Michelin star for his work as executive chef at the Four Seasons in
Berlin. Here, Deckman serves dishes in three portion sizes so that
guests can experiment with the many flavors and textures on his menu,
which include beautiful presentations of oysters from northern Baja in
a yuzu, tobiko, and mint mignonette; octopus and pork belly paired
with cauliflower, Meyer lemon, and chili; and Spanish mackerel with
littleneck clams. Three-, five-, and seven-course tastings are offered at
slightly higher prices, paired with the many Mexican wines that shape
the list, which is the best way to appreciate all that the Deckman's
kitchen has to offer. ⑤ *Average main: $18* ⊠ *Hwy. 1, just outside San
Jose del Cabo* ☎ *624/172–6269* ⊕ *www.deckmans.com* ⊘ *Closed Mon.
and Aug. and Sept.* ✛ *1:A6*

$ ✕ **El Ahorcado.** By day it looks like a hole-in-the-wall, but when the
MEXICAN sun goes down, the rummage-sale-meets-taco stand atmosphere of this
open-air local favorite truly comes to life. Get beyond the ghoulish
silhouette logo—*ahorcado* means "hangman" in Spanish—and you'll
find out that the food is pretty good. One of the few area restaurants
open late, it's packed until closing, usually around midnight. Old pots,
baskets, antique irons, sombreros, and other tchotchkes hang from the
walls and rafters. Quesadillas come with vegetarian fillers such as *flor
de calabaza* (squash blossom), *nopales* (cactus), and *rajas* (poblano
chilies), while meatier house specialties include beef tongue tacos in
mustard sauce, *cochinita pibil* tacos, Cantonese-style beef rib tacos,
and *cuchiviriachis*—a tostada filled with cheese and meat and roasted
for a perfect melt. Bring your own *cerveza*; El Ahorcado doesn't have
a liquor license. ⑤ *Average main: $4* ⊠ *Paseo Pescadores and Marinos*
☎ *624/172–2093* ▬ *No credit cards* ⊘ *Closed Mon.* ✛ *1:A3*

$$ ✕ **El Comal.** Nestled in "La Casa de don Rodrigo" building, this beauti-
MEXICAN ful garden restaurant off of Boulevard Mijares becomes atmospheric
and romantic once the sun sets. Relying on authentic ingredients and
traditional recipes, El Comal is one of the more affordable Mexican
options serving both classic and modern dishes such as cactus and Oaxacan cheese salads, black bean *gorditas*, carne asada à la Tampiqueña,
chicken *tamales*, and *cabrilla* (sea bass) with grilled tomatoes. ⑤ *Average main: $14* ⊠ *Blvd. Mijares 1357, across the street from Tropi-
cana Inn, Centro* ☎ *624/142–5508* ⊕ *www.restaurantelcomal.com*
⊘ *Closed Sun.* ✛ *1:D3*

$$ ✕ **Flora's Field Kitchen.** Gloria and Patrick Greene's Flora's Field Kitchen
ECLECTIC is an alfresco dining experience that exemplifies farm to table. Just out-
Fodor's Choice side of San Jose del Cabo, near La Playita, Flora's is built right in the
★ center of the self-sustaining "Flora Farm." Meals are created solely from
homemade bread, and produce and meat (chicken and pork) grown on
the property. Meander through the many rows of vegetables, then sit
down to a beautifully crafted plate featuring those same ingredients.

4

Flora's Field Kitchen is situated in the middle of a self-sustaining farm.

Casiano's offers innovative dishes.   Jean-Georges Vongerichten opened Market in 2008.

Wholly organic meals are served family style at communal tables, and the generous portions include favorites like fried chicken with mashed potatoes and gravy, massive pork chops fired in the wood-burning oven, beet carpaccio laced with *fromage blanc*, and a selection of pizzas and seasonal salads. The adjacent Farm Bar serves unique takes on classic cocktails, like the heirloom-carrot Farmarita, Flora Farm's spin on the traditional margarita. Flora's is a wonderful learning experience for family by day and a romantic spot for couples by night. ⑤ *Average main: $18* ✉ *Flora Farms, Las Animas Bajas* ☎ *624/355–4564* ⊕ *www. flora-farms.com* ⊗ *Closed Mon. and Oct. No breakfast or lunch in Sept.* ✣ *1:D5*

$ ✕**French Riviera Bakery.** We challenge you to try to ignore the smell of
CAFÉ fresh baked French baguettes, or the picture-perfect display of croissants and éclairs, or the selection of colorful candies and refreshing ice creams at this café-bistro just off San José del Cabo's main square. In the creperie area, the cook tucks delicate crepes around eggs and cheese, ground beef and onions, or shrimp and pesto. If you choose to sit down, salads, quesadillas, and other standard fare are offered. The patisserie has a well-designed drink menu of fine wines and tequilas and a full list of coffee and tea-based drinks. ⑤ *Average main: $5* ✉ *Manuel Doblado al Av. Hidalgo, Centro* ☎ *624/142–3350* ⊕ *www.frenchrivieraloscabos. com* ✣ *1:D2.*

$$ ✕**La Dolce.** This popular Italian restaurant, right in the center of San
ITALIAN José on the town's *zócalo* (square), is known for authentic and affordable Italian fare. Locals and visitors alike flock to this reasonably priced perennial favorite for antipasti and wood-fired-oven pizzas, a never-ending selection of pastas, and steaks and seafood dishes. Another outpost can be found in Cabo San Lucas. ⑤ *Average main: $12* ✉ *Av. Zaragoza and Av. Hidalgo, Plaza Jardin Mijares, Centro* ☎ *624/142–6621* ⊕ *www.ladolcerestaurant.com* ⊗ *Closed Mon.* ✣ *1:D2*

$$$ ✕**La Panga Antigua.** A 170-year-old wooden *panga* (small skiff) hangs
MEXICAN above the door at this seafood-heavy, atmospheric restaurant, located just across from San José's historical mission. The setting is a series of tropical patios, one with a faded mural, another with a burbling fountain, romantically lighted by dim fixtures, and a view of the stars above. Chili-infused olive oil accompanies the bread basket that starts the meal, while a roving mariachi band unobtrusively entertains diners with song. Menu highlights focus on seafood; the catch of the day is drizzled with cilantro oil and served with mashed potatoes and *huitlacoche*, or corn truffle, while regional Mexican dishes like *pollo con mole*, gazpacho, and shrimp pozole round out the list. ⑤ *Average main: $30* ✉ *Av. Zaragoza 20, Centro* ☎ *624/142–4041* ⊕ *www. lapanga.com* ✣ *1:C2.*

$ ✕**Las Guacamayas Taqueria.** The outdoor-garden setting of Las Gua-
MEXICAN camayas is a bit kitschy, with trees sprouting up from the floor, and
★ Christmas lights strung from branch to branch. Painted murals run along the walls, and wooden chairs surround tables with plastic coverings. Massive globes of mediocre margaritas and a Mexican guitarist singing American covers makes this a magnet for tourists, but, surprisingly, it also draws locals—a good sign. If you're looking for cheap,

4

CLOSE UP

Dining In

Eating every meal in a Los Cabos restaurant can devour your dollars quickly. Most food and liquor is shipped from the mainland or imported from the United States, resulting in higher prices than the rest of Mexico. Many hotel rooms have small refrigerators and coffeemakers, and more and more of the popular time-share units becoming available in Los Cabos are equipped with completely stocked kitchens. By stocking up on groceries you can save your pesos for some of our splurges like Casiano's or El Farallon. Watch out for the prices on imported goods—a box of imported cereal can cost $5 or more. Stick with Mexican brands, or the many U.S. brands that are manufactured in Mexico. (It'll look just like the Kellogg's Corn Flakes box, but it will say "hojuelas de maíz".)

Supermarkets, such as Cabo San Lucas's longtime standby **Aramburo** (⌂ *Av. Cárdenas across from Hard Rock Cafe, Cabo San Lucas* ☎ *624/143–1450*) and neighborhood markets, sell the basics for quick meals. Aramburo keeps a good stock of items that appeal to foreigners.

A Mexican supermarket chain that resembles a Walmart superstore, **Soriana** (⌂ *Hwy. 19 just outside Cabo San Lucas* ☎ *624/105–1290*) has terrific prices and a great produce selection, but fewer U.S. brands than at Aramburo. At **Costco** (⌂ *Hwy. 1, Km 4.5, just outside Cabo San Lucas* ☎ *624/146–7180*), members can stock up on inexpensive supplies. With a great selection of beer and wines— more than 450 different labels from Australia, California, Chile, Italy, and Spain—as well as organic and frozen foods, healthy and low-calorie offerings, and cheese, **Tutto Bene** (⌂ *Blvd. Marina and Camino del Cerro, at the western end of Marina San Lucas, Cabo San Lucas* ☎ *624/144–3300*) also has prices that can be even lower than those at Costco. Tutto Bene offers free delivery throughout Cabo San Lucas, and people even drive in from La Paz to shop here. Located in the Puerto Paraíso Mall, on the lower level facing the marina, **La Europea Deli and Grocery** (⌂ *Puerto Paraíso, Lower Level, Cabo San Lucas* ☎ *624/105–1818*) has good prices for food, drinks, grocery items, beer, wine, champagne, and spirits.

good Mexican food, you've come to the right place. Tacos stuffed with chorizo, marinated pork, and flank steak pervade the menu, though it's the quesadillas, with fillings like pumpkin flower, poblano pepper and onion, and pork skin that shine. *Chilangas*, or fried, folded-over quesadillas with melted cheese, also merit the trip, while the volcanoes (hard-shell taco cups filled with cheese and your choice of meat) are not to be missed. ⑤ *Average main: $6* ⌂ *Calle Paseo de los Marinos, Centro* ▭ *No credit cards* ✛ *1:A3.*

$$ ✕ **Mi Cocina.** Traveling foodies favor this chic outdoor restaurant at
ECLECTIC   Casa Natalia, San José del Cabo's loveliest boutique hotel. Torches
Fodor's Choice glow on the dining terrace, which is surrounded by palm trees and
★   gently tinkling waterfalls, blending the four elements: earth, wind, fire, and water. Tables are spaced far enough apart so that you don't have to share your whispered sweet nothings with neighbors. Chef-owner Loic Tenoux experiments with his ingredients, calling his approach

"Euro-Mexican Bistro." He mixes marinated octopus with Chinese noodles in a to-die-for salad, grills baby scallops over a vegetable tartare, and stuffs poblano chilies with lamb and Oaxacan cheese. Catch of the day is served with your choice of saucing—Veracruz, Mediterranean, or Provençal style—and the seafood-infused risotto is always a hit. A generous wine list pairs well with the menu, while the hotel's adjoining martini bar offers more colorful drink selections. $ *Average main: $19* ✉ *Casa Natalia, Blvd. Mijares 4, Centro* ☎ *624/146–7100* ⊕ *www.casanatalia.com* ⚲ *Reservations essential* ⏱ *Closed Tues. during summer season* ✢ *1:D2.*

$$
MEXICAN

✕ **Salsitas.** This Mexican cantina-style bar and restaurant is well positioned for people-watching along San José's main drag. Decorated with cozy stone-and-stucco walls, the fare is standard but consistent, and reasonably priced. Choose from shrimp and fish tacos, chicken tostadas, enchiladas, or enormous burritos. To wet your whistle, there's a full bar, but you might consider washing down your meal with a refreshing *agua de Jamaïca* (hibiscus-flavored drink). There's also a small artisan shop in the restaurant, so feel free to browse while you wait for either your meal or your table. $ *Average main: $12* ✉ *Obregón 1732, Centro* ☎ *624/142–6787* ⊕ *www.salsitascocinaycantina.com.mx* ✢ *1:C2.*

4

$
MEXICAN
★

✕ **Taqueria Rossy.** Don't be fooled by the bare-bones atmosphere: Taqueria Rossy serves some of the best tacos in San José. Fish tacos are the thing at this no-frills joint brimming with local families who munch on everything from peel-and-eat shrimp to ceviche and chocolate clams. Served breaded and fried, the shrimp, scallop, and fish (flounder) tacos here are cheap and delicious. Dress them up however you like at a condiment bar that offers avocados, chilies, cabbage slaw, onions, and an assortment of sauces from tomatillo to habanero. $ *Average main: $8* ✉ *Hwy. 1, Km 33, Centro* ☎ *624/142–6755* ✢ *1:A2.*

$$
ECLECTIC

✕ **Tequila Restaurante.** A beautifully redone adobe home sets the stage for this classy dining experience. A lengthy tequila list tempts diners to savor the finer brands of Mexico's national drink, and an extensive wine cellar will give you plenty of choices for what to sip as you sup. The menu is a blend of Mediterranean and Mexican influences; select from excellent regional salads made from produce grown on the restaurant's organic farm, then move on to seafood choices like clams or shrimp soaked in the restaurant's namesake tequila, catch of the day in ginger and cilantro, or beef tenderloin or lamb in Cabernet sauce. $ *Average main: $19* ✉ *Manuel Doblado 1011, Centro* ☎ *624/142–1155* ⊕ *www.tequilarestaurant.com* ✢ *1:C3.*

$$
INTERNATIONAL

✕ **Tropicana Inn.** Start the day with coffee and French toast at this enduringly popular restaurant set in central San José hotel of the same name. The back garden patio quickly fills up with a loyal clientele for every meal; the front sidewalk seating is a great place to survey the world going by. The menu includes U.S. cuts of beef along with fajitas, *chiles rellenos*, and a variety of seafood platters and lobster—always in demand. Latin bands and other musicians play nightly. Service can be slow at times, so be prepared to be patient, especially when you're trying to get the bill. $ *Average main: $13* ✉ *Blvd. Mijares 30, Centro* ☎ *624/142–4146* ⊕ *www.tropicanainn.com.mx* ✢ *1:D2.*

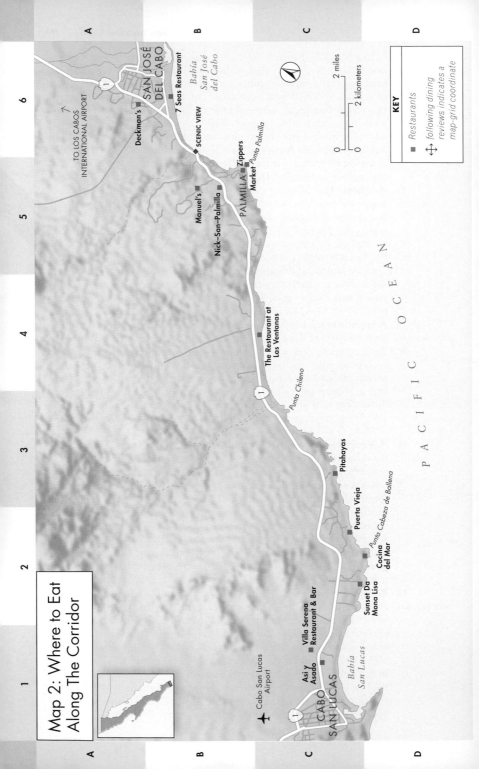

Map 2: Where to Eat Along The Corridor

TO LOS CABOS
INTERNATIONAL AIRPORT

SAN JOSÉ
DEL CABO

Bahía
San José
del Cabo

Deckman's

7 Seas Restaurant

SCENIC VIEW

Manuel's

Nick-San-Palmilla

PALMILLA

Zippers

Market · Punta Palmilla

The Restaurant at
Las Ventanas

Punta Chileno

Pitahayas

Puerta Vieja

Punta Cabeza de Ballena

Cocina
del Mar

Sunset Da
Mona Lisa

Villa Serena
Restaurant & Bar

Asi y
Asado

CABO
SAN LUCAS

Cabo San Lucas Airport

Bahía
San Lucas

P A C I F I C   O C E A N

KEY

■ Restaurants

⬩ following dining
reviews indicates a
map-grid coordinate

0 ___ 2 miles

0 ___ 2 kilometers

$$ ✕ **Voilà Bistro.** Sharing a space and
ECLECTIC creative environment with an art
gallery and an interior decorator
has rubbed off on this restaurant,
sin duda (without a doubt). Here
you'll find an anything-goes style
of Mexican fusion cuisine. You
could order *sopa de tortilla* or a
traditional Caesar salad, but opt
instead for the lobster burrito,
served with avocado, chipotle, and
mango, along with rice and black
beans. For dessert, a pistachio
crème brûlée or a coconut tart,
perhaps? Live Latin music reigns
supreme on Friday night from 7:30 to 10:30, and happy hour from
noon to 5, Monday through Saturday. ⑤ *Average main: $20* ✉ *1705
Comonfort at Morelos, Centro* ☎ *624/130–7569* ⊕ *www.voila-events.
com* ✛ *1:C2.*

> ### MORE ON TEQUILA
>
> The real stuff comes from the
> Tequila region in mainland Mexico,
> but there's nothing stopping local
> Los Cabos folks from putting their
> labels on the bottles. Cabo Surf
> Hotel now offers its own Cabo
> Surf Hotel tequila, available only
> at the hotel. Other tequila brands
> offered with Los Cabos labels
> are Cabo Wabo, Hotel California
> tequila, and Las Varitas brand.

THE CORRIDOR

Dining along the Corridor between San José del Cabo and Cabo San
Lucas used to be restricted to the ever-improving hotel restaurants. But
with the addition of the Tiendas de Palmilla shopping center, just across
from the One&Only Palmilla resort, top-notch eateries are establish-
ing a new dining energy along this stretch of highway, giving drivers
along the Corridor a tasty reason to slow down, and maybe even stop.

$ ✕ **7 Seas Restaurant.** It's quite soothing to sit in this restaurant, in the
ECLECTIC Cabo Surf Hotel, at the ocean's edge, smelling the sea breezes. Stop
off after your morning surf session to munch on *machaca con huevos*
(eggs scrambled with shredded beef) washed down with a fresh-fruit
smoothie; grab some fish tacos after a hearty surf workout, or drop in
to watch the sunset and dine on blue crab tostadas and tri-color shrimp
ravioli. Your entertainment is simple: a wonderful view that never stops
changing. ⑤ *Average main: $11* ✉ *Cabo Surf Hotel, Acapulquito Beach,
Km. 28* ☎ *624/142–2666* ⊕ *www.7seasrestaurant.com* ✛ *2:B6.*

$$$$ ✕ **Cocina del Mar.** Argentinean chef Gonzalo Cerda is changing things
SEAFOOD up at Cocina del Mar, the elegant restaurant in the exquisite Esperanza
Resort. Using daily market ingredients and focusing on simple seafood
and lush presentation, Cerda reinterprets classics like tortilla soup, here
made with seafood, and presents inventive dishes such as ahi tuna–and-
lobster salad accompanied by a seaweed salad and sriracha rémoulade,
or perfect parrot fish enhanced by a lump purée and seafood cream
sauce. The dining room is under a thatched-roof palapa overlooking
the Pacific for a setting that can't be beat. When you're finished with
your meal, retire to El Bar for either a cigar, a nightcap, or a flight of
some very fine tequila. ⑤ *Average main: $35* ✉ *Hwy. 1, Km 7, Punta
Ballena* ☎ *624/145–6400* ⊕ *www.esperanzaresort.com* ⌖ *Reservations
essential* ✛ *2:D2.*

4

Enjoy out-of-this-world sushi at Nick-San–Palmilla, in the Tiendas de Palmilla shopping center.

Sunset Da Mona Lisa offers up a romantic atmosphere, amazing views of El Arco, and an inventive Italian menu.

$$$
INTERNATIONAL
✕ **Manuel's.** With a delightfully eclectic menu, owner-chef Manuel Arredondo is giving Nick-San—a favorite restaurant in the Shoppes' at Palmilla—some serious competition. Start with duck empanadas or a goat cheese salad, then sample shrimp fettuccine with saffron, free-range chicken with orange habanero sauce, or a cacao-and-coffee-marinated pork fillet. Menu selections change daily depending on market availability, so if you're having trouble deciding on what's most appealing, the tasting menu lets you sample eight appetizer-size portions—an especially good option if you come here with a group. $ *Average main: $24* ✉ *The Shoppes at Palmilla, Carretera Transpeninsular Km. 27.5* ☎ *624/144–6171* ⊕ *www.manuelsrestaurant.com.mx* ⊘ *Closed Sun.* ✛ *2:B5*

$$$$
ECLECTIC
Fodor's Choice
★
✕ **Market.** The first Latin American restaurant opened by three-star Michelin chef Jean-Georges Vongerichten resides in the One&Only Palmilla. It's one of the priciest spots in Los Cabos, but it's also one of the best. Described as Eurasian with Mexican influences, the elegant yet comfortable restaurant is accented with deep red and rich burgundy details, and original artwork. Entrées include thoughtful presentations of roast veal chops with chipotle glaze, Chilean salmon with lemon and dill, crab-stuffed squash blossoms, and cornmeal ravioli with cherry tomatoes. You can bring your bill down slightly by opting for a fine Baja wine from the extensive wine list rather than a European one. Feeling more casual? Adjacent to Market, also overseen by Jean-Georges, is Suviche Bar, which offers fresh sushi and Mexican ceviches incorporating both local and Asian flavors, and chic cocktails. $ *Average main: $40* ✉ *One&Only Palmilla, Hwy. 1, Km 27.5* ☎ *624/146–7000* ⊕ *palmilla.oneandonlyresorts.com* ⚓ *Reservations essential* ✛ *2:B5.*

$$
SUSHI
Fodor's Choice
★
✕ **Nick-San–Palmilla.** For fresh, out-of-this-world-inventive sushi, there's no question that the Nick-San franchise corners the market, and this outpost in the Tiendas de Palmilla shopping mall wins the prize. Pair each of your selections with wine or sake, and let chef Eddie Carvajal and floor manager Alma help you make the best choices from the vast menu. Favorites include the lobster roll (with cilantro, mango, mustard, and roe), lobster *sambal* (marinated in sake with soy, ginger, and garlic), and the tuna tostadas served on rice crackers with avocado. The seared tuna with black and white sesame seeds and spicy *serranito*—fresh catch laced with serrano chili pepper—also find their way on most of the tables. Hot dishes like the *chile age*, a California chili stuffed with spicy crab and sesame sauce, and a sea bass in miso and white mushroom sauce, offer even the most fickle diners plenty to marvel at. $ *Average main: $18* ✉ *The Shoppes at Palmilla, Hwy. 1, Km. 27.5* ☎ *624/144–6262* ⊕ *www.nicksan.com* ✛ *2:B5.*

$$$
ASIAN FUSION
✕ **Pitahayas.** Chef Volker Romeike blends Thai, Polynesian, and Chinese ingredients with local ingredients for a menu that showcases well-executed Pacific Rim fusion. Above the beach in the Sheraton's Hacienda del Mar resort in Cabo del Sol, Pitahayas is set under a soaring palapa overlooking the rollicking surf. Seafood-heavy dishes are the specialty. Try soft shell crabs with a wasabi, pineapple, and balsamic glaze, blackened salmon accompanied by mango-papaya relish, lobster laced with

vanilla-bean sauce, and scallops delicately sautéed in grapefruit beurre blanc. Also on offer is one of the largest wine selections in all of Mexico with near 3,000 bottles, as well as private dining in the wine cellar for 8 to 10 people. $ *Average main: $30* ✉ *Sheraton Hacienda del Mar, Hwy. 1, Km 10* ☏ *624/145–8010* ⊕ *www.pitahayas.com* ✛ *2:C3.*

$$$
INTERNATIONAL

✗ **Puerta Vieja.** Puerta Vieja translates into "Old Door" and the beautiful door you walk through to enter this restaurant is actually 750 years old and was imported from India. Though Puerta Vieja serves lunch, we suggest dinner at sunset, when the view of El Arco is the most impressive. The cuisine pulls from Continental, Latin, and Mexican traditions, with a touch of Asian flavorings. Entrées feature lobster, shrimp, and Sonoran cuts of meat. There's live music on Wednesday, Friday, and Sunday from 6:30 to 10 pm. $ *Average main: $22* ✉ *Hwy. 1, Km 6.3* ☏ *624/104–3252 or 624/104–3334* ⊕ *www.puertavieja.com* ✛ *2:C2.*

$$$$
MEXICAN

★

✗ **The Restaurant at Las Ventanas.** It's well known that Las Ventanas is one of the best hotels in Mexico, and The Restaurant on the property does not disappoint. Chef Fabrice Guisset has unveiled a new Mexican menu that pays homage to the country's culinary traditions. With a focus on local ingredients and traditional recipes, highlights include Ensenada-sourced mussels cooked in dark Negra Modelo beer, chipotle, tomatillo, and *acuyo* (an herb that tastes like anise); and braised beef ribs in *pascalito* sauce (mole made from roasted pumpkin seeds and serrano chilies) and *epazote* (a Mexican herb)—with homemade tortillas. Also recommended is the suckling pig presented in an updated interpretation of the classic Mayan *cochinita pibil*. The desserts are as varied as the main courses, so save room for The Restaurant's version of *tres leches* cake, churros, flan, and an excellent house-made tequila ice cream. $ *Average main: $35* ✉ *Hwy. 1, Km 19.5* ☏ *624/144–2800* ⊕ *www.rosewoodhotels.com/en/lasventanas* ⌂ *Reservations essential* ✛ *2:C4.*

$$$
ITALIAN
Fodor's Choice
★

✗ **Sunset Da Mona Lisa.** Stunning views of El Arco from cocktail tables along the cliffs make this restaurant just outside Cabo San Lucas the best place to toast the sunset. If the breeze is still, stay outside and enjoy dining alfresco; if not, move into the candlelit dining room under a palapa. Italian chef Salvatore Messina's menu offers traditional Italian fare like veal Milanese and linguine with shellfish, but how does ravioli filled with seafood in white-truffle sauce sound? If you can't decide, go for the three-pasta sampler. For seafood, try the seared halibut with crunchy polenta and smoked organic vegetables. Or splurge on the Sea Lovers or Grand Mona Lisa tasting menus, which include five or seven courses, respectively. Make sure to check out the Mona Lisa's tile artwork flooring. If you arrive without a reservation, you can always head upstairs to the more casual Sunset Point, a wine and pizza lounge with daily tapas specials from 5 to 6 pm. $ *Average main: $23* ✉ *Hwy. 1, Km 5.5* ☏ *624/145–8160* ⊕ *www.sunsetmonalisa.com* ⌂ *Reservations essential* ✛ *2:C2.*

$$
AMERICAN

✗ **Villa Serena Restaurant & Bar.** Open for more than 20 years in the Villa Serena neighborhood along the main highway, this quiet, open-air, palapa-covered restaurant offers standard fare, from shrimp cocktail to chicken Caesar salad and T-bone steak, with some Mexican specialties thrown in. If you grab an ocean-facing table, you can watch the cruise ships glide past. This restaurant has what most don't: a pool—perfect for dipping your feet while sipping a fruity concoction. ⑤ *Average main: $17* ✉ *Hwy. 1, Km 7.5* ☎ *624/145–8244* ⊕ *www.villaserenarestaurant.com* ✛ *2:C1.*

$$
AMERICAN
☾

✗ **Zippers.** Popular with the surfing crowd this palapa-covered joint is on Cabo Azul beach, just south of San José del Cabo. Though their burger is the reason to come, the aroma of grilling lobster and tacos, and a sound track of surf tunes are good reasons to return. Casual doesn't begin to describe the crowd, which can get downright rowdy. But hey, have fun, *amigo*, you've entered the Los Cabos Surf Zone! There's no question that owner "Big Tony" feeds you well for your pesos. With half-pound burgers, slabs of prime rib, or steak and lobster for two at under $40, you'll leave the beach a glutton, albeit a jolly one. Bring the kids in the daytime; they'll enjoy running from the dining table to the sand between every couple of bites. Sporting events sometimes blare on the TV, and Friday nights bring live music. ⑤ *Average main: $12* ✉ *Hwy. 1, Km 28.5* ☎ *624/172–6162* ⊕ *zippersbarandgrill.com* ⊟ *No credit cards* ✛ *2:B5.*

CABO SAN LUCAS

Cabo San Lucas is known for its rowdy nightlife, and, though much of the fine-dining scene has moved to the Corridor and San José, there are still some solid choices in Cabo. A pedestrian walkway lined with restaurants, bars, and shops anchored by the sleek Puerto Paraíso mall curves around Cabo San Lucas harbor, itself packed with yachts. The most popular restaurants, clubs, and shops are along Avenida Cárdenas (the extension of Highway 1 from the Corridor) and Boulevard Marina, paralleling the waterfront.

$$
ITALIAN

✗ **Alcaravea.** One diner called this spot "the parking-lot restaurant," and, yes, this eatery is carved out of such a space. But put in a raised floor, a roof, some heavy cloth hangings to serve as walls, some plants, and approximately 10 tables, and you've got a surprisingly intimate and cozy place that makes you forget this was a parking lot. On the menu are salads, fresh pastas, chicken, seafood like *pescado con champiñones* (fish with mushroom sauce) and meats such as scalloped beef with prosciutto, plus a good selection of wine and beer. It's small and modest, but what is done here, is done well. But diners beware; there is no air-conditioning. ⑤ *Average main: $17* ✉ *Zaragoza and 16 de Septiembre, Centro* ☎ *624/143–3730* ⊕ *www.alcaraveagourmet.com* ⊟ *No credit cards* ✛ *3:B4.*

$$$
EUROPEAN

✗ **Alexander's Restaurant.** Ideally located along Cabo San Lucas's busy marina walkway, Alexander's is where Switzerland meets Mexico. Pull up a chair at one of the sidewalk tables and start with a meat-and-cheese fondue, a treat for which Swiss chef and owner Alex Brulhart is known. You could finish with the chateaubriand in béarnaise sauce or tempura prawns served in a half coconut—but it's the flambéed tequila shrimp and duck a l'orange that draw other diners' eyes in wonder and awe. ⑤ *Average main: $22* ✉ *Marina Walkway, Plaza Bonita 8, Marina* ☎ *624/143–2022* ⊕ *www.alexandercabo.com* ✛ *3:B4.*

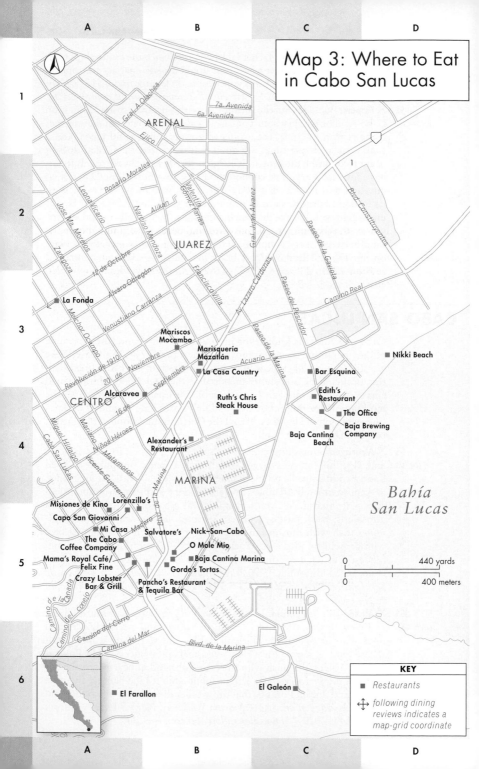

Map 3: Where to Eat in Cabo San Lucas

ARENAL

7a. Avenida
6a. Avenida

Elico

Gral. A Olachea

Leona Vicario

Jose Ma. Morelos

Rosario Morales

Narciso Mendoza

Alikan

Valentin Gomez Farias

JUAREZ

Zaragoza

12 de Octubre

Alvaro Obregón

Francisco Villa

Gral. Juan Alvarez

Av. Lázaro Cárdenas

Paseo de la Gaviota

Blvd. Constituyentes

1

■ La Fonda

Melchor Ocampo

Venustiano Carranza

Camino Real

Paseo del Pescador

Revolución de 1910

20 de Noviembre

Septiembre

■ Mariscos Mocambo

■ Marisquería Mazatlán

Acuario

Paseo de la Marina

■ Nikki Beach

■ La Casa Country

CENTRO

Alcaravea ■

16 de

Niños Héroes

Mariano Matamoros

Miguel Hidalgo

Cabo San Lucas

Vicente Guerrero

■ Ruth's Chris Steak House

■ Bar Esquina

■ Edith's Restaurant

■ The Office

■ Baja Brewing Company

Baja Cantina Beach ■

Alexander's Restaurant ■

MARINA

Bahía San Lucas

Misiones de Kino ■   Lorenzillo's ■

Capo San Giovanni ■

■ Mi Casa

Madero

Salvatore's ■   ■ Nick-San-Cabo

The Cabo Coffee Company ■

■ O Mole Mio

Mama's Royal Café/ Felix Fine ■

■ Baja Cantina Marina

Crazy Lobster Bar & Grill ■

Gordo's Tortas ■

Camino de la Cañada

Camino del corizo

Pancho's Restaurant & Tequila Bar

Camino del Cerro

Camino del Mar

Blvd. de la Marina

0 ─────── 440 yards

0 ─────── 400 meters

■ El Farallon

El Galeón ■

$$ ✕ **Baja Brewing Company.** This branch of the established San José del
AMERICAN   Cabo microbrewery features the same menu—burgers, soups, salads,
and pizza—same prices, and the same tasty selection of freshly brewed
beers as the locations in San José del Cabo and Cabo Marina. The
beers are still brewed in San José, meaning what you get here is "20
minutes fresh." No quibbles with the system; the seven house brews
and seasonal additions are a flavorful change from the ubiquitous
Tecate. The location of this outpost on the rooftop of the Cabos Vil-
las hotel on Médano Beach, however, ups the ante with a semi-open-
air venue and view of the ocean. ⑤ *Average main: $13* ✉ *Cabo Villas
Hotel, Callejon del Pescador, Playa Médano* ☎ *624/143–9199* ⊕ *www.
bajabrewingcompany.com* ✛ *3:C4.*

$ ✕ **Baja Cantina Beach.** Lighted by torches at night with a killer view of
MEXICAN   Los Arcos, this restaurant on busy Médano Beach (with another outpost
in Cabo Marina) is warm, casual, and even slightly romantic. Serving
mesquite grilled seafood, USDA cuts of meats, Mexican staples from
nachos to quesadillas, and sushi bar specials, it's calmest during break-
fast, and most festive on Wednesday nights when Mexican music takes
center stage. Live beachfront jazz is on the schedule on Tuesday and
Thursday. Ladies night is on Friday. Wi-Fi available. ⑤ *Average main:
$8* ✉ *Playa Médano, Next to Cabo Villas, Playa Médano* ☎ *624/143–
1111* ⊕ *www.bajacantina.com.mx* ✛ *3:C4.*

$ ✕ **Baja Cantina Marina.** This large, casual, sportfishing-oriented cantina,
MEXICAN   just around the corner from the Wyndham Hotel, draws a lot of guys
who come for the all-day drink specials. Boasting a top marina location
near M Dock, an excellent view of the sportfishing and megayachts,
$2 cervezas all day, affordable eats, and American sports on multiple
TVs, it's a favorite of the sportfishing deckhands and boat captains for
the rock-bottom prices. You can enjoy a Captain's breakfast special
for $2.99, a $3 afternoon appetizer menu, or splurge a bit more for
daily seafood and steak specials. Most meals can be had for under
$10. Friday night is Ladies' Night —ladies drink free from 9:30 to
11:30 pm—and if you stay late, you'll catch the live DJ and dancing.
Free Wi-Fi is accessible throughout the restaurant. ⑤ *Average main:
$8* ✉ *Cabo Marina, Dock L-M, Marina* ☎ *624/143–1111* ⊕ *www.
bajacantina.com.mx* ✛ *3:C4.*

$$ ✕ **Bar Esquina.** Set in Cabo San Lucas's swank Bahia Hotel, Bar Esquina
ECLECTIC   is making a name for itself as Medano Beach's best new restaurant.
★   Whether you're craving eggs Benedict in the morning to help you
absorb last night's party; pizza or ceviche; or a burger while you lie by
the pool, La Esquina is the spot to fit your mood. For dinner try the
highly recommended tuna tartare, steak, chicken, or risotto. With tall
cocktail tables in the bar, a bi-level, open-air dining room, chalkboard
menus written on columns that front an open kitchen, and live music
five days a week, this very cool spot is where it's at on Medano Beach.
For a quick refuel, there's Esquina Coffee Shop right next door. Open
at 7 am, it sells muffins, coffee, and bagels for takeaway. ⑤ *Average
main: $16* ✉ *Av. El Pescador, Medano Beach* ☎ *624/143–1890* ⊕ *www.
bahiacabo.mx* ✛ *3:C3.*

4

$ ✕ **The Cabo Coffee Company.** We think we've found Los Cabos' best cof-
CAFÉ   fee and best coffeehouse, and it's a twofer, depending on your mood.
Locals hang out at the original branch on Hidalgo. A second, newer
installment at Plaza Nautica draws the tourists. Either way, you get
a terrific selection of gourmet coffee drinks that are made with beans
from the Mexican state of Oaxaca and roasted fresh at Cabo Coffee's
own facility just outside town. Bring your laptop; there's free Wi-Fi.
⑤ *Average main: $2* ✉ *Hidalgo at Madero, Marina* ☎ *624/105–1130*
⊕ *www.cabocoffee.com* ⑤ *Average main: $2* ✉ *Plaza Nautica Blvd.*
Marina, Marina ⊕ *www.cabocoffee.com* ✛ *3:A5.*

$$ ✕ **Capo San Giovanni's Mari e Monti.** At this intimate Italian restaurant the
ITALIAN   smell of rich sauces simmering in the open kitchen blends with strains
of opera. Owner and Executive Chef Gianfranco Zappala and his wife,
Hilda, the sommelier, perform a culinary concert that keeps you coming
back for encores. Try the green salad with lobster, cioppino Calabrese,
spaghetti with crab, or the *taglioni del barcaiolo*—pasta with octopus,
salmon, and shrimp in pesto sauce. For dessert, the chocolate mousse or
the *mela,* an apple-and-nut pastry topped with caramel cap off a lovely
meal. For a romantic evening, dine on the starlit back patio, where soft
music plays on most evenings. ⑤ *Average main: $18* ✉ *Vicente Guerrero*
5 between Av. Cárdenas and Madero, Centro ☎ *624/143–0593* ⊕ *www.*
caposangiovanni.com ⊗ *Closed Sun.* ✛ *3:A5*

$ ✕ **Crazy Lobster Bar & Grill.** Lobster's the thing here, but daily specials like
MEXICAN   surf-and-turf combos round out the list. Open for breakfast, lunch, and
★   dinner, this typical Mexican sit-down locale has a happy hour that runs
from 8 am to 6 pm—and prices are supercheap. You can get a lobster
tail for less than 10 bucks; Cuervo tequila shots are a mere 70¢; and
Don Julio tequila shots are less than $3! As you sit under the open-air
palapa enjoying this feast fit for a king, strolling mariachis will pass by,
providing your dining sound track. ⑤ *Average main: $8* ✉ *Hidalgo and*
Zapata, Centro ☎ *624/143–6535* ⊗ *Closed Sept.* ✛ *3:A5*

$$$ ✕ **Edith's Restaurant.** One of the more upscale choices near hectic Medano
MEXICAN   Beach, Edith's is the sister restaurant to the popular The Office on the
☾   Beach. The Caesar salad and flambéed banana crepes are prepared
tableside at this colorful and popular restaurant. Wally's Special, including with lobster, shrimp, and fish is also a hit with the tourist set that
tends to dine here. The focus here is on Mexican ingredients—quesadillas feature Oaxacan cheese and are filled with seasonal zucchini flowers;
meat and fish dishes are doused in local chili or tropical fruit sauces.
Edith's air-conditioned wine cellar offers a large selection of domestic
and imported wines and is ideal for hosting small intimate dinner parties of up to 10. Families dine in early evening, so come in later if you're
looking for a less crowded experience. ⑤ *Average main: $28* ✉ *Paseo*
del Pescador, Playa Médano ☎ *624/143–0801* ⊕ *www.edithscabo.com*
⊗ *Closed Sept.* ✛ *3:A5*

$$$$ ✕ **El Farallon.** Atop a bluff in the Capella Pedregal hotel, El Farallon
SEAFOOD   provides one of the most breathtaking vantage points from which to
Fodor's Choice   have a meal in Cabo San Lucas. Chef Marco Bustamante presents a
★   seafood-heavy menu with a "fresh fish market" displaying the catch of
the day. Customize your dish from an array of fish and meats—from

yellowtail, parrot fish, spiny lobster, steak, chops, and sea bass to the irresistible local chocolate clams. All dishes come with a tasting of the day's three appetizers, which can include anything from tuna ceviche to crab-and-chipotle soup, as well as two sides that range from asparagus to grilled

> **FRUITY FLAN**
>
> Flan is usually sinfully, sweetly, caramel flavored. But guava? Guava flan is *delicioso*, and can be found at hot-spot La Fonda restaurant, in Cabo San Lucas.

corn to cilantro-infused rice. Fish and meats are simply prepared on a flat grill with fine herbs and a drop of butter. They're so well executed that you may forego the accompanying sauces. It's challenging, but save room for desserts like Mexican doughnuts, then digest over an after-dinner drink while you ogle the view. ⑤ *Average main: $37 ⊠ Capella Pedregal Hotel, Camino Del Mar 1, Marina* ☎ *624/163–4300* ⊕ *www.capellahotels.com/cabosanlucas* ⚲ *Reservations essential* ⊹ *3:A6.*

$$ ✕ **El Galeón.** One of the older dining rooms in town in desperate need
ITALIAN of a remodeling, El Galeón has been around for more than 20 years. Serving traditional Italian fare, the place has its fans, though it lacks any real vibe or local flavor. The "choice" seats look out on the marina and the space is decorated with heavy wooden furnishings and white linens, lending a sense of outdated formality. Stop off at the piano bar afterwards, and enjoy some music over a late-night brandy or an over-the-top Mexican coffee. ⑤ *Average main: $14 ⊠ Blvd. Marina, near Finisterra Hotel, Marina* ☎ *624/143–0443* ⊹ *3:C6.*

$ ✕ **Gordo Lele's Tacos & Tortas.** Ready for a floor show along with your
MEXICAN tacos or *tortas*? Listen for the blaring Beatles' tunes, then watch Javier don his tattered Beatles wig and strum his battered, two-stringed ukulele to "I Wanna Hold Your Hand." You've found Gordo Lele's tiny sidewalk stand. Javier's tacos and *tortas* (sandwiches) are made with loving care, and his fans are loyal enough to chow down while standing, as there are only two small plastic tables by the stand. You can have two or three ham-and-cheese tortas for the price of one anywhere else, plus an assortment of generously sized tacos. ⑤ *Average main: $4* ⊠ *Guerrero at Zapata down the street from Cabo Wabo, Centro* ▭ *No credit cards* ⊹ *3:B5.*

$$ ✕ **La Casa Country.** For a good steak in a rustic atmosphere accented by
STEAKHOUSE wood tables and leather stools, head to La Casa Country, recently relocated at the Marina. Serving breakfast, lunch, and dinner, complete with sports games on oversized TVs, La Casa is the spot for some toothsome *carne* at reasonable prices and a wide variety of Mexican fare, against the bustling backdrop of the Marina's many boats. ⑤ *Average main: $14 ⊠ Cabo Marina, next to Puerto Paraiso, Marina* ☎ *624/105–1999* ⊕ *lacasacountry.com* ⊹ *3:B3.*

$$ ✕ **La Fonda.** Here's a restaurant that's all about genuine Mexican reci-
MEXICAN pes. La Fonda's chef and owner Christophe Chong Boone has searched high and low, including through his mother's extensive recipe book, to offer traditional Mexican fare, down to the maguey worms, ant eggs, and grasshoppers. You'll receive an education in Mexican gastronomy

here. A graduate of the Culinary Institute of America, Boone is also working towards his Master Chef Degree. Try the *tortas horgadas* (a Mexican sandwich filled with carnitas and dipped in tomato sauce) from Guadalajara, *chalupas* from Puebla, or several incarnations of mole. Adventurous palates may enjoy the slightly crunchy maguey worms, wrapped in tortillas with guacamole and lime, which are surprisingly tasty, as are the ant eggs (*escamoles*) and grasshoppers (*chapulines*). Ⓢ *Average main: $12* ✉ *Av. Hidalgo near 12 de Octubre, Centro* ☎ *624/143–6926* ✛ *3:A3.*

$$$ ✕ **Lorenzillo's.** Gleaming hardwood floors and polished brass give a nau-
SEAFOOD   tical flair to this second-floor dining room, where fresh lobster is king. Lorenzillo's has long been a fixture in Cancún, where lobster is raised on the company's farm. That Caribbean lobster is shipped to Los Cabos and served 18 ways (the simpler preparations—steamed or grilled with lots of melted butter—are best). Menu items are named after pirates and Caribbean marine history, so Sir Francis Drake is the rib-eye steak, El Barlovento is abalone sashimi with chipotle soy sauce, and El Doblón is a giant chop on the bone. Various sized lobsters and lobster tails are served with spinach puree and linguine or potato, while other options like Alaska king crab, conch, coconut shrimp, or beef medallions round out the menu. The dessert list is lengthy and mouthwatering, and if you're in the mood for a less formal meal, an oyster bar with a limited selection of the same menu sits on the pier near the entrance. Ⓢ *Average main: $22* ✉ *Av. Cárdenas at Marina, Marina* ☎ *624/105–0212* ⊕ *www. lorenzillos.com.mx* ✛ *3:A5.*

$ ✕ **Mama's Royal Café/Felix Fine Mexican & Seafood Restaurant.** Claiming to
MEXICAN   have "the best damn breakfast restaurant in the entire country," Mama's is a casual, lively, indoor-outdoor spot in Cabo San Lucas that serves up bountiful plates of omelets and poached eggs with avocado and ham, and finger-licking fried potatoes. Also claiming to serve the "World's Best French Toast"—a treasure stuffed with cream cheese, strawberries, mangoes, bananas, pecans, and topped with orange liqueur, Mama's have a right to this claim. At night, the colorful restaurant morphs into Felix and serves traditional Mexican dishes like *chiles en nogada* (chilies in walnut sauce), *pozole* (pork soup with hominy, onion, garlic, dried chilies, and cilantro), along with a lineup of more than 30 unusual salsas. Owner Spencer Moore, the amiable salsa guru, shares all his cooking and salsa "secrets" on the restaurant's website. Ⓢ *Average main: $8* ✉ *Hidalgo at Zapata, Marina* ☎ *624/143–4290* ⊕ *www.mamascabosanlucas. com, www.felixcabosanlucas.com* ☯ *Closed Sun. and Sept.* ✛ *3:A5*

$$ ✕ **Mariscos Mocambo.** Veracruz—a region known for its seafood prepa-
SEAFOOD   rations—meets Los Cabos in an enormous dining room packed with appreciative locals. The menu has such regional dishes as octopus ceviche, shrimp empanadas, and a heaping mixed-seafood platter that includes sea snails, clams, octopus, lobster, and shrimp. Musicians stroll among the tables and the chatter is somewhat cacophonous, but you're sure to have a great local dining experience here. Ⓢ *Average main: $14* ✉ *Leona Vicario at Calle 20 de Noviembre, Centro* ☎ *624/143–2122* ⊕ *www.mariscosmocambo.com* ✛ *3:B3.*

MENU GLOSSARY

Aguacate	avocado
Ajo	garlic
A la parrilla	cooked on the grill
Almuerzo	lunch
Arrachera	flank steak
Arroz	rice
Atún	tuna
Azúcar	sugar
Barra de ensaladas	salad bar
Cabrilla	sea bass
Camarones	shrimp
Carnes	meats
Carta de vinos	wine list
Cebolla	onion
Chalupas	stuffed tortillas
Champiñones	mushrooms
Cocida en horno de Lena	cooked in a wood-burning oven
Con queso	with cheese
Cuchara	spoon
Cuchillo	knife
Desayuno	breakfast
Enegrecido	blackened
Ensalada	salad
Frijoles	beans
Frito	fried
Fruta	fruit
Helados	ice cream
Hielo	ice
Huitlacoche	corn fungus
Langosta	lobster
Leche	milk
Mariscos	seafood
Menu degustación	tasting menu
Ostiones	oysters
Pescado	fish
Picante	hot sauce, spicy
Pollo	chicken
Postres	desserts, sweets
Servilletas	napkins
Tenedor	fork
Totopos y salsa	chips and salsa

$
SEAFOOD
★
✕**Marisquería Mazatlán.** Ask a local where he or she goes for dinner, and they inevitably mention Marisquería Mazatlán, and the crowds of Mexicans lunching at this simple seafood restaurant lend credibility to the claim. Huge glass cases packed with fresh shrimp, ceviche, and other seafood cocktails abound. You can dine inexpensively and quickly on wonderful seafood soup, or spend a bit more for tender *pulpo ajillo* (marinated octopus with garlic, chilies, onion, and celery) and enjoy

some great people-watching as you eat. $ *Average main: $8* ⊠ *Mendoza at Calle 16 de Septiembre, Centro* ☎ *624/143–8565* ✛ *3:B3.*

$$ ✕ **Mi Casa.** One of Cabo San Lucas' top restaurants is in a cobalt-blue

MEXICAN adobe building painted with murals. Interior decorations range from

☾ Day of the Dead statues and silver crosses and hearts, to T-shirts and tequilas. The place seats up to 450 and is often full of tourists, but Chef Edgar Roman Chavez does his best to keep his menu authentic. Using local products and fresh catch (which changes daily), standouts include an original *mole* made from organic flowers, and *chiles en nogada* (poblano chilies stuffed with a meat-and-fruit mixture and covered with white walnut sauce and pomegranate seeds). Try the pork short ribs with tamarind and pasilla pepper adobo, or the creamless lobster bisque with shrimp, scallop, and octopus. Mi Casa also offers 20 different fruit margaritas and a wine list focused on Mexican, California, and South American wines. The large back courtyard glows with candlelight at night, and mariachis provide entertainment. $ *Average main: $20* ⊠ *Av. Cabo San Lucas at Lazaro Cardenas, Centro* ☎ *624/143–1933* ⊕ *www. micasarestaurant.com.mx* ✛ *3:A5.*

$$ ✕ **Misiones de Kino.** You may feel like you've discovered a well-kept

ITALIAN secret when you find, and enter, this palapa-roof house with adobe walls, just a few blocks off the main strip and around the corner from the Mar de Cortez Hotel. Sit on the front patio or in a backyard hut strung with weathered lanterns and photographs of the Mexican Revolution. Menu highlights include *cabrilla con salsa de frambuesa* (sea bass with raspberry sauce), *camarón coco* (coconut shrimp with mango sauce), and the crab or fish with garlic sauce. A second menu, called Pasta Bella, offers a wide range of pastas and Italian dishes. $ *Average main: $15* ⊠ *Guerrero and 5 de Mayo, Centro* ☎ *624/105–1408* ⊕ *www.misionesdekino.com* ☾ *Closed Sun.* ✛ *3:A5*

$$ ✕ **Nick-San–Cabo.** Dare we make such a claim: Nick-San may very well

SUSHI be Cabo San Lucas's top restaurant. Owner Angel Carbajal is an artist

Fodor's Choice behind the sushi counter (he also has his own fishing boats that collect

★ fish each day), and his creative fusion menu of Japanese and Mexican cuisines truly sets his masterpieces apart. The sauce on the cilantro sashimi is so divine that some say diners sneak in bread to sop up the sauce (rice isn't the same), while all of the tuna specialties—from seared sashimi with sesame seeds to tuna tostadas—are exquisite. Beware; you can run up a stiff tab ordering sushi here, though it's worth the splurge. The mahogany bar and minimalist dining room are packed most nights, but the vibe is upbeat. If you're staying in the Corridor, you're in luck; there's also a second Nick-San in the Tiendas de Palmilla shopping center. Reservations are recommended, especially on weekend nights and during high season. Otherwise, be prepared for a wait. $ *Average main: $18* ⊠ *Blvd. Marina, next to Wyndham Hotel, Marina* ☎ *624/143–4484* ⊕ *www.nicksan.com* ✛ *3:B5.*

$$ ✕ **Nikki Beach.** Undoubtedly one of the hippest places in Cabo, by day

ECLECTIC or by night, this restaurant by the pool of the ME Cabo Hotel is really more than a place to eat—it's a scene in and of itself. Surrounded by sometimes chill, sometimes pulsing music and many scantily clad revelers, you'll be tempted by appetizers such as tuna sashimi, an assortment

Enjoy creative seafood and meat dishes, lively salsas, and expertly made margaritas at Mi Casa.

of ceviches, calamari rings, and tomato bruschetta. Kobe beef sliders, tacos, chicken sandwiches, and quesadillas are offered at lunchtime. At dinner you can choose from chicken satay, as assortment of fajitas, surf and turf, and Pacific salmon. Those who want to eat light will find an additional sushi menu. This is not, however, a quiet spot for dinner; the restaurant becomes a full-blown club as the evening wears on. $ *Average main: $16 ⊠ Playa Médano, in ME Cabo Hotel ☎ 624/145–7800 ⊕ www.nikkibeach.com ✛ 3:D3.*

$$
MEXICAN

✕ **The Office.** At least once during your visit to Los Cabos, you should visit The Office, the original breakfast spot on Médano Beach's sandy shore. The Office screams "tourist-trap," bedecked with tiki torches and colorful rainbow tablecloths, but it's all in good fun, and it's always packed with revelers enjoying the near-perfect views of El Arco. Start your morning with a lobster omelet, fresh-fruit smoothie, and powerful cup of Mexican coffee. The French toast is another favorite. Service is super-friendly but the menu a bit expensive. Later in the day, decent, if not stellar, ceviche, nachos, fish tacos, seafood, and burgers are served in large portions that justify the high prices. Dinners of grilled shrimp or fish with garlic, and steaks are popular, especially when paired alongside cold beers and goblet-size margaritas. $ *Average main: $18 ⊠ Playa Médano ☎ 624/143–3464 ⊕ www.theofficeonthebeach.com ⌕ Reservations essential ✛ 3:C4.*

$$
MEXICAN

✕ **O Mole Mío.** O Mole offers contemporary Mexican fare from fajitas to enchiladas to tacos and, of course, moles. The bi-level space near the marina is filled with traditional arts and crafts, and its walls are lined with tequila bottles. Inexpensive breakfasts are $3 to $5; quick appetizers such as *quecas de tingas*, small quesadillas, are tasty ways

CLOSE UP

Budget Bites

You can dine reasonably in Los Cabos if you're not scared by the myth that the food at mom-and-pop operations or at street stands will send you running for the bathroom. These places usually cook to order, so you can tell if something has been sitting out too long or hasn't been cooked well. If there's a crowd of locals, the food is probably fresh and well prepared. Safe bets include quesadillas, fish tacos, corn on the cob, and *tortas* (sandwiches). Some restaurants have a *comida corrida* (prepared lunch special), a three-course meal that consists of soup or salad, an entrée with rice and vegetables, coffee, and a small dessert. It's not gourmet, but you'll be sated, and at a reasonable price.

In Cabo San Lucas, head for the taco stands in the couple of blocks behind Squid Roe and Avenida Cárdenas, and the backstreets inland from the marina.The best tacos in Cabo can be found off Highway 1, just outside Cabo San Lucas between Cabo Cielo and the Go-Kart track, at **Asi y Asado** (⊠ *Hwy 1, Km. 3.8* ☎ *624/105–9500* ✛ *2:C1).* There are more than 14 types of tacos, including marinated skirt steak, grilled octopus, and smoked tuna, but it's the Vampiros, served in a hard corn shell and filled with cheese and the meat of your choice, that takes the prize. Pair with made-to-order juices, such as watermelon or lime with chia seeds. **Carnitas El Michoacano** (⊠ *Leona Vicario between Carranza and Obregon*) sells savory roasted pork served in tacos or tortas for about $3 each and is beloved by locals and tourists in the know. With branches in both San Jose and Cabos San Lucas, **Los Claros** (⊠ *Zaragoza at*

16 de Septembre) is the place for a quick taco fix; $2 (fish and shrimp) or $5 (lobster) gets you some serious tacos, while $6 will buy you a killer breakfast. Two for one margaritas are served all day and five beers (Corona or Pacifico) can be had for $10. At **Pollo de Oro** (⊠ *Morelos at Av. Cárdenas*), a half-chicken meal costs about $5.

For inexpensive Mexican eateries close to the marina and hotels, try the juice stands. **Rico Suave** (⊠ *Av. Cárdenas between Av. Hidalgo and Calle Guerrero* ☎ *624/143–1043*) makes great smoothies with yogurt, as well as cheese tortas. **Café Europa** (⊠ *Blvd. Marina*) has a big breakfast burrito for $5 and quesadillas for $1.50. In San José del Cabo, there are at least a dozen stands at the **Mercado Municipal** (⊠ *Calle Coronado at Vicente Ibarra*), a couple of blocks west of the heart of San José. You may be the only gringo at the tables—a great way to practice your Spanish. Stock up on fresh papayas, mangoes, melons, and other fruits.

Look for reasonably priced restaurants on Zaragoza and Doblado by the market. Good taco stands line streets on the inland side of Highway 1. **Super Tacos Indios** has filling baked potatoes. **Las Ranas,** a *taquería* (taco eatery), has a full bar, and **Los Claros** has a few locations serving fish tacos and all-day-margarita and Mexican beer specials.

¿Y LO DESEA CON PAPAS FRITAS?*

Translation: And would you like fries with that?

We understand. Sometimes the siren's call of a U.S. chain is too tempting to ignore, especially if you're traveling with kids. Several have set up shop here in Los Cabos.

Applebee's (✉ *Plaza Península, Hwy. 1, Km 29.5, San José del Cabo* ☎ *624/172–6472*).

Burger King (✉ *Blvd. Marina 17* ☎ *624/143–5727* ✉ *Aeropuerto Internacional de Los Cabos, San José del Cabo* ☎ *624/146–5452*).

Dairy Queen. Dairy Queen (✉ *Plaza de la Danza, Blvd. Marina, San José del Cabo* ☎ *624/143–2858*).

Domino's (✉ *Centro Comercial Posada, Cabo San Lucas* ☎ *624/143–3999*).

Johnny Rocket's (✉ *Puerto Paraíso at San Lucas Marina, Marina* ☎ *624/143–9891* ⊕ *www.johnnyrockets.com*).

McDonald's. (✉ *Av. Lázaro Cárdenas and Paseo de Marina* ☎ *624/143–8101* ✉ *San José Mega Mall, San José del Cabo* ☎ *624/130–7526*).

Subway (✉ *Plaza Nautica, Blvd. Marina* ☎ *624/143–0924* ✉ *Aeropuerto Internacional de Los Cabos, San José del Cabo* ☎ *624/146–5283*)

4

to start; and dinners such as O Mole Mío (The Dance of O Mole Mío), a chicken-mole concoction, will delight your taste buds. This spot is also great for just a quick cocktail while shopping in downtown Cabo, and it's a favorite with the cruise crowd. ⑤ *Average main: $13* ✉ *Plaza del Sol shopping center, Francisco Madero and Blvd. Marina, Marina* ☎ *624/143–7577* ✛ *3:B5.*

$$
MEXICAN
☺

✕ **Pancho's Restaurant & Tequila Bar.** Owner John Bragg has an enormous collection of tequilas, and an encyclopedic knowledge of the stuff. His restaurant is something of a tequila museum, with a colorful array of hundreds of the world's top tequilas—many no longer available—displayed behind the bar. Sample one or two of the nearly 1,000 labels available, and you'll appreciate the rainbow-colored Oaxacan tablecloths, murals, painted chairs, and streamers even more than you did when you first arrived. Hungry, too? Try regional specialties like tortilla soup, chiles rellenos, or *chamorro* (pork shank in wine sauce). For larger appetites, the Pancho's combo, which includes steak, quesadilla, chile relleno, and a chicken enchilada, is the way to go. Though dinner is pricier, the breakfast and lunch specials are a bargain. Pancho's offers special and private tequila tastings, which will give you a greater appreciation of this piquant liquor from Jalisco. ⑤ *Average main: $19* ✉ *Hidalgo between Zapata and Serdan, Centro* ☎ *624/143–2891* ⊕ *www.panchos.com* ☾ *Closed Sept.* ✛ *3:B5*

$$$
STEAKHOUSE

✕ **Ruth's Chris Steak House.** If you've eaten enough fish tacos for a while, and are hankering for a steak like they cook 'em back home, then Ruth's at the Puerto Paraíso mall, facing the Marina, is your best bet. It's known for its wide range of meaty cuts from fillets to porterhouse, and also serves veal, chicken, fish, and lamb. Not finished yet? There's crème brûlée and key lime pie, both freshly baked, and specialty cocktails from martinis to Manhattans. Lunch isn't served until 1 pm. ⑤ *Average main: $28* ⊠ *Puerto Paraíso, 1st floor, Marina San Lucas, Marina* ☎ *624/144–3232* ⊕ *www.ruthschris.com* ✛ *3:B4.*

$$
ITALIAN

✕ **Salvatore's.** The local gringo cadre has nothing but *bueno* things to say about this affordable and dependable little Italian spot, located by the pool at the Siesta Suites Hotel in downtown Cabo San Lucas. Mussels in marinara sauce, osso buco, chicken parmigiana, lasagna, and calamari are just some of the many Italian staples offered at this funky little spot. Portions are large and prices are reasonable. Finish dinner off with a chocolate flan before hitting the main drag for some serious nightlife. ⑤ *Average main: $12* ⊠ *Zapata between Guerrero and Hidalgo, Centro* ☎ *624/105–1044* ✛ *3:B5.*

Where to Stay in Los Cabos

WORD OF MOUTH

"I would classify Cabo San Lucas as a spring break crowd—think bars like Cabo Wabo, El Squid Roe, Mango Deck, The Monkey Bar. Fun for one or two nights. San Jose del Cabo—much more "refined" town—smaller. Nice shopping, art galleries, and restaurants."

—jbass

THE SCENE

Updated by
Marie Elena
Martinez

Expect high-quality accommodations wherever you stay in Los Cabos—whether at a huge resort or a small bed-and-breakfast. Much of the area's beaches are now backed by major properties, all vying to create the most desirable stretch on the sand; for the privilege of staying in these hot properties, you'll pay top dollar—and more for oceanfront rooms with incredible views.

Prices at accommodations off the beach reflect the popularity of the area and may surprise travelers used to spending much less in other areas of Mexico—even in the hot summer months which are, technically, the low season.

Sprawling Mediterranean-style resorts of generally 200 to 400 rooms dominate the coastline of Los Cabos, especially on the 29-km-long (18-mile-long) Corridor, but also on the beaches in Cabo San Lucas and San José (the town of San José is not on the coast, but inland just a bit). These resorts have lavish pools and lush grounds in addition to their beachfront access, although the majority of beaches on the densely developed coastline, with the notable exception of Playa Médano in Cabo San Lucas, can have an oddly deserted appearance because of the dangerous currents in the water and the predominance of luxurious pools.

Many of the resorts along the Corridor offer all-inclusive plans if you want to check into your hotel and stay put for the duration of your stay, but choosing that option means you'll have little reason to venture out and taste some of the diverse and remarkable food available in this region. These huge resorts offer high-quality facilities and pleasant service, to be sure, but guests looking to get a feel for the local culture may find the generic, chain-hotel atmosphere frustrating. For those wanting less Westernized slickness, and a more intimate experience of Mexican hospitality, checking into one of the many excellent smaller properties is the way to go.

If you're inclined to go beyond the beach-and-party vibe of Cabo San Lucas, it's well worth spending time in Todos Santos (⇨ *see Los Cabos Side Trips chapter*) and San José del Cabo. Both towns offer exceptional independent hotels and inns, as well as burgeoning arts scenes, great restaurants, and ambience you won't find elsewhere.

PLANNING

WHEN TO GO

With its growing popularity, Los Cabos has a high season that seems to keep gaining months. It's been said that high season is now mid-November through May, though the crowds are a bit more manageable in October and after mid-April. Summers can be scorchers in this desert landscape, reaching temperatures in the 90s and above. Book early—as many as six months in advance for top holidays such as Thanksgiving, Christmas, New Year's, and Easter, and at least three months in advance for other high-season stays.

WHAT TO EXPECT

Bargains here are few; rooms generally start at $200 a night and can climb into the thousands. For groups of six or more planning an extended stay, condos or villas can be a convenient and economical option, though you should always book early.

Hotel rates in Baja California Sur are subject to a 10% value-added tax and a 2% hotel tax for tourism promotion. Service charges (at least 10%) and meals generally aren't included in hotel rates. Several of the high-end properties include a daily service charge in your bill; be sure you know the policy before tipping (though additional tips are always welcome). We always list the available facilities, but we don't specify extra costs; so always ask about what's included.

CHOOSING THE RIGHT REGION

San José del Cabo is the closest to the international airport, and it's here that you'll be farthest from the crowds that gravitate toward downtown Cabo San Lucas's fiesta atmosphere. These towns have retained their Mexican colonial roots and are the most charming of Los Cabos region. Some small hotels and bed-and-breakfasts lie in or near the town centers of these very walkable towns, and others are more remote. For high-season stays, try to make reservations at least three months in advance, and six months in advance for holidays. Precious few lodgings serve travelers on a budget.

The Corridor—the stretch that connects San José with Cabo San Lucas—has seen the growth of several megaresorts. These microcosms contain two or more hotels, throughout which golf courses, private villas, and upscale condo projects are interspersed. ⚠ If you are planning a vacation in Los Cabos, do keep in mind that most of the beaches at the resorts along the Corridor are not swimmable.

Cabo San Lucas continues its meteoric climb into the five-star stratosphere. Nearly every hotel in Cabo has undergone some kind of renovation, from minor to complete makeovers. The ME Cabo by Meliá is one such example. When Casa Dorada Resort opened, smack in the middle of busy El Médano Beach, it raised the bar in regards to rooms, services, and pampering, and Capella Pedregal has set a new high standard.

The rate of development in the area is astonishing, and begs the question of sustainability. As developable space in Los Cabos region diminishes and becomes prohibitively expensive, the newest expansions are moving beyond the Sea of Cortez coastline north of San José del Cabo, known as the "East Cape," and north of Cabo San Lucas along the Pacific coast. For years, building restrictions have been discussed, but money talks in every language. The only "restrictions" seem to be how much actual land is left.

ALL ABOUT ALL-INCLUSIVES

All-inclusives are like all-you-can-eat buffets—with all the positive and negative aspects included. You fork over the cash and just have at it, from the food and drink to an expansive pool complex and often water sports and excursions, too. You might consider this as one way for first-time visitors (especially families) to experience Los Cabos and not break the bank. The all-inclusive concept has come a long way since Club Med launched the concept decades ago. These days, all-inclusive properties are becoming more and more sophisticated, offering an impressive array of restaurants, bars, activities, and entertainment—and often striving to keep some local flavor present in the process.

WEDDINGS

If you decide to get married in Los Cabos, you'll be able to enjoy nuptials with friends and family in a gorgeous setting, and there'll be no worries about heading out for the honeymoon the morning after—you're already there. Los Cabos has a bevy of choices, and prices, for dream destination weddings. If money is no object, look into the big-name properties such as One&Only Palmilla, Las Ventanas al Paraíso, Esperanza, and the Secrets Marquis Los Cabos, where celebs often say "I do." Palmilla even has an official Director of Celebrations to assist. At Las Ventanas, hire its *caballero anillo*, "ring bearer on horseback." But the true champion of weddings has got to be the Dreams Los Cabos property, where as many as five couples get hitched each week. Let anyone concerned about the legitimacy of a Mexican wedding know that as long as you satisfy a few easy requirements, the ceremony will be legally binding.

CABOS WITH KIDS

If you're heading down to Los Cabos with the little ones in tow, you're in luck, because many properties are kid-friendly. A number of them welcome children with Kids' Clubs, including the Royal Solaris in San José del Cabo and the Hilton Los Cabos in the Corridor. In Cabo San Lucas, the time-share properties Villa del Palmar, Villa del Arco, and neighboring Club Cascadas will keep your little ones busy with fun activities. *The properties that go out of their way to provide entertainment for kids are marked with* ○ *in this chapter.* Many of the independent hotels listed don't restrict children, but their size and arrangement suggest more adult-oriented accommodations. We've mentioned these factors in our reviews.

BEST BETS FOR LOS CABOS LODGING

Fodor's offers a selective listing of quality lodging experiences in every price range, from the city's best budget beds to its most sophisticated luxury hotels. Here, we've compiled our top recommendations by price and experience. The very best properties—in other words, those that provide a particularly remarkable experience in their price range—are designated in the listings with the Fodor's Choice logo.

Fodor's Choice ★

Cabo Azul, $$$ p. 114

Cabo Cush, $ p. 124

Capella Pedregal, $$$$ p. 124

Casa Dorada Los Cabos Resort & Spa, $$$$ p. 124

Casa Natalia, $$ p. 114

Esperanza, $$$$ p. 117

Hilton Los Cabos, $$ p. 118

Las Ventanas al Paraíso, $$$$ p. 118

Marbella Suites, $ p. 118

One&Only Palmilla, $$$$ p. 120

Posada Terranova, $ p. 115

Pueblo Bonito Pacifica Holistic Retreat & Spa, $$$$ p. 128

Secrets Marquis Los Cabos, $$$$ p. 120

Villa del Arco Beach Resort & Spa, $ p. 129

Best by Price

$

The Bungalows, p. 122

Cabo Cush, p. 124

Marbella Suites, p. 118

Posada Terranova, $ p. 115

Sheraton Hacienda del Mar Resort, p. 120

Tropicana Inn, p. 117

$$

Casa Natalia, p. 114

Hilton Los Cabos, p. 118

$$$

Cabo Azul, p. 114

$$$$

Capella Pedregal, p. 124

Casa Dorada Los Cabos Resort & Spa, p. 124

Esperanza, p. 117

Las Ventanas al Paraíso, p. 118

One&Only Palmilla, p. 120

Pueblo Bonito Pacifica Holistic Retreat & Spa, p. 128

Best by Experience

BEST OVERALL

Cabo Surf Hotel, $$ p. 117

El Encanto, $ p. 114

Las Ventanas al Paraíso, $$$$ p. 118

One&Only Palmilla, $$$$, p. 120

BEST SPA

Capella Pedregal, $$$$ p. 124

Esperanza, $$$$ p. 117

Las Ventanas al Paraíso, $$$$ p. 118

One&Only Palmilla, $$$$ p. 120

Secrets Marquis Los Cabos, $$$$ p. 120

Villa del Arco Beach Resort & Spa, $ p. 129

MOST KID-FRIENDLY

Casa Dorada Los Cabos Resort & Spa, $$$$ p. 124

Hilton Los Cabos, $$ p. 118

Playa Grande Resort, $ p. 128

Sheraton Hacienda del Mar, $ p. 120

BEST FOR ROMANCE

Casa Natalia, $$ p. 114

Esperanza, $$$$ p. 117

Las Ventanas al Paraíso, $$$$ p. 118

Pueblo Bonito Pacifica, $$$$ p. 128

Secrets Marquis Los Cabos, $$$$, p. 120

Zoetry Casa del Mar, $$$$ p. 122

BEST VIEWS

Capella Pedregal, $$$$ p. 124

Casa Dorado Los Cabos, $$$$ p. 124

ME Cabo, $$$ p. 128

One&Only Palmilla, $$$$ p. 120

Villa del Arco, $ p. 129

MOST LUXURIOUS

Capella Pedregal, $$$$ p. 124

Esperanza, $$$$ p. 117

Las Ventanas al Paraíso, $$$$ p. 118

One&Only Palmilla, $$$$ p. 120

5

CABO CONDOS

If you're planning to stay a week or more, renting a condo can be more economical and convenient than a hotel. Los Cabos has countless condominium properties, ranging from modest homes to ultra-luxurious villas in such exclusive areas as Palmilla near San José del Cabo and the hill-clinging Pedregal neighborhood above Cabo San Lucas and its marina. Many private owners rent out their condos, either through the development's rental pool or property management companies. The price is the same for both, but with the latter you might get a better selection.

Nearly all condos are furnished and have a fully equipped kitchen, a television, bed and bath linens, laundry facilities, and maid service. Most are seaside and range from studios to three-bedroom units. A minimum stay of one week is typically required, though rules can vary by property. Start the booking process at least four months in advance, especially for high-season rentals.

CONTACTS

Cabo Homes and Condos. Cabo Homes and Condos ☎ *866/321– CABO(2226) from U.S.* ⊕ *www.cabohomesandcondos.com.*

Cabo Villas. Cabo Villas represents several properties including the high-end homes at Villas del Mar in the One&Only Palmilla compound, and other five-star properties throughout Los Cabos. ☎ *800/745–2226 in U.S./Canada* ⊕ *www.cabovillas.com.*

SAN JOSÉ DEL CABO

If being in Mexico, not the thick of a hopping resort scene, is more your speed, Cabo San Lucas's sister city San José del Cabo is the place to base your stay. Its restored downtown, with century-old buildings and many elevated sidewalks, is a delight to explore on foot. Plaza Mijares, the open and popular *zócalo*, is graced by a "dancing waters" fountain, lighted at night, and a stage where live music takes place frequently for the crowds who gather to stroll, enjoy ice cream, and relax after the heat of the day has let up. Several streets fronting the square are pedestrian-only, giving this historic downtown a lush and leisurely feel. Just beyond the center of town, and a bit farther south, is the ever-expanding Zona Hotelera, where a dozen or so new hotels, time-shares, and condo projects face the long stretch of beach (also referred to as Playa Hotelera) on the usually placid Sea of Cortez.

For expanded hotel reviews and current deals, visit Fodors.com.

$$
ALL-INCLUSIVE

⊡ **Barcelo Los Cabos Palace.** The latest addition to San José del Cabo's hotel zone, Barcelo Los Cabos Palace is a massive deluxe property that is making a name for itself in the all-inclusive category. **Pros:** great à la carte restaurant selection for an all-inclusive; spacious suites; kids club and adjacent water park offer diversion for little ones. **Cons:** resort's size is bit overwhelming; daily rate for Internet; airport shuttle is also at a charge. ⑤ *Rooms from: $275* ⊠ *Paseo Malecon, Zona Hotelera* ☎ *624/163–7730, 800/BARCELO toll free, US* ⊕ *www.barcelo.com* ⇌ *619 suites* ⊠⊙⊠ *All-inclusive* ✛ *1:B5.*

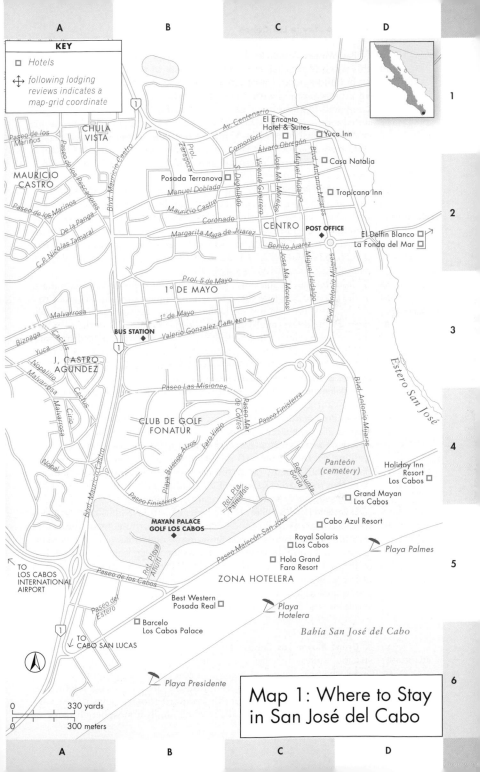

Map 1: Where to Stay
in San José del Cabo

$ 🖵 **Best Western Posada Real.** One of the better values in the hotel zone,
HOTEL   this tranquil beachside property consists of two tri-level, Santa Fe–
style buildings, and nice cactus gardens. **Pros:** the hotel maintains
an intimate feeling with a friendly staff; the price is very reasonable
compared to all of its neighbors. **Cons:** fairly standard, slightly outdated rooms, many of which have a lingering smell of cigarette smoke;
staff isn't well trained in handling booking errors or other snafus.
⑤ *Rooms from: $75* ✉ *Malecón, Zona Hotelera* ☎ *624/142–0155,*
800/448–8355 in U.S. ⊕ *www.posadareal.com.mx* ◊ *140 rooms, 8*
suites †○† *No meals* ✛ *1:B5.*

$$$ 🖵 **Cabo Azul Resort.** On the beach in San José del Cabo, this chic, white-
RESORT   washed property is so peaceful that it could be destined to be one of Los
Fodor's Choice   Cabos' top hotels. **Pros:** huge villas; excellent customer service; well-
★   maintained amenities **Cons:** lobby is under construction; spotty Internet
connectivity ⑤ *Rooms from: $350* ✉ *Paseo Malecón, Zona Hotelera*
☎ *624/163–5100, 877/216–2226 in the U.S.* ⊕ *www.caboazulresort.*
com ◊ *152 villas* †○† *No meals* ✛ *1:C5.*

$$ 🖵 **Casa Natalia.** An intimate, graceful boutique hotel, Casa Natalia is
HOTEL   in the heart of San José's downtown and opens onto the zócalo. **Pros:**
Fodor's Choice   lovely, oasis-like location in the heart of downtown; fantastic compli-
★   mentary breakfast; excellent staff. **Cons:** no bathtubs in the standard
rooms; noise from music and fiestas on Plaza Mijares can be disturbing;
beach shuttle only runs twice per day. ⑤ *Rooms from: $215* ✉ *Blvd.*
Mijares 4, Centro ☎ *624/146–7100* ⊕ *www.casanatalia.com* ◊ *14*
rooms, 2 suites †○† *No meals* ✛ *1:C2.*

$ 🖵 **El Delfin Blanco.** This is an affordable alternative for travelers who
B&B/INN   don't want all the hoopla of a highly developed, all-inclusive–style
resort. **Pros:** natural surroundings make this a great place to get away
from it all; the shared kitchen is super for cooking your catch of the
day; wonderfully attentive innkeepers; a few restaurants are within
walking distance. **Cons:** 10-minute drive to San José del Cabo; taxis
only by arrangement; saggy mattresses; slightly ramshackle facilities.
⑤ *Rooms from: $67* ✉ *Pueblo La Playita, La Playita* ☎ *624/142–1212*
⊕ *www.eldelfinblanco.net* ◊ *4 casitas, 1 cabana* ✛ *1:D2.*

$ 🖵 **El Encanto Hotel & Suites.** In the heart of San José's Historic Arts Dis-
HOTEL   trict, and near many bars and great restaurants, this gorgeous and comfortable inn has two separate buildings—one looks onto the verdant
gardens and pool; the other one, across the street, is in a charming, historic building with a narrow courtyard. **Pros:** lush, Mexican-hacienda
feeling; sunny pool area; excellent location that is central but quiet; local
restaurants will deliver room service. **Cons:** service may be friendly, but
staffing is minimal. ⑤ *Rooms from: $99* ✉ *Calle Morelos 133, Cen-*
tro ☎ *624/142–0388* ⊕ *www.elencantoinn.com* ◊ *12 rooms, 14 suites*
†○† *No meals* ✛ *1:C1.*

$$ 🖵 **Grand Mayan Los Cabos.** This glitzy, exotic resort offers vibrant,
ALL-INCLUSIVE   spacious suites, all with a view of the enormous pool and, if you're
☾   lucky, the Sea of Cortez beyond. **Pros:** children's programs; Grand
Mayan golf course; guests can opt out of all-inclusive plan. **Cons:** no
coffeemakers or refrigerators in standard rooms; views of sea vary
from panoramic to none at all; bustling family atmosphere because of

time-share element is sometimes chaotic. ⑤ *Rooms from: $250* ✉ *Paseo Malecón, Zona Hotelera* ☎ *624/163–4000, 800/292–9466 from U.S.* ⊕ *thegrandmayan.com* ⌁ *82 rooms, 90 suites* ⏚. *9-hole course* Ⓞ *All-inclusive* ✢ *1:D4.*

$ **Hola Grand Faro Los Cabos.** Another all-inclusive on Playa del Sol,
ALL-INCLUSIVE along San José del Cabo's hotel zone, this five-story hotel caters to both
business and fun, with five restaurants, five pools, four bars, and massive meeting rooms. **Pros:** friendly service and reasonable rates for the beach; La Tortuga kids' club keeps tots busy; no time-shares, hence no time-share salespeople. **Cons:** food is standard, American-buffet style; housekeeping can be an issue; daily fee for Internet access. ⑤ *Rooms from: $199* ✉ *Paseo Malecón, Zona Hotelera* ☎ *624/142–9292, 866/400–2692 in U.S.* ⊕ *www.holaloscabosresort.com* ⌁ *333 rooms, 22 suites* Ⓞ *All-inclusive* ✢ *1:C5.*

$ **Holiday Inn Resort Los Cabos.** At the former home of the Presidente
RESORT InterContinental Los Cabos, the familiar Holiday Inn brand has taken
over this sprawling property featuring cactus gardens that surround low-lying terra-cotta-color buildings. **Pros:** Chiqui Kids' Club (ages 5–12); adults-only restaurant and pool; generally mellow atmosphere is good for families and those looking for a getaway; free Wi-Fi. **Cons:** rooms tend to be basic, without refrigerators; food is run-of-the-mill buffet style restaurants, except at Napa. ⑤ *Rooms from: $160* ✉ *Blvd. Mijares and Paseo San José, cul-de-sac at end of hotel zone, Zona Hotelera* ☎ *624/142–9229* ⊕ *www.holidayinnresorts.com/loscabos* ⌁ *390 rooms, 7 suites* ✢ *1:D4.*

$ **La Fonda del Mar.** If you're looking for a peaceful back-to-nature
B&B/INN retreat, check out this hotel on a long, secluded beach that straddles
the line between desert and ocean. **Pros:** beautiful beachfront property; excellent full breakfast included in room rate. **Cons:** located past La Playita which is far from town; difficult to find; shared shower facilities. ⑤ *Rooms from: $75* ✉ *Old East Cape Rd., La Playita* ☎ *624/145–2139 cell* ⊕ *www.buzzardsbar.com* ⌁ *3 cabañas, 1 suite* ⊟ *No credit cards* Ⓞ *Breakfast* ✢ *1:D2.*

$ **Posada Terranova.** People return to San José's best inexpensive hotel
HOTEL over and over again. **Pros:** friendly staff; immaculate rooms; easy walk
Fodor'sChoice to Plaza Mijares. **Cons:** no pool; check the bed if a firm mattress is
★ a necessity for you. ⑤ *Rooms from: $67* ✉ *Calle Degollado at Av. Zaragoza, Centro* ☎ *624/142–0534* ⊕ *www.hterranova.com.mx* ⌁ *21 rooms* Ⓞ *Breakfast* ✢ *1:C2.*

$ **Royal Solaris Los Cabos.** This was the first all-inclusive in Los Cabos—it
ALL-INCLUSIVE runs smoothly, although the resort feels a bit like an amusement park
and is a bit dated. **Pros:** Kids' Club entertains kids 4–12 years old from 9 to 9; there is something for everyone at this busy resort, from cooking classes to dancing lessons; this is the best value for the money of the all-inclusives. **Cons:** the accommodations and food veer toward only adequate here, despite the volume of options; this is not the place to go for romance-seeking couples; time-share salespeople are pushy. ⑤ *Rooms from: $150* ✉ *Paseo Malecon, Lote 10, Colonia Campo de Golf, Zona Hotelera* ☎ *624/145–6800, 877/270–0440 in U.S.* ⊕ *www. hotelessolaris.com* ⌁ *387 rooms, 2 suites* Ⓞ *All-inclusive* ✢ *1:C5.*

5

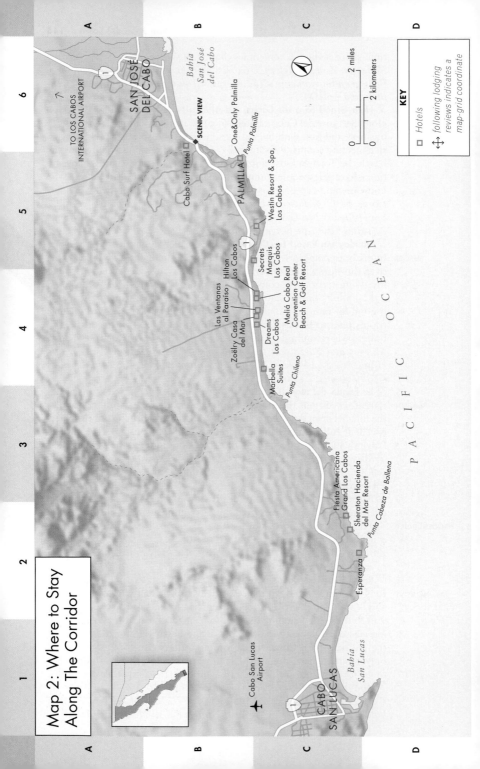

Map 2: Where to Stay Along The Corridor

A
TO LOS CABOS INTERNATIONAL AIRPORT ↑

SAN JOSÉ DEL CABO

Bahía San José del Cabo

SCENIC VIEW

PALMILLA

One&Only Palmilla
Punta Palmilla

Cabo Surf Hotel

Westin Resort & Spa, Los Cabos

Hilton Los Cabos

Secrets Marquis Los Cabos

Las Ventanas al Paraíso

Zoëtry Casa del Mar

Dreams Los Cabos

Meliá Cabo Real Convention Center Beach & Golf Resort

Marbella Suites

Punta Chileno

Fiesta Americana Grand Los Cabos

Sheraton Hacienda del Mar Resort

Punta Cabeza de Ballena

Esperanza

CABO SAN LUCAS

Cabo San Lucas Airport ✈

Bahía San Lucas

PACIFIC OCEAN

0   2 miles
0   2 kilometers

KEY

☐ *Hotels*

⬄ *following lodging reviews indicates a map-grid coordinate*

$ ▣ **Tropicana Inn.** It's not on the beach, but this hotel in a quiet enclave
HOTEL   along one of San José's main boulevards is a delightful, reasonable find.
★   **Pros:** bustling on-site restaurant and bar with live entertainment on the
weekends; rooms are immaculate, and beds extremely comfortable; staff
is attentive and courteous. **Cons:** kids are allowed, even though the hotel
is clearly oriented to adults seeking peace and relaxation; Wi-Fi is only
available around the pool. ⑤ *Rooms from: $127* ⊠ *Blvd. Mijares 30,
Centro* ☎ *624/142–1580* ⊕ *www.tropicanainn.com.mx* ⤳ *36 rooms, 4
suites* ⎮⊙⎮ *Breakfast* ✛ *1:D2.*

$ ▣ **Yuca Inn.** Basic accommodations at this friendly, funky place are clean
B&B/INN   and simple, and each room has a private bathroom. **Pros:** unbeatable
price; just steps away from the zócalo; the gregarious manager, Rogelio,
is happy to advise on activities and sights. **Cons:** mattresses can be soft;
this is not the choice for those looking for any kind of luxury accommodations—this is strictly a budget hotel. ⑤ *Rooms from: $50* ⊠ *Al-
varo Obregón #1 L-B, by Casa de la Cultura, Centro* ☎ *624/142–0462*
⊕ *www.yucainn.com.mx* ⤳ *9 rooms, 1 suite* ⎮⊙⎮ *Breakfast* ✛ *1:D1.*

THE CORRIDOR

Even before the Corridor had an official name or even a paved road,
the few hotels here were ritzy and elite; one even had its own private
airstrip. As the saying goes, the more things change, the more they stay
the same—developers have deliberately kept this area high-end and private. The Corridor is the most valuable strip of real estate in the region,
with guard-gated exclusivity, golf courses, luxury developments, and
unsurpassed views of the Sea of Cortez.

$$ ▣ **Cabo Surf Hotel.** Legendary and amateur surfers alike claim the prime
HOTEL   break-view rooms in this small hotel on the cliffs above Playa Costa
Azul. **Pros:** if surfing is your thing, then you can't get any closer than
this while having all your basic needs covered; celebrity sightings are
frequent; in-room iPod players. **Cons:** traffic from the highway can be
noisy; musty smells in the rooms. ⑤ *Rooms from: $265* ⊠ *Hwy. 1, Km
28* ☎ *624/142–2676, 858/964–5117 in U.S.* ⊕ *www.cabosurfhotel.com*
⤳ *22 rooms* ⎮⊙⎮ *No meals* ✛ *2:B6.*

$$$ ▣ **Dreams Los Cabos.** If there's one Los Cabos property that gets a nod
ALL-INCLUSIVE   for the most weddings per year, it would have to be the all-inclusive
☺   Dreams, which averages as many as five per week. **Pros:** Explorer's Club
for kids ages 3–12; access to Cabo Real golf course; golf concierge; com-
plimentary shuttle to and from the airport. **Cons:** resort can feel overrun
with children; food is abundant but cuisine is only average; staff often
seems overwhelmed and uninterested in service; daily charge for Internet
access, unless staying at the Preferred level of accommodation. ⑤ *Rooms
from: $350* ⊠ *Hwy. 1, Km 18.5* ☎ *866/237–3267 or 624/145–7600*
⊕ *www.dreamsresorts.com* ⤳ *308 suites* ⎮⊙⎮ *All-inclusive* ✛ *2:C4.*

$$$$ ▣ **Esperanza.** One of the most exquisite resorts in Los Cabos, focused
RESORT   on privacy and impeccable service, and home to one of the best spas
Fodor's Choice   in the region, Esperanza is a true luxury. **Pros:** service and amenities
★   are virtually flawless; the physical setting is exquisite; every room
has an ocean view; resort is for adults and children 16 and over only

5

(families with younger children are welcome in the Villas). **Cons:** the high cost of incidentals can get exhausting; wind can be fierce on the rocky cliffs that the resort is set on. Ⓢ *Rooms from: $695* ✉ *Hwy. 1, Km 7* ☎ *624/145–6400, 866/311–2226 in U.S.* ⊕ *www. esperanzaresort.com* ↘ *57 suites, 60 villas* ♚ *No meals* ✛ *2:C2.*

$

RESORT

☷ **Fiesta Americana Grand Los Cabos.** The dramatic lobby of the Fiesta is eight stories above the beach, and every room looks out onto the Sea of Cortez. **Pros:** a good choice for couples wanting a relaxing getaway; though the beach is rocky, this is one of the few hotels on a

stretch of water that is safe to swim and snorkel in. **Cons:** not the place for people looking for Cabo's infamous party scene; expensive to get back and forth to town, whether in a cab or the resort's shuttle; food quality doesn't match expensive dining costs; service is notoriously spotty. Ⓢ *Rooms from: $125* ✉ *Cabo del Sol, Hwy. 1, Km 10.3* ☎ *624/145–6200 or 866/927–7666* ⊕ *www.fiestamericanagrand.com* ↘ *249 rooms* ♞ *Jack Nicklaus Ocean Golf Course at Cabo del Sol* ♚ *No meals* ✛ *2:C3.*

$$

RESORT

♻

Fodor's Choice

★

☷ **Hilton Los Cabos.** Rooms are spacious at this hacienda-style Hilton built on one of the Corridor's few swim-friendly beach lagoons. **Pros:** professional, attentive staff stands out among Corridor hotels in this price range; the infinity pool is dramatic and relaxing; excellent golf concierge service can make arrangements at area's best courses. **Cons:** spa services aren't up to par with the rest of the resort; resort is not within walking distance to any towns or other sights. Ⓢ *Rooms from: $209* ✉ *Hwy. 1, Km 19.5* ☎ *624/145–6500 or 800/HILTONS* ⊕ *www. hiltonloscabos.com* ↘ *309 rooms, 66 suites* ♚ *No meals* ✛ *2:B4.*

$$$$

RESORT

Fodor's Choice

★

☷ **Las Ventanas al Paraíso.** Las Ventanas is one of the leading hotels in the world, making it a standout not only in Los Cabos, but throughout Mexico. **Pros:** this is the place to escape the often-hectic Cabos scene; exceptional service and attention to guests; children under 12 not allowed. **Cons:** there can be a minimum night stay for weekends depending on the season; the resort tends to feel more formal than others in the area. Ⓢ *Rooms from: $968* ✉ *Hwy. 1, Km 19.5* ☎ *624/144–2800, 888/ROSEWOOD in U.S.* ⊕ *www.lasventanas.com* ↘ *71 suites* ♚ *No meals* ✛ *2:B4.*

$

HOTEL

Fodor's Choice

★

☷ **Marbella Suites en la Playa.** With all the sophisticated properties in Los Cabos, it's a treat to discover little Marbella Suites, one of the oldest hotels in Cabo, and one which still retains the flavor of the peaceful and romantic East Cape properties. **Pros:** large rooms with kitchenettes; gracious, friendly staff; homey, relaxed atmosphere; free Wi-Fi. **Cons:** lobby is three floors above lowest level; not accessible for guests with

The Hilton Los Cabos, on the Corridor, offers up a swimmable beach and attentive service.

The name Esperanza is synonymous with total luxury and seclusion for those in the know.

One of San José's true gems, Casa Natalia is decorated with authentic Mexican flair.

wheelchairs; most rooms open onto a central garden courtyard with only minimal ocean views; rental car is mandatory, though a bus stop is located right outside the property. ⑤ *Rooms from: $83* ✉ *Trans. Hwy. 17* ☎ *624/144–1060* ⊕ *www.marbellasuites.com* ⇱ *41 suites* ⦿ *No meals* ✛ *2:C4.*

$$$$
ALL-INCLUSIVE

🖼 **Meliá Cabo Real Convention Center Beach & Golf Resort.** Whether you're traveling for a business meeting or a family get-together, this all-inclusive property is fun. **Pros:** near golf courses; low prices make this attractive for budget-oriented travelers looking for an all-inclusive; swimmable beach. **Cons:** basic accommodations; housekeeping standards tend to be lax, at best; daily Internet charge ⑤ *Rooms from: $400* ✉ *Hwy 1, Km 19.5* ☎ *624/144–2218 or 866/43–MELIA* ⊕ *www.meliacaboreal. com* ⇱ *350 rooms* ⦿ *All-inclusive* ✛ *2:C4.*

$$$$
RESORT
Fodor's Choice
★

🖼 **One&Only Palmilla.** Built in 1956 by the son of the then-president of Mexico, the One&Only was the first resort introduced to the Los Cabos area, and it retains an old-world ambience and elegance that is without match in the region. **Pros:** from beginning to end, Palmilla has already thought of everything, even offering "Air to Go" meals: quality, custom-made box lunches to take along with you on the flight home. **Cons:** prices are high; increasing numbers of large, boisterous groups in the past few years mar the otherwise genteel atmosphere. ⑤ *Rooms from: $695* ✉ *Hwy. 1, Km 27.5* ☎ *624/146–7000, 866/829– 2977 in U.S.* ⊕ *www.oneandonlyresorts.com* ⇱ *61 rooms, 91 junior suites, 20 one-bedroom suites* ⚓ *Jack Nicklaus designed 18-hole course* ⦿ *No meals* ✛ *2:B5.*

$$$$
ALL-INCLUSIVE
Fodor's Choice
★

🖼 **Secrets Marquis Los Cabos.** Stunning architecture, a property-wide art collection of unique pieces, noticeable attention to detail, and loads of luxurious touches make the Marquis a standout. **Pros:** adults only; tranquillity prevails for complete escape; exceptional full-service spa. **Cons:** weddings (and wedding parties) are frequently taking place on the premises; surf is unswimmable. ⑤ *Rooms from: $1,040* ✉ *Carretera 1, Km. 21.5* ☎ *624/144–2000 or 877/238–9399* ⊕ *www.secretsresorts. com/marquis* ⇱ *208 suites, 26 casitas* ⦿ *All-inclusive* ✛ *2:C5.*

$
RESORT
☉
★

🖼 **Sheraton Hacienda del Mar Resort.** Small tiled domes painted red, orange, and pink top eight buildings at this lovely, hacienda-style resort. **Pros:** rooms, whether on the golf course or with a view of the ocean, are serene and quiet; as part of the Cabo del Sol development, the Sheraton has access to amazing local golf courses. **Cons:** beach is not usually good for swimming; the mostly mediocre restaurants are expensive; daily Internet fee; shared facilities with time-share guests brings an otherwise excellent facility down a notch and salespeople can get pushy. ⑤ *Rooms from: $175* ✉ *Cabo del Sol, Hwy. 1, Km 10* ☎ *624/145–8000, 800/325–3535 in U.S.* ⊕ *www.sheratonloscabos. com* ⇱ *270 rooms, 31 suites* ⚓ *All Cabo del Sol's courses are available to guests* ✛ *2:C2.*

$
RESORT
☉

🖼 **Westin Resort & Spa, Los Cabos.** Built by prominent Mexican artist Javier Sordo Madaleno, the colorful architecture makes this Westin more memorable than some of the others in the Corridor. **Pros:** the children's center is clean and well staffed; great gym; multiple pools including an adults-only option. **Cons:** it's a trek from the parking

The intimate, 40-suite Marbella Suites is known for its laid-back atmosphere.

Las Ventanas al Paraíso is stylish and ultra-luxurious, with in-room fireplaces and an unforgettable spa.

lot and lobby to the rooms and pools, making this a poor choice for those with disabilities; daily Internet surcharge. ⑤ *Rooms from: $189* ⊠ *Hwy. 1, Km 22.5* ☎ *624/142–9000, 888/625–5144 in U.S.* ⊕ *www.starwood.com/ westin* ⟳ *243 rooms, 14 suites* ⊙ *No meals* ✢ *2:B5.*

$$$$
ALL-INCLUSIVE

⌖ **Zoëtry Casa del Mar.** It's all about comfort and privacy at this award-winning, hacienda-style hotel. **Pros:** access to the fantastic Cabo Real golf course; gorgeous views of the Sea of Cortez; adults-only Beach Club with pool and restaurant. **Cons:** the hotel is technically 63 rooms/suites, but it's surrounded by 220 time-share condos; time-share salespeople can be annoyingly pushy and omnipresent. ⑤ *Rooms from: $500* ⊠ *Hwy. 1, Km 19.5* ☎ *624/145–7700, 888/4–ZOETRY in U.S.* ⊕ *www.zoetryresorts.com* ⟳ *63 suites* ⊙ *All-inclusive* ✢ *2:C4.*

> **STARRY STARRY NIGHT**
>
> Every Friday night, customized desert vehicles transport One&Only Palmilla guests and the hotel's astronomer into the desert mountain region to enjoy the Baja desert at night under the star-filled sky. The unique mountain background sets the stage for an evening of exciting entertainment including fire dancing and song as well as a sumptuous Mexican feast.

CABO SAN LUCAS

In Cabo San Lucas, there's a massive hotel on every available plot of waterfront turf. A pedestrian walkway lined with restaurants, bars, and shops anchored by the sleek Puerto Paraíso mall curves around the entire perimeter of Cabo San Lucas harbor, itself packed with wall-to-wall sportfishing and pleasure yachts. Unfortunately, a five-story hotel complex at one edge of the harbor blocks a small portion of the water view and sea breezes from the town's side streets, but it can't be denied that Cabo is a carnival and a parade, all at once. The short Pacific coast beach just over the rocky hills at the west end of the marina has a more peaceful ambience, though monstrous hotel projects have gobbled up much of the sand here, too. If being right on the water isn't a primary concern, it is well worth checking out some of the smaller, independently owned hotels sprinkled around the downtown area. Several offer gracious, hacienda-style accommodations with a personal touch that huge hotels cannot match.

$
B&B/INN

⌖ **The Bungalows Hotel.** Forget the five-star accommodations; this quaint little inn situated just above the Marina in Cabo San Lucas exudes budget-friendly charm. **Pros:** oasis-like property is a nice way to escape the constant hustle of Cabo; caring, personalized service encourages lingering and relaxation. **Cons:** hot water can be in short supply; there is noise from traffic and surrounding neighborhood; a bit off the beaten path. ⑤ *Rooms from: $95* ⊠ *Blvd. Miguel Angel Herrera* ☎ *624/143–5035* ⊕ *thebungalowshotel.com* ⟳ *16 suites, 2 bungalows* ⊙ *Breakfast* ✢ *3:A4.*

One&Only Pamilla is a stunning seaside resort.

Luxury and natural beauty abound at Secrets Marquis Los Cabos.

$ ⊡ **Cabo Cush.** By far one of the most affordable hotels in Cabo, this
HOTEL   little gem is reminiscent of courtyard hotels in mainland Mexico, with
Fodor's Choice   a central breezeway running between the low-slung two-story build-
★   ings in the heart of town. **Pros:** fantastic price for a simple, comfortable
room; easygoing, friendly staff will offer all sorts of recommendations;
cheap, tasty meals available from the on-site eatery; free Wi-Fi and long
distance calls to the U.S. **Cons:** no swimming pool or gardens—not
really a hangout spot; no view. ⑤ *Rooms from: $70 ⊠ Calle Zaragoza
between Revolucion and Carranza* ☎ *624/143–9300* ⊕ *www.cabocush.
com* ↪ *22 rooms* ⑴ *No meals* ✛ *3:A3.*

$ ⊡ **Cabo Inn.** The small, comfortable rooms at this affordable palapa-
B&B/INN   roof, cactus-lined, and jungle-like hotel have tangerine-and-cobalt
sponge-painted walls and stained-glass windows above the headboards.
Pros: very affordable hotel right in the thick of things and only a few
minutes' walk to the beach; communal kitchen, barbecue, and dining
area mean you can cook here and save on expensive meals out. **Cons:**
some rooms are dark and cramped; upper rooms can get very noisy during high season when downtown revelers are at their wildest. ⑤ *Rooms
from: $39 ⊠ Calle 20 de Noviembre and Vicario, Centro* ☎ *624/143–
0819, 619/819–2727 in U.S.* ⊕ *www.caboinnhotel.com* ↪ *20 rooms*
⑴ *No meals* ✛ *3:A3.*

$$$$ ⊡ **Capella Pedregal.** Just when we thought there was no more room
RESORT   for a top resort in Cabos' five-star universe, along comes the swank
Fodor's Choice   Capella Pedregal, Cabos San Lucas' premiere accommodation. **Pros:**
★   hidden away through a tunnel, but still quite near Cabo San Lucas
town and marina; every room has a plunge pool; stellar restaurant El
Farallon is on-site. **Cons:** Pacific-side beach is not swimmable. ⑤ *Rooms
from: $595 ⊠ Camino del Mar 1, Marina* ☎ *877/247–6688* ⊕ *www.
capellapedregal.com* ↪ *52 rooms, 14 suites* ⑴ *No meals* ✛ *3:A5.*

$ ⊡ **Casa Bella.** The Ungson family had been in Cabo for more than four
B&B/INN   decades before turning their home across from Plaza San Lucas into
a spacious, tranquil inn. **Pros:** no TVs or phones in the rooms; property feels totally secluded, though it's in the middle of town; ambience
suggests a stay at a private home rather than a hotel. **Cons:** no TVs or
phones in the rooms; local roosters crow in the mornings. ⑤ *Rooms
from: $160 ⊠ Calle Hidalgo 10, Centro* ☎ *624/143–6400, 626/209–
0215 in U.S.* ⊕ *www.casabellahotel.com* ↪ *11 rooms, 3 suites* ⊙ *Closed
Aug. and Sept.* ⑴ *Breakfast* ✛ *3:A4.*

$$$$ ⊡ **Casa Dorada Los Cabos Resort & Spa.** Through the dramatic, drawbridge-
RESORT   like entry on the stone facade you'll find this seven-floor, all-suites com-
↻   bination hotel–time-share has it all. **Pros:** beautifully appointed rooms;
Fodor's Choice   huge jetted tubs in bathrooms; ocean views from every room; located at
★   the heart of Playa Médano; great online deals for up to 50% off adver-
tised rates. **Cons:** the beach in front of the hotel is host to noisy bars and
clubs; time-share salespeople are aggressive. ⑤ *Rooms from: $400 ⊠ Av.
del Pescador, Medano Beach* ☎ *624/163–5757, 866/448–0151 toll free
from U.S.* ⊕ *www.casadorada.com* ↪ *186 suites* ⑴ *No meals* ✛ *3:C3.*

$ ⊡ **Club Cascadas de Baja.** While surrounding properties have gone up,
HOTEL   up, up, the two-story, palapa-roof villas of Club Cascadas haven't
changed a bit. **Pros:** nice location on Playa Médano; tropical grounds

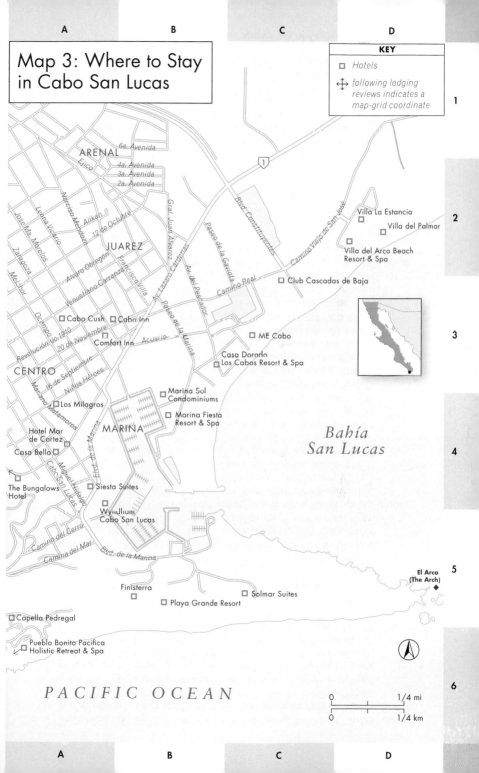

are lush and much quieter than those at larger hotels. **Cons:** rooms near the back of the property, in the building where the lobby is, tend to be noisy and are more run-of-the-mill. ⑤ *Rooms from: $199* ✉ *Camino Viejo de San José* ☎ *624/143–1882* ⊕ *www.clubcascadasdebaja.com* ⌨ *110 villas* ⦿ *No meals* ✛ *3:C3.*

$ ⊡ **Comfort Inn.** Located several blocks from the marina and about a
HOTEL   five-minute walk to the beach, there is nothing fancy here, but the rooms are clean, the beds are comfortable, and the interior courtyard with pool has lush palms and flowers in addition to a palapa-roof swim-up bar. **Pros:** very safe-feeling hotel; attentive staff; reliable budget option. **Cons:** rooms are small; furnishings somewhat flimsy and basic. ⑤ *Rooms from: $73* ✉ *Leona Vicario and Revolucion 20 de Noviembre* ☎ *624/143–7501* ⊕ *www.comfortinn.com* ⌨ *103 rooms* ⦿ *Breakfast* ✛ *3:A3.*

$ ⊡ **Finisterra.** One of the first hotels built in Cabo, the Finisterra, perched
RESORT   on a hill overlooking the marina and the Pacific, was an architectural marvel back in the 1960s. **Pros:** fantastic location; short walk to the marina and Cabo's action, but very quiet, as well; great beach access for walking on the Pacific side; attentive but unobtrusive staff. **Cons:** restaurants (except at the pool) and older sections of the hotel are closed during the summer months; beach is not swimmable because of rough waves and undertow. ⑤ *Rooms from: $125* ✉ *Blvd. Marina* ☎ *624/143–3333* ⊕ *www.finisterra.com* ⌨ *287 rooms* ⦿ *No meals* ✛ *3:B5.*

$ ⊡ **Hotel Mar de Cortez.** Another one of Cabo's original hotels, this colo-
HOTEL   nial-style property has been operating for over 30 years, and remains one of the most affordable in all of Los Cabos. **Pros:** clean rooms and pleasant surroundings; refreshing pool; free Internet. **Cons:** noisy air-conditioning units; surrounding streets are busy and loud; beds and pillows are too hard; towels are limited. ⑤ *Rooms from: $57* ✉ *Lazaro Cardenas and Guerrero* ☎ *624/143–0032, 800/347–8821 in U.S.* ⊕ *www.mardecortez.com* ⌨ *72 rooms, 16 suites* ☾ *Closed Sept.* ⦿ *Breakfast* ✛ *3:A4.*

$ ⊡ **Los Milagros.** A mosaic sign (crafted by co-owner Ricardo Rode) near
HOTEL   the entrance hints at the beauty inside this small inn. **Pros:** quaint, quiet inn located close to everything in Cabo; one room is accessible to travelers with disabilities; free Wi-Fi. **Cons:** air-conditioning units in rooms can be loud; pool is small and not heated. ⑤ *Rooms from: $85* ✉ *Matamoros 116* ☎ *718/928–6647 in U.S., 624/143–4566* ⊕ *www. losmilagros.com.mx* ⌨ *12 rooms* ⦿ *No meals* ✛ *3:A4.*

$ ⊡ **Marina Fiesta Resort & Spa.** Though this colonial-style building is not
RESORT   ocean-side, most rooms have a pleasant view of the cloverleaf-shape pool and out to the yacht-filled marina. **Pros:** close to popular bars and shops, and a quick walk from popular Playa Médano. **Cons:** staff is not trained to deal with problems or guest concerns; there is no buffer between guests and aggressive time-share salespeople. ⑤ *Rooms from: $160* ✉ *Marina, Lot 37, Marina* ☎ *624/145–6020, 877/243–4880 toll free from U.S.* ⊕ *www.marinafiestaresort.com* ⌨ *155 rooms* ⦿ *No meals* ✛ *3:B4.*

$ ⊡ **Marina Sol Condominiums.** Good bargains can be found here—espe-
RESORT   cially for groups. **Pros:** only a few blocks from the town center and just

Casa Dorada Los Cabos Resort & Spa is home to the 7,000-square-foot Saltwater Spa.

The designers of Pueblo Bonito Pacifica Holistic Retreat & Spa incorporated feng shui elements throughout the resort.

a quick walk to Playa Médano, this is a good spot if you like being close to the action. **Cons:** be sure to ask for an "inside" garden condo, as the outside rooms are noisy, due to the never-ending construction and traffic in this, one of the busiest parts of town; Internet connectivity is spotty; this property may just have the pushiest time-share salespeople in the area. ⑤ *Rooms from: $129* ⊠ *Paseo del Pescador* ☎ *624/143–3231* ⊕ *www.marinasolresort.com* ⤵ *128 condos* ⫶❍⫶ *No meals* ✛ *3:B4.*

> ### WHALE-WATCHING FROM UP ON HIGH
>
> The **Finisterra's** tower is about as high you can get, geographically, and it's the best spot in Cabo San Lucas to watch the gray whales in their winter home.

$$$
RESORT

⬚ **ME Cabo.** In the middle of the most popular Médano beach is where you'll find the ME, the Meliá brand's posh offering in Cabos San Lucas. **Pros:** great for adults and singles looking for a hopping social scene; ME's Passion Night Club (open Thursday–Saturday) is a popular Cabo destination; iPod docking stations and plasma TVs in every room. **Cons:** rooms in the high $200s are limited and rates jump up quickly after that; rooms anywhere near the Passion club are noisy; though not advertised as "adults only," this is not the hotel to take children. ⑤ *Rooms from: $350* ⊠ *Playa Médano* ☎ *624/145–7800, 877/954–8363 in U.S.* ⊕ *www.me-cabo.com* ⤵ *88 rooms, 62 suites* ✛ *3:C3.*

$
RESORT
☾

⬚ **Playa Grande Resort.** This large, multicolor all suite hotel complex on the beach next to the original Solmar property (which is now a luxury all-inclusive) looks a bit Las Vegas, even by Cabo standards but, it's got all kinds of activities and facilities, making it a great family vacation option. **Pros:** the Thalasso Spa is huge and gets rave reviews; putt-putt golf course and play structures, in addition to fabulous pools, will keep your kids entertained. **Cons:** fitness center and Internet charges apply for use; getting to and from rooms in the Ridge is time-consuming and confusing; ongoing construction on all Solmar properties is both noisy and detracts from the charm. ⑤ *Rooms from: $187* ⊠ *Av. Playa Grande #1* ☎ *624/145–7524, 800/344–3349 in U.S.* ⊕ *www.solmar.com* ⤵ *358 rooms* ⫶❍⫶ *No meals* ✛ *3:B5.*

$$$$
ALL-INCLUSIVE
Fodor$Choice
★

⬚ **Pueblo Bonito Pacifica Holistic Retreat & Spa.** Soothing waterfalls, glass-domed ceilings, and pebbled floors bring nature indoors to complement this holistic approach to vacationing. **Pros:** adults only; truly tranquil lodgings. **Cons:** the extremely sedate atmosphere can be shocking for guests; charges apply for use of beach beds and gym; beach is not swimmable; you must have a car or take a cab to get to town. ⑤ *Rooms from: $600* ⊠ *Predio Paraiso Escondido* ☎ *624/142–9696, 800/990–8250 in U.S.* ⊕ *www.pueblobonitopacifica.com* ⤵ *140 rooms, 14 suites* ⫶❍⫶ *All-inclusive* ✛ *3:A6.*

$$
RESORT
☾

⬚ **Pueblo Bonito Rosé.** A bit dated to compete with some of Cabos' more luxe properties, Mediterranean-style buildings curve around seemingly never-ending grounds. Imitations of Roman busts guard reflecting pools, and Flemish tapestries adorn the lobby—this is definitely not your typical Cabo hotel. Even the Rosé's smallest suites can accommodate four people, and all have private balconies. Staff is gracious and attentive, and many guests return year after year because of this. You can opt for an all-inclusive plan should you choose. **Pros:** a shuttle bus travels between the two Pueblo Bonito hotels on El Médano Beach and the more upscale Pueblo Bonito Pacifica Holistic Resort and Pueblo Bonito Sunset on the Pacific coast; guests have signing privileges at all four hotels; booking online often gets significant discounts on rates. **Cons:** outdated furnishings; thin walls mean you may have to endure the noises of your neighbors; charge for Wi-Fi. $ *Rooms from: $200* ✉ *Playa Médano* ☎ *624/142–9898, 800/990–8250 in U.S.* ⊕ *www. pueblobonito-rose.com* ⤴ *258 suites* ⚌ *No meals.*

$ **Ⓣ Siesta Suites.** The owners keep a close eye on this four story hotel—a
HOTEL calm refuge two blocks from the marina—and dispense great insider advice to visitors. **Pros:** great rates; friendly staff really takes care of guests; barbecue area great for cooking up the catch of the day; free Wi-Fi. **Cons:** town noise can sometimes be disturbing; limited off-street parking; pool is small and is surrounded by tables from Salvatore's restaurant at night. $ *Rooms from: $69* ✉ *Calle Zapata at Guerrero, Centro* ☎ *624/143–2773, 866/271–0952 toll free in U.S.* ⊕ *www. cabosiestasuites.com* ⤴ *5 rooms, 15 suites* ⚌ *No meals* ✢ *3:A4.*

$ **Ⓣ Solmar Resort.** The whitewashed, modern Solmar sits against the rocks
ALL-INCLUSIVE at Land's End facing the surging Pacific and has recently undergone a renovation. **Pros:** secluded location; 10-minute walk to town; great spa. **Cons:** ongoing construction at all Solmar properties is both distracting and noisy. $ *Rooms from: $145* ✉ *Av. Solmar at Blvd. Marina, Apdo. 8* ☎ *624/145–7524, 800/344–3349 in U.S.* ⊕ *www.solmar.com* ⤴ *102 suites* ⚌ *All-inclusive* ✢ *3:C5.*

$ **Ⓣ Villa del Arco Beach Resort & Spa.** As with its sister properties, del Arco
RESORT offers comfortable, stylishly decorated one-, two- and three-bedroom
Ⓒ suites and penthouses with all the amenities, including full kitchens,
Fodor's Choice and the bustling pools are anchored by a pirate ship/restaurant docked
★ within that delights kids of all ages. **Pros:** an on-property deli and market lets you stock up the kitchen, saving money on meals out; rooms are large and very comfortably furnished. **Cons:** service can be spotty; time-share salespeople can be pushy. $ *Rooms from: $190* ✉ *Camino Viejo a San José, Km 0.5* ☎ *624/145–7200, 877/845–5247 in U.S.* ⊕ *www. villagroupresorts.com* ⤴ *220 suites* ⚌ *No meals* ✢ *3:D2.*

$ **Ⓣ Villa del Palmar.** The large marble-floored entry here welcomes you
RESORT into a property that is as comfortable and casual as a vacation home—if
Ⓒ vacation homes came with a full-time staff on hand. **Pros:** large rooms with kitchenettes; great location on Playa Médano and near all of Cabo's offerings; recent room renovation; great for kids and families. **Cons:** the oldest of the Villa Group properties on Playa Medano; surcharge for Wi-Fi $ *Rooms from: $159* ✉ *Camino Viejo a San José, Km 0.5* ☎ *800/823–4488 in Mexico, 877/845–5247 in U.S.* ⊕ *www. villagroupresorts.com* ⤴ *460 suites* ⚌ *No meals* ✢ *3:D2.*

$$ **Ⓣ Villa La Estancia.** It's apparent that this is the Villa Group's top
RESORT property as soon as you enter its suites. **Pros:** beautifully maintained grounds; located on swimmable Playa Médano; small deli-market on the premises to stock up on snacks. **Cons:** restaurants on this property are expensive, and food quality varies widely; pushy time-share

5

TIME-SHARE BEWARE

For some families who frequently like to get away to resorts, the time-share concept can be a good, and economical, way to vacation. Time-shares are a big business in Los Cabos, and the offers are incessant, especially as you walk through the town of Cabo San Lucas. Indeed, pushy, in-your-face time-share representatives at the airport and in many hotel lobbies will try to entice you to attend a presentation by offering free transportation, breakfast, and activities, or even attractive amounts of cash. These aggressive salespeople are a major downside to many

expensive lodgings where you might assume that you won't be harassed. Don't feel obligated to accept—presentations often last two hours or more, and can be physically and emotionally draining. If you're staying in a hotel that has time-share units, aggressive salespeople may call your room every morning asking you to attend a free breakfast. If you're not interested, nicely demand to be taken off their call list.

■TIP→ If you want those time-share "sharks" off your back pronto, simply say "I live here"— and they'll leave you alone.

salespeople; charge for Wi-Fi. ⑤ *Rooms from: $250* ⊠ *Camino Viejo a San José, Km 0.5* ☎ *624/145–6900, 877/845–5247 toll free in U.S.* ⊕ *www.villagroupresorts.com* ⇥ *156 villas* |◎| *No meals* ✛ *3:D2.*

$ ⌕ **Wyndham Cabo San Lucas.** The Wyndham has taken over what was
HOTEL   formerly known as the Tesoro Hotel, located in a plum spot on the Cabo Marina. **Pros:** the Wyndham is the most centrally located hotel for fishing, restaurants, and Cabo's overall party atmosphere—it's literally surrounded by dozens of fun bars and restaurants; best close-up view of Marina Cabo San Lucas; free shuttle to Playa Medano. **Cons:** charge for Wi-Fi in rooms; this is not a lounge-around-a-luxurious-pool resort, nor is it on the beach. ⑤ *Rooms from: $111* ⊠ *Calle Marina San Lucas* ☎ *624/173–9300, 866/998–3767 in U.S.* ⊕ *www.wyndham.com* ⇥ *135 rooms, 151 suites* |◎| *No meals* ✛ *3:A4.*

Shopping

WORD OF MOUTH

"Other places we liked in San Josè were the art galleries—definitely a notch above average, the delicious croissants at French Riviera, a few of the shops, the local market where the kids did all their souvenir shopping and the Baja Brewing Co. which had live music in the evening."

—carrom

Updated by
Marie Elena
Martinez

Los Cabos may not have a whole lot of homegrown wares, but the stores are filled with beautiful and unusual items from all over mainland Mexico. You can find hand-painted blue Talavera tiles from Puebla; blue-and-yellow pottery from Guanajuato; black pottery from San Bartolo Coyotepec (near Oaxaca); hammocks from the Yucatán; embroidered clothing from Oaxaca, Chiapas, and the Yucatán; silver jewelry from Taxco; fire opals from Queretaro; and the fine beaded crafts of the Huichol tribe from Nayarit and Jalisco.

Los Cabos manufactures good times under plenty of sunshine but very few actual products. One exception is glassware from Fábrica de Vidrio Soplado (Blown-Glass Factory). In addition, a burgeoning arts scene has national and international artists opening galleries and, in fact, a large number of galleries now abound throughout Los Cabos, with many in San José del Cabo's rapidly evolving city center and more dotted throughout Todos Santos's historic downtown. Dozens of shops will custom-design gold and silver jewelry for you, fashioning pieces in one to two days. Liquor shops sell a locally produced liqueur called *damiana*, which is touted as an aphrodisiac. A few shops will even create custom-designed bathing suits for you in a day or so.

No longer hawking only the requisite T-shirts, belt buckles, and trinkets, Cabo's improved shopping scene has reached the high standards of other Mexican resorts. Its once-vacant streets are today lined with dozens of new shops, from open-air bazaars to souvenir shops and fine designer boutiques. To be sure, there's something for everyone here.

PLANNING

HOURS OF OPERATION

Many stores are open as early as 9 am, and often stay open until 9 or 10 pm. A few close for siesta at 1 pm or 2 pm, then reopen at 4 pm. About half of Los Cabos' shops close on Sunday; those that do open usually close up by 2 or 3 in the afternoon.

It's not uncommon to find some shops and galleries closed in San José del Cabo or Todos Santos during the hot season (roughly June to September), though very few shops close in Cabo San Lucas. We've noted this whenever possible; however, some shops simply close up for several weeks if things get excruciatingly slow or hot. In any case, low-season hours are usually reduced, so call ahead during that time of year.

BUYER BEWARE

One of the benefits of traveling in Los Cabos is the low crime rate, thanks in part to the large population of expats and year-round tourists, and the *tranquilo* nature of locals. That being said, it's always wise to pay attention to what's going on when money is changing hands. Some tips: Watch that your credit card goes through the machine only once, so that no duplicates of your slip are made. If there's an error and a new slip needs to be drawn up, make sure the original is destroyed. Don't let your card leave a store without you. One scam is to ask you to wait while the clerk runs next door ostensibly to use another business's phone or to verify your number—but really to make extra copies. Again, this area is refreshingly safe and incident-free compared to many areas on the mainland, but it's always wise to be aware.

BEST BRING-BACKS

If you travel Los Cabos with a few extra pesos in your pocket it's likely you'll want to return home with a memento, or 10, that reminds you of the spirit and vibrancy of this region.

Works of art by local artists make great treasures to take back home—and galleries will usually ship the items for you. For more packable take-home goodies, the clothing options are nearly endless: T-shirts, resort wear, and clothing from hip Mexican designers will all compete for space in your suitcase. Cabo San Lucas is a great shopping town; if you've got time and some money, there's no need to worry about purchasing your beach vacation clothing before leaving home.

If you're looking for something truly authentic and *hecho en Cabo* (made in Cabo), then check out the blown glass at the intriguing **Fábrica de Vidrio Soplado**. Other fun souvenirs include the new labels of tequila offered from such outlets as Cabo Wabo, Hotel California in Todos Santos, the Cabo Surf Hotel, and Las Veritas, a popular Cabo dance club and bar.

WHAT YOU CAN'T BRING HOME

Don't buy items made from tortoiseshell or any sea turtle products: it's illegal (Mexico's turtle species are endangered or threatened, and these items aren't allowed into the United States, Canada, or the United Kingdom). Cowboy boots, hats, and sandals made from the leather of endangered species such as crocodiles may also be taken from you at customs,

6

as will birds, or stuffed iguanas or parrots. It isn't uncommon for U.S. Customs agents to seize seashells, so those and all sea creatures are best left where you find them.

Both the U.S. and Mexican governments also have strict laws and guidelines about the import–export of antiquities. Check with customs beforehand if you plan to buy anything unusual or particularly valuable.

Although Cuban cigars are readily available, American visitors aren't allowed to bring them into the United States and will have to enjoy them while in Mexico. However, Mexico produces some fine cigars from tobacco grown in Veracruz. Mexican cigars without the correct Mexican seals on the individual cigars and on the box may be confiscated.

SHOPPING IN SPANISH

bakery: *panadería*

bookseller: *librería*

candy store: *dulcería*

florist: *florería*

grocery store: *abarrotes*

health-food store: *tienda naturista*

jewelry store: *joyería*

market: *mercado*

notions store: *mercería*

stationery store: *papelería*

tobacconist: *tabaquería*

toy store: *juguetería*

TIPS AND TRICKS

Better deals are often given to cash customers—even though credit cards are nearly always accepted—because stores must pay a commission to the credit-card companies. If you are paying in cash, it is perfectly reasonable to ask for a 5%–10% discount—though you shouldn't assume you'll be given one.

U.S. dollars are widely accepted in Los Cabos, although most shops pay a lower exchange rate than a bank (or ATM) or *casa de cambio* (money exchange).

Bargaining is common in markets and by beach vendors, who may ask as much as two or three times their bottom line. Occasionally an itinerant vendor will ask for the real value of the item, putting the energetic haggler into the awkward position of offering far too little. One vendor says he asks *norteamericanos* "for twice the asking price, since they always want to haggle." The trick is to know an item's true worth by comparison shopping. It's not necessary to bargain for already inexpensive trinkets like key chains or quartz-and-bead necklaces or bracelets.

SENDING STUFF HOME

Better stores and galleries offer shipping services for large or unwieldy items.

If you are an avid shopper, it won't hurt to pack a duffel bag for all your new treasures to check as luggage on your way home.

For more shipping info, ⇨ *see Travel Smart Los Cabos.*

SAN JOSÉ DEL CABO

Cabo San Lucas's sister city has a refined air, with many shops in old colonial buildings just a short walk from the town's *zócalo* (central plaza). Jewelry and art are great buys—this is where you'll find the best shopping for high-quality Mexican folk art. Many of the most worthwhile shops are clustered within a few of blocks around Plaza Mijares, where Boulevard Mijares and Avenida Zaragoza both end at the remodeled zócalo at the center of San José. Thursday nights from November through April are designated Art Nights, when galleries stay open until 9 serving drinks and snacks, with various performances, demonstrations, and dancing—it's a fun night out!

ART WALKS

Thursday art walks happen in downtown San José from November through June. Participating galleries and shops stay open until 9 pm and serve drinks and snacks, and many arrange for special events or openings. There is usually music on Plaza Mijares, and it's not uncommon for the streets to be full of people, locals and tourists alike. "Historic Art District" brochures are in most galleries and shops (⊕ www.artcabo.com).

ART GALLERIES

Amber Gallery & Fine Art Annex. Amber Gallery & Fine Art Annex is the store to visit if you're a fan of amber jewelry, sculptures, abstract art, and collector perfume bottles. ⊠ *Obregón 18 B* ☎ *624/105–2332* ⊕ *www.amberart.net* ✣ *1:A3.*

Arenas Gallery. Arenas Gallery displays fine jewelry, oil and acrylic paintings, and intricately painted, handmade pottery from Mata Ortiz, a small town in the state of Chihuahua that's famous for its Mesoamerican pottery revival. ⊠ *Obregón and Morelos* ☎ *624/142–4969* ✣ *1:B2.*

Casa Dahlia Fine Art Gallery. Casa Dahlia Fine Art Gallery features contemporary artists from Mexico and abroad, and invites visitors to linger in its beautifully renovated historic building with organic teas and coffee—some people even enjoy a cigar in the gallery's gardens. ⊠ *Morelos and Zaragoza* ☎ *624/132–2647, 503/922–3434 in U.S.* ⊕ *www.casadahlia.com* ✣ *1:B3.*

★ **Frank Arnold Gallery.** Frank Arnold Gallery has two big draws: arguably the best gallery space in town, in a great new building by local architect Alfredo Gomez, and Frank Arnold's dramatic, widely acclaimed contemporary paintings that have been compared to de Kooning, Gorky, and Hans Hofmann. ⊠ *1137 Calle Comonfort* ☎ *624/142–4422, 559/301–1148 in U.S.* ⊕ *www.frankarnoldart.com* ✣ *1:B2.*

Fodors Choice **Galería Corsica.** Galería Corsica is in a spectacularly dramatic space.
★ The gallery, which has three sister galleries in Puerto Vallarta, shows museum-quality fine art with an emphasis on paintings and large, impressive sculpture pieces. ⊠ *Obregón 15* ☎ *624/146–9177* ⊕ *www.galeriacorsica.com* ✣ *1:B2.*

6

SELF-GUIDED GALLERY WALK IN SAN JOSÉ

A good number of galleries are closed, or have greatly reduced operating hours, during the hottest months of the year, usually late June through September. If there is one gallery you are particularly interested in, it's worth calling ahead to check on hours.

The Thursday art walks start at 5 pm, with galleries open until 9 pm. Start your walk on Hidalgo and Obregón, and wander down Obregón through the six or so galleries scattered on the next two blocks. Turning left on to Guerrero, you'll want to stop in to see **Galería de Ida Victoria** and

Casa Don Pablo. Turn right out of the galleries and walk a block over to Comonfort, where you'll connect to Morelos in another block to find the galleries in **Casa Paulina** awaiting, and the **Frank Arnold Gallery** a half block farther up on Comonfort. If you're hungry at this point, **Voilà Bistro** in Plaza Paulina and **Baan Thai**, across the street from each other on Morelos at Comonfort, are both excellent. Finish up by heading back to the zócalo and wandering among the shops on Plaza Mijares—making sure not to miss **Galería Veryka** and **silvermoon**.

Galería de Ida Victoria. Galería de Ida Victoria has been designed with skylights and domes to show off the international art contained within its three floors, which includes paintings, sculpture, photography, and prints. ⊠ *Guerrero 1128* ☎ *624/142–5772* ⊕ *www.idavictoriaarts.com* ✛ *1:A3.*

★ **Galería Veryka.** Galería Veryka is one of the best folk art shops in the region, with gorgeous embroidered clothing, masks, wood carvings, jewelry, and hand-molded black and green pottery. Most of the goods are from Oaxaca. Check out the seasonal displays, especially the Day of the Dead altar. ⊠ *Plaza Mijares 418* ☎ *624/142–0575* ✛ *1:D3.*

Gallery Casa Don Pablo. Gallery Casa Don Pablo has a little bit of everything: original Mexican art, Talavera earthenware, wood carvings, fine silver, local historic photographs, and traditional works in forged steel. ⊠ *Guerrero 12, near Obregón* ☎ *624/142–2539* ✛ *1:A3.*

La Dolce Art Gallery. La Dolce Art Gallery, near San José's classic cathedral on the zócalo, specializes in modern painting styles. ⊠ *Hidalgo between Zaragoza and Obregón* ☎ *624/142–6621* ⊕ *www.alejandrinacalderoni. com* ✛ *1:C2.*

Fodor'sChoice
★ **Patricia Mendoza Gallery.** Explore works of art by Mexico's top contemporary artists such as Lucille Wong, Javier Guadarrama, Eric Perez, and Joao Rodriguez, among others. All of the artists represented here are known nationally and internationally in important collections and museums. ⊠ *Obregón at Hidalgo* ☎ *624/158-6497* ⊕ *ww. patriciamendoza-gallery.com* ✛ *1:C2.*

Fodor'sChoice
★ **silvermoon gallery.** Silvermoon gallery is remarkable in the Los Cabos region both for the assortment and the quality of art contained within its walls. Mexican folk art makes up most of the inventory here. Treasures include Carlos Albert's whimsical papier-mâché sculptures, Mata Ortiz pottery from the Quezada family, Huichol yarn "paintings," Alebrijes (colorful wooden animal sculptures) from Oaxaca, and fine

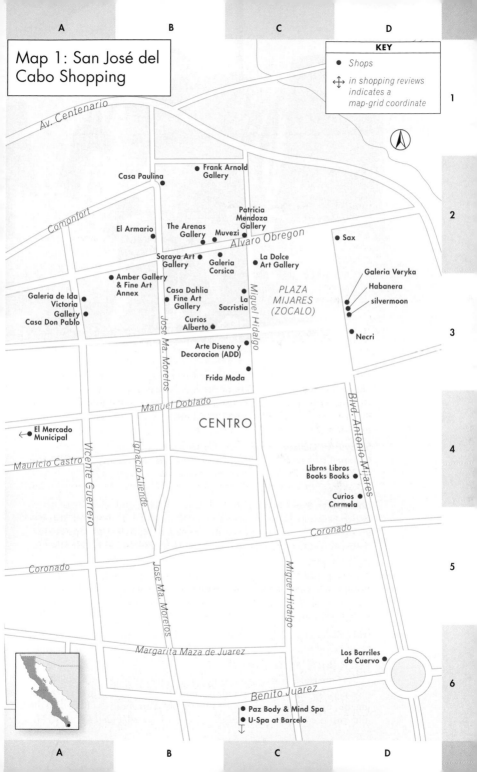

A shop in San José del Cabo displays its colorful handmade wares.

jewelry. Owner Armando Sanchez Icaza is gracious and knowledgeable; he knows volumes about the artists whose work he carries. His silversmiths can also make custom jewelry for you within a day or two. ⊠ *Plaza Mijares No. 10* ☎ *624/142–6077* ⊕ *silvermoongallerycabo. com* ⊹ *1:D3.*

Soraya Art Gallery. Soraya Art Gallery sells murals, faux finish, and trompe l'oeil art by local artists. ⊠ *Obregón and Morelos* ☎ *624/355–2819* ⊹ *1:B2.*

BOOKS

Libros Libros, Books Books. This bookstore stocks a good selection of newspapers, such as the *Wall Street Journal* and *USA Today,* and also has an extensive selection of English-language magazines, plus postcards, maps, and souvenirs. ⊠ *Blvd. Mijares 41* ☎ *624/142–4433* ⊹ *1:D4.*

CLOTHING

Curios Alberto. Curios Alberto carries beautiful embroidered dresses for young girls amid all sorts of other fun goodies, curios, knickknacks, and clothing items to pick up for folks at home. ⊠ *Zaragoza in front of Plaza Mijares* ⊹ *1:B3.*

Frida Moda. Frida Moda offers a range of mostly American sportswear, casual clothing, and jeans. ⊠ *Blvd. Mijares* ☎ *624/142–2870* ⊹ *1:C3.*

FOLK ART, AND CERAMICS

Curios Carmela. Curios Carmela displays an array of Mexican textiles, pottery, glassware, hammocks, and souvenirs that can be nearly overwhelming, but never fear: the prices are reasonable. You could easily find all the gifts you need right here. ⊠ *Blvd. Mijares 43* ☎ *624/142–1117* ⊹ *1:D4.*

El Armario. El Armario which calls itself "the cutest shop in town," offers a selection of Mexican folk art, ceramic pottery, candles, clay figurines, papier-mâché—plus fresh coffee out on the patio. ⊠ *Obregón and Morelos* ☎ *624/105–2989* ✥ *1:B2.*

★ **La Sacristia.** La Sacristia has a fine selection of Talavera pottery, traditional and contemporary Mexican jewelry, blown glass, and contemporary paintings. The glassware is incredible. ⊠ *Hidalgo near Obregón* ☎ *624/142–4007* ⊕ *www.lasacristiaart.com* ✥ *1:C3.*

Muvezi. Muvezi presents the unexpected here in Baja Sur: fine Shona sculptures from Zimbabwe in a variety of breathtaking stones. This gallery is the public face of an economic development project working to keep the ancient tradition of stone carving alive in Zimbabwe, and to provide desperately needed funds for health care at the grassroots level there. Don't worry about the weight of the stone: sculptures come in a variety of sizes and Muvezi will ship pieces to your home. Muvezi donates 20% of the revenues to help fight malaria throughout Africa. Buy a piece of art and affect positive change. ⊠ *Alvaro Obregón 15* ☎ *624/157–2428* ⊕ *www.muvezi.com* ✥ *1:C2.*

Necri. Necri carries Talavera ceramics, handicrafts, pottery, and pewter pieces and hot sauce made by the owner. ⊠ *Calle Alvaro Obregón #17, between Morelos & Hidalgo* ☎ *624/130–7500* ✥ *1:D3.*

HOME FURNISHINGS

Arte, Diseno y Decoracion (ADD). ADD is an interior-design shop that has hand-painted dishes from Guanajuato, carved wood furniture from Michoacán, fine Oaxacan embroidery, and an impressive selection of tempting housewares from all over Mexico. ⊠ *Zaragoza at Hidalgo* ☎ *624/142–3090* ✥ *1:C3.*

Casa Paulina. Casa Paulina is more than just an art gallery, it's a wealth of decorating ideas and items for the home that will hold your attention for hours. If you get hungry, Plaza Paulina is also home to the gourmet Voilá Bistro, which serves up creative Mexican fare. ⊠ *Plaza Paulina, Morelos and Comonfort* ☎ *624/142–5555* ⊕ *www. casapaulina.com* ✥ *1:B2.*

JEWELRY

Sax. Sax, owned by two talented sisters, is a great place to find exceptional, eclectic silver jewelry designs. The artists will create a design of your choice in 24 hours. Prices are very good here and there is another location in the Shoppes at Palmilla. ⊠ *Plaza Mijares 2* ☎ *624/142–6053* ⊕ *www.saxstyle.com* ✥ *1:D2.*

MARKETS

El Mercado Municipal. El Mercado Municipal is San José's traditional market area, where you can stock up on fresh meats and produce, or visit the market's **Viva Mexico** stand for clothes, belts, spices, jewelry, and other curios—all at excellent prices. ⊠ *Castro and Coronado, off Calle Doblado* ✥ *1:A4.*

6

SPAS

Paz Body and Mind Spa. Surrounded by natural stone walls, all of the treatment rooms at Cabo Azul's Paz Spa are named after semiprecious stones such as onyx, pearl, opal, lapis, jade, sapphire, and amber. Specialties include 50-minute massages to 210-minute complete experiences, as well as exfoliations, wraps, facials, manicure, and pedicure. A terrace suite can accommodate up to four treatments at one time for those looking for group relaxation. Eight other rooms round out the spa itself, and two double cabanas on the beach are available for those seeking the sound of the waves as backdrop to their treatment. Popular therapies include a Papaya Sugar Polish and Shea Butter Massage, as well as an Aloe Cooling Massage. An on-site salon is open Monday to Saturday from 9 to 5. ⊠ *Cabo Azul Resort, Paseo Malecón s/n Lote 11 Fonatur* ☎ *624/163–5100* ⊕ *www.caboazulresort.com* ☞ *Body treatments: $170–$250. Facials: $120–$190* ✛ *1:C6.*

U-Spa at Barcelo Los Cabos Palace. The spa's design was inspired by the contrast of the water and desert of Baja's landscape. Lounge by the communal pool, or duck into one of 19 treatment rooms for revitalizing massages, romantic packages, anti-aging facials, detoxifying body wraps, and deep-cleansing scrubs using local, natural ingredients. For those interested in a quick fix, manicures and pedicures are popular, and the on-site salon can help turn a bad-hair day into something grand. ⊠ *Barcelo Los Cabos Palace Deluxe, Paseo Malecon s/n Lote 5* ☎ *624/163–7730* ⊕ *www. barcelo.com* ☞ *Body treatments: $110–$280. Facials: $75–$240* ✛ *1:C6.*

SUNDRIES AND LIQUOR

Los Barriles de Cuervo. Los Barriles de Cuervo specializes in rare tequilas, and their selection is complemented by a good collection of Cuban cigars. ⊠ *Blvd. Mijares and Juárez* ☎ *624/142–5322* ✛ *1:D6.*

THE CORRIDOR

There are shopping options along the Corridor—the stretch of land between San José del Cabo to the east and Cabo San Lucas to the west—but the shops cater more to resort guests and American expats than travelers looking to experience Los Cabos. Unless you are intent on something specific at one of the shops on the Corridor, you'll have much more fun shopping in San José del Cabo, Cabo San Lucas, or Todos Santos.

HOME FURNISHINGS

★ **Artesanos.** Artesanos is where home owners and restaurateurs go from throughout the area to shop for Mexican furnishings, dishes, and glassware, along with colorful handicrafts and ornaments. ⊠ *Hwy. 1, Km 2.5* ☎ *624/143–3850.*

Villa Valentina. Villa Valentina is the most notable shop on the Corridor, with impressive and unique home furnishings, from rustic antiques to custom-made pieces that will delight any home decor enthusiast. ⊠ *Hwy. 1, Km 31.5* ☎ *624/142–6612* ⊕ *www.vvalentina.com.*

MALL

Las Tiendas de Palmilla. Las Tiendas de Palmilla is across from the posh Palmilla Resort. There are a smattering of shops and galleries, a couple of restaurants, a coffee shop, a nice terrace with a peaceful fountain, and a view of the Palmilla development with the tranquil, turquoise Sea of Cortez beyond. **Antigua de México** is a branch of the famous Tlaquepaque store, and shoppers will discover distinctive furniture and bedding supplies, and many Mexican-flavor interior-decorating items. **Pez Gordo Art Gallery** is artist Dana Leib's second location, and offers her pieces, as well as those by other artists. You'll find beautifully designed silver tableware pieces from Taxco at **Prestige Designs.** Tiki Lounge is one of the Tommy Bahama "lifestyle" boutiques for men only, with silk and other natural-fiber clothing in relaxed styles. Stop in Casa Vieja for beautiful women's apparel by Mexican designers, including Pineda-Covalin—you'll find a wide range of styles in fibers such as cotton, silk, linen, and even cactus. If you need to fuel up during your time here, there's an outpost of popular Nick-San, and Mexican-fusion restaurant, Manuel's. ✉ *Hwy. 1, Km 27.5* ☏ *624/144–6999* ⊕ *www. lastiendasdepalmilla.com.*

SPAS

★ **One&Only Palmilla Spa.** Treatment villas are tucked behind white stucco walls, ensuring privacy. Therapists lead you through a locked gate into peaceful palm-filled gardens with a bubbling hot tub and a daybed covered with plump pillows. There are 13 private treatment villas, for either one or two people; 6 are equipped with an outdoor shower, bathtub, and thatched-roof daybed, for relaxing in between or after treatments. There's a blend of Mexican and Asian, and other global accents; treatments use cactus, lime, and a variety of Mexican spices. Each treatment begins with a Floral Footbath—a symbolic Balinese ritual, which represents a cleansing of life's tensions to prepare you for total relaxation. One signature treatment is the Aztec Aromatic Ritual, a spicy body wrap with an ancient recipe of clove, ginger, and cinnamon.

Body Treatments: *Massage*: Aromatherapy, Balinese, chocolate synergy, deep-tissue, essential oil, hot stone, pregnancy, reflexology, sports, Swedish, Thai. *Exfoliation*: Body polish, dry brush, salt glow. *Wraps/baths*: Floral bath, herbal wrap, milk bath. *Other*: Anticellulite, colon therapy, pools, sauna, steam room.

Beauty Treatments: Anti-aging, peels, facials, hairstyling, scalp conditioning, makeup, manicure, pedicure, waxing.

✉ *Hwy. 1, Km. 27.5* ☏ *624/146–7000* ⊕ *palmilla.oneandonlyresorts. com/* ↪ *Body treatments: $250–$450. Facials: $175–$250. Mani/Pedi: $55–$150. Parking: Valet (free).*

Secrets Marquis Los Cabos Spa. You'll enjoy the open-air hot tubs that face the Cape's blue sky and overlook the Sea of Cortez. Lounge chairs draped with thick towels tempt you to linger by the hot tubs, but floors inlaid with stones will lead you to the spa's treatment rooms and the amazing experiences within. Noteworthy is the Quetzalcoatl Oxygenating Experience: a eucalyptus foot bath, marine-salt exfoliation, herbal

6

purification bath, and light massage with cucumber-milk lotion. A hallway connects the spa with the Marquis's fitness center, with its sky-high ceiling and wall-to-wall windows looking out to the pool, sand, and sea.

Body Treatments: *Massage*: Aromatherapy, ayurvedic, deep-tissue, essential oil, hot stone, pregnancy, reflexology, shiatsu, sports, Thai. *Exfoliation*: Salt glow. *Wraps/baths*: Herbal bath, mud wrap, thalassotherapy. *Other*: Ayurvedic treaments, hot tub, sauna, steam room.

Beauty Treatments: Facials, mani/pedi, waxing.

✉ *Secrets Marquis Los Cabos Resort, Hwy. 1, Km 21.5* ☎ *624/144–0906* ⊕ *www.secretsresorts.com/marquis* ☞ *Body treatments: $35–$189. Facials: $85–$220. Mani/Pedi: $39–$79. Waxing: $19–$79. Parking: Valet (free).*

SOMMA Wine Spa. This concept spa uses grapes from the up-and-coming Valle de Guadalupe wine region just outside of Ensenada. It's an unusual experience blended with classical treatments, focusing on the calming, cosmetic, and antioxidant properties of grapes and wine, or vinotherapy.

SOMMA is the only spa of its kind in Mexico, with only six others throughout the world. It towers high above the Sea of Cortez with 15 treatment rooms, both indoor and open-air, and offers more than 30 facial and body treatments from a Champagne Mud Wrap to a Le Vine Massage.

Body Treatments: *Massage*: Classic, sports, aromatherapy, hot stone, relaxing, Chardonnay foot, Swedish. *Exfoliation*: Salt body scrub. *Wraps/baths*: Mud wrap, chocolate wrap, Chardonnay wrap, clay wrap, honey and fruit wrap, seaweed wrap, green coffee wrap, water lily wrap. *Other*: Facials, cellulite firming.

Beauty Treatments: Hair/scalp conditioning, hairstyling, mani/pedi, waxing.

✉ *Fiesta Americana Grand Resort, Hwy. 1, Km. 10.3, Cabo del Sol* ☎ *624/145–6200* ⊕ *www.fiestamericanagrand.com/mx-los-cabos/hotel-grand-los-cabos* ☞ *Body treatments: $100–$250. Facials: $140–$290. Mani/Pedi: $40–$60. Parking: Valet and self-parking.*

Fodor's Choice **The Spa at Esperanza.** Luxury soars to even greater heights at this exclu-
★ sive 17-acre resort between Cabo San Lucas and San José del Cabo. At check-in you're presented with an *agua fresca*, a healthy drink made with papaya or mango, or other fruits and herbs. Before your treatment, linger in the grotto, enjoying the *Pasaje de Agua* (water passage) therapy, which includes steam caves and a waterfall. Treatments incorporate local ingredients, tropical fruits, and ocean-based products. Look for such pampering as the papaya-mango body polish, the grated-coconut-and-lime exfoliation, and the Corona beer facial. Two free yoga classes are held at 9 and 10:15 each morning.

Body Treatments: *Massage*: Agua, hot stone, essential oil, Thai (stroke techniques vary). *Exfoliation*: Body polish, salt glow. *Wraps/bath*: Aloe wrap, floral bath, herbal bath, mud bath, thalassotherapy. *Other*: Outdoor shower, steam room, warm soaking pool, waterfall rinse.

Beauty Treatments: Facials, hair/scalp conditioning, manicure, pedicure, peels.

Vibrant, hand-painted masks make for memorable souvenirs and gifts.

✉ *Esperanza Resort, Hwy. 1, Km 7* ☎ *624/145–6406* ⊕ *www. esperanzaresort.com* ☞ *Body treatments: $160–$335. Facials: $185– $295. Mani/Pedi: $45–$200. Parking: Valet (free).*

Fodor's Choice **The Spa at Las Ventanas al Paraíso.** The resort's bi-level spa was renovated
★ in 2011 to double its size. It has both indoor and outdoor facilities. It's known for its innovative treatments—skin resurfacing facials, nopal (cactus) anticellulite and detox wrap, crystal healing massages, and raindrop therapy.

Some of the eight treatment rooms have private patios, and the two couples' suites come with a private butler. Healing rituals like the Holistic Twilight Ceremony are performed daily. Salt glows and massages are available in a pavilion by the sea; and body wraps and massages are also performed on the hotel's 55-foot yacht.

Body Treatments: *Massage:* Aromatherapy, ayurvedic, deep-tissue, hot stone, reflexology, Reiki, shiatsu, shirodhara, sports, Swedish, watsu. *Exfoliation:* Body polish, dry brush, loofah scrub, salt glow. *Wraps/baths:* Herbal wrap, milk bath, mud wrap, cactus wrap. *Other:* Acupuncture, anticellulite, crystal therapy, hydrotherapy pool, sauna, steam room.

Beauty Treatments: Facials, hairstyling, mani/pedi, waxing.

✉ *Las Ventanas al Paraíso Resort, Hwy. 1, Km. 19.5* ☎ *624/144–0300* ⊕ *www.lasventanas.com* ☞ *Body Treatments: $145–$300. Facials: $180–$275. Mani/Pedi: $45–$145. Parking: Valet (free).*

SUNDRIES

La Europea. La Europea carries a wide selection of imported wines and deli products. ⊠ *Hwy. 1, Km 6.7* ☎ *624/145–8755.*

Trader Dick's. Trader Dick's, located along the Costa Azul surf coast near the popular Zipper's Restaurant, is a favorite with Americans seeking newspapers from home, along with familiar deli meats and cheeses. ⊠ *Hwy. 1, Km 29.5* ☎ *624/142–2828.*

CABO SAN LUCAS

Cabo San Lucas has the widest variety of shopping options in Los Cabos area, with everything from intriguing Mexican folk art and designer clothing to beer holsters and touristy T-shirts. Bargains on typical Mexican tourist items can be found in the dozens of shops between Boulevard Paseo de la Marina and Avenida Lazaro Cárdenas.

Get hungry when you're shopping? Worth trying in this zone are the very inexpensive taco and juice stands tucked into the mini–flea markets that stretch between streets.

Many of the shops in malls like Puerto Paraiso are typical of those you'd find in any mall in the United States—with prices to match. All over the downtown and marina areas, however, are great shops and galleries with unique and compelling items.

ART GALLERIES

Fodor's Choice ★ **Arte de Origen.** Arte de Origen is a standout among the shops on the increasingly hip Madero Street. Pan-American cultural traditions inform the original decorative art in this richly colored open space. Painting, ceramics, and inventive, painting-like collages are applied to a wide variety of objects like boxes, tables, and mirror frames. Small sculptures, jewelry, and some textiles are also part of a collection of art that is clearly meant to be part of your living space. Another location can be found at the Puerto Paraíso Mall. ⊠ *Madero between Guererro and Blvd. Marina* ☎ *624/105–1965* ⊕ *www.artedeorigen.com* ✢ *2:B4.*

Galería La Grande. Galería La Grande claims to be "the largest gallery in Baja California" and we won't challenge them. There's truly a huge selection of fine Mexican art—more than 1,500 pieces—and if something catches your eye and you'd like to make a purchase, they'll pack it up and ship it home for you. ⊠ *Plaza Nautica* ☎ *624/143–1415* ⊕ *www. galerialagrande.com* ✢ *2:B4.*

★ **Golden Cactus Gallery.** The Golden Cactus Gallery, run by painter Celyne Poupart, has been showcasing local artists' work (paintings, lithographs, and many colorful gifts) since 1997. Bill Clinton has been a customer. ⊠ *Hidalgo and Zapata* ☎ *624/147–5287, 619/272–3737 from U.S.* ⊕ *www.goldencactusgallery.com* ✢ *2:B4.*

Fodor's Choice ★ **Sergio Bustamante.** The talented artist from Guadalajara now has a shop in the Puerto Paraíso Mall. Bustamante's works initially focused on painting and papier-mâché. His recent sculptures in wood and bronze, many reflecting animal themes, can be purchased at this wonderful gallery and store. Ceramic sculptures and an extensive line of exquisite

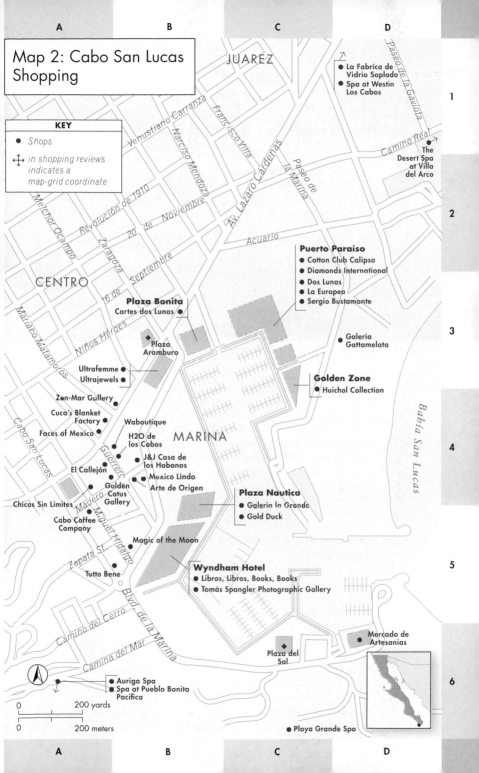

Map 2: Cabo San Lucas Shopping

KEY

● *Shops*

✛ *in shopping reviews indicates a map-grid coordinate*

JUAREZ

Venustiano Carranza
Narciso Mendoza
Francisco Villa
Paseo de la Marina
Av. Lázaro Cárdenas
Paseo de la Gaviota
Camino Real

● La Fábrica de Vidrio Soplado
● Spa at Westin Los Cabos

The Desert Spa at Villa del Arco

Melchor Ocampo
Revolución de 1910
Zaragoza
20 de Noviembre
16 de Septiembre
Acuario

CENTRO

Mariano Matamoros
Niños Héroes

Puerto Paraíso
● Cotton Club Calipso
● Diamonds International
● Dos Lunas
● La Europea
● Sergio Bustamante

Plaza Bonita
Cartes dos Lunas ●

◆ Plaza Aramburo

● Galería Gattamelata

Ultrafemme ●
Ultrajewels ●

Golden Zone
● Huichol Collection

Zen-Mar Gallery ●
Cuca's Blanket Factory ●
Faces of Mexico ●

Cabo San Lucas

Waboutique ●
H2O de los Cabos ●

MARINA

Guerrero
J&J Casa de los Habanos ●
El Callejón ●
Mexico Lindo ●
Arte de Origen ●
Madero
Golden Catus Gallery ●

Plaza Náutica
● Galería la Grande
● Gold Duck

Chicas Sin Limites ●
Miguel Hidalgo
Cabo Coffee Company ●

Magic of the Moon ●

Zapata St.
Tutto Bene ●

Wyndham Hotel
● Libros, Libros, Books, Books
● Tomás Spangler Photographic Gallery

Blvd. de la Marina

Camino del Cerro
Camino del Mar

Bahía San Lucas

● Mercado de Artesanías

◆ Plaza del Sol

● Auriga Spa
● Spa at Pueblo Bonita Pacífica

0 ___ 200 yards
0 ___ 200 meters

● Playa Grande Spa

The inviting Plaza Bonita Shopping Mall in Cabo San Lucas.

jewelry in bronze, gold, and silver, many set with precious and semiprecious stones, are found here as well. Bustamante has recently expanded to handbags and shoes, both of which are also on sale here. Don't balk at the price tags: each piece belongs to a limited edition and is created by hand. ⊠ *Puerto Paraíso Mall* ☎ *866/300–8030 In U.S.* ⊕ *www.sergiobustamante.com.mx* ✛ *2:C3.*

Tomás Spangler Photographic Gallery. Tomás Spangler Photographic Gallery is owned by an accomplished art photographer who has accumulated a number of stunning images from his travels throughout Mexico and the world; several are matted and mounted and on display at the Wyndham Hotel, and information about upcoming exhibitions can be obtained here, as well. ⊠ *Wyndham Hotel Lobby* ☎ *831/480–4411 from U.S.* ⊕ *www.fotomas.com* ✛ *2:B5.*

BOOKS

Libros Libros, Books Books. Libros Libros, Books Books carries a vast number of Spanish- and English-language newspapers, novels, magazines, plus fun souvenirs. ⊠ *Blvd. Marina at Plaza de la Danza* ☎ *624/143–3173* ✛ *2:B5.*

CLOTHING

Chicas Sin Limites. Chicas Sin Limites translates to "girls without limits," which describes the apparel services here. Need your own custom-designed bathing suit—and fast? Select the fabric and cut, and your suit will be ready in 24 hours. ⊠ *Hidalgo at Plaza Amelia* ☎ *624/143–1500* ✛ *2:A4.*

Cotton Club-Calipso. "Cotton" might be in the name, but the Cotton Club stocks women's resort wear made from all sorts of natural fibers, crafted by both Mexican and international designers. The adjacent Calipso sells bathing suits and resort wear. ⊠ *Puerto Paraíso, Av. Cárdenas* ☎ *624/105–1168* ✛ *2:C3.*

Dos Lunas. Dos Lunas is full of trendy, colorful sportswear and straw hats, as well as a large selection of handcrafted accessories and gifts. ⊠ *Plaza Bonita, Blvd. Marina* ☎ *624/143–1969* ⊕ *www.cabowebcreators.com/ doslunas.* ✛ *2:C3*

H2O de los Cabos. H2O de los Cabos offers bathing suits ranging from skimpy thongs to modest one-piece suits, all with a bit of Mexican flair. ⊠ *Madero and Guerrero* ☎ *624/143–1219* ✛ *2:B4.*

Magic of the Moon. Magic of the Moon is a favorite among locals and Cabo regulars, featuring clothing designed by Pepita Nelson, the owner. If you can't find anything that fits you or your style, she will design an outfit for you and finish it in three days. Also check out the handmade ceramic jewelry, beaded bustiers, and colorful bathing suits. ⊠ *Hidalgo off Blvd. Marina* ☎ *624/144–6133* ⊕ *www.pepitadesigns.com* ✛ *2:B5.*

FOLK ART

Faces of Mexico. Faces of Mexico is one of the oldest folk-art shops in the area; it has a selection of masks from Oaxaca and Guerrero, though the owner's wonderful collection of handmade masks at the back of the tiny shop may be the biggest draw of all. ⊠ *Av. Cárdenas, beside Mar de Cortéz hotel* ☎ *624/143–2634* ✛ *2:A4.*

Huichol Collection. Huichol Collection carries the Huichol Indian tribe's beautiful beaded crafts, as well as posters, postcards, and T-shirts in the vibrant colors and patterns typical of this ancient culture. ⊠ *Blvd. Marina and Ocampo* ☎ *624/143–4055* ✛ *2:C3.*

Mercado de Artesanías. Mercado de Artesanías is at the far western end of Marina San Lucas, where the fishing boats drop anchor to weigh and photograph the few fish still brought in. This crafts market sells pottery, blankets, jewelry, and Mexican sombreros. It's a great place to find souvenirs for the folks at home. ⊠ *South end of Blvd. Marina* ✛ *2:D6.*

Zen-Mar Gallery. Zen-Mar Gallery is a friendly place that carries hundreds of masks, Day of the Dead figures, rugs, glassware, bark-paper wall hangings from Puebla, and all sorts of other fun and captivating items. This is one of Cabo's more comprehensive folk-art shops. ⊠ *Cárdenas between Matamoros and Ocampo* ☎ *624/143–0661* ⊕ *www.zen-mar.com.mx* ✛ *2:B4.*

FOOD

★ **Cabo Coffee Company.** Cabo Coffee Company sends forth the aroma of roasting coffee beans and lures java junkies to its shop. The organic green coffee beans are flown fresh from Oaxaca, where they are roasted and bagged for sale. The store sells a number of Starbucks-like flavored coffee drinks, chai tea, as well as ice cream. ⊠ *Madero and Hidalgo* ☎ *624/105–1130* ⊕ *cabocoffee.com* ✛ *2:A5.*

La Europea. La Europea has a great deli and selection of wines, champagne, beers, and nibblies for the home, fiesta, or even picnic with box lunches for those on the go. ⊠ *Puerto Paraíso Mall, near Ruth Chris Steakhouse* ☎ *624/145–8755* ⊕ *laeuropea.com.mx* ✛ *2:C3.*

Continued on page 154

THE ART OF THE HUICHOL

Updated by
Georgia de Katona

The intricately woven and beaded designs of the Huichols' art are as vibrant and fascinating as the traditions of its people, best known as the "Peyote People" for their traditional and ceremonial use of the hallucinogenic drug. Peyote-inspired visions are thought to be messages from God and are reflected in the art.

Like the Lacandon Maya, the Huichol resisted assimilation by Spanish invaders, fleeing to inhospitable mountains and remote valleys. There they retained their pantheistic religion in which shamans lead the community in spiritual matters and the use of peyote facilitates communication directly with God.

Roads didn't reach larger Huichol communities until the mid-20th century, bringing electricity and other modern distractions. The collision with the outside world has had pros and cons, but art lovers have only benefited from their increased access to intricately patterned woven and beaded goods. Today the traditional souls that remain on the land—a significant population of perhaps 6,000 to 8,000—still create votive bowls, prayer arrows, jewelry, and bags, and sell them to finance elaborate religious ceremonies. The pieces go for as little as $5 or as much as $5,000, depending on the skill and fame of the artist and quality of materials.

(left) Huichol yarn painting, National Museum of Anthropology, (top) Huichol art, Puerto Vallarta

UNDERSTANDING THE HUICHOL

When Spanish conquistadors arrived in the early 16th century, the Huichol, unwilling to work as slaves on the haciendas of the Spanish or to adopt their religion, fled to the Sierra Madre. They lived there, disconnected from society, for nearly 500 years. Beginning in the1970s, roads and electricity made their way to tiny Huichol towns. Today, about half of the population of perhaps 12,000 continues to live in ancestral villages and *rancheritas* (tiny individual farms).

THE POWER OF PRAYER
They believe that without their prayers and offerings the sun wouldn't rise, the earth would cease spinning. It is hard, then, for them to reconcile their poverty with the relative easy living of "free-riders" (Huichol term for non-spiritual freeloaders) who enjoy fine cars and expensive houses thanks to the Huichols efforts to sustain the planet. But rather than hold our reckless materialism against us, the Huichol add us to their prayers.

THE PEYOTE PEOPLE
Visions inspired by the hallucinogenic peyote plant are considered by the Huichol to be messages from God and to help in solving personal and commu-

Huichol artisans and beadwork

nal problems. Indirectly, they provide inspiration for their almost psychedelic art. Just a generation or two ago, annual peyote-gathering pilgrimages were done on foot. Today the journey is still a man's chief obligation, but they now drive to the holy site at Wiricuta, in San Luis Potosi State. Peyote collected is used by the entire community—men, women, and children—throughout the year.

SHAMANISM
A Huichol man has a lifelong calling as a shaman. There are two shamanic paths: the path of the wolf, which is more aggressive, demanding, and powerful (wolf shamans profess the ability to morph into wolves); and the path of the deer, which is playful—even clownish—and less inclined to prove his power. A shaman chooses his own path.

Huichol bird, Jalisco

HOW TO READ THE SYMBOLS

Spiders that come out at dawn are thought to welcome the rising sun.

The deer is the animal manifestation of the god Kahumari, who intercedes in heaven on earthlings' behalf.

Anything with horns or antlers symbolizes communion and oneness with God.

Yarn painting

■ The trilogy of corn, peyote, and deer represents three aspects of God. According to Huichol mythology, peyote sprang up in the footprints of the deer. Depicted like stylized flowers, peyote represents communication with God. Corn, the Huichol's staple

Corn symbol

food, symbolizes health and prosperity. An image drawn inside the root ball depicts the essence of God within it.

■ The double-headed eagle is the emblem of the omnipresent sky god.

Peyote

■ A nierika is a portal between the spirit world and our own. Often in the form of a yarn painting, a nierika can be round or square.

■ Salamanders and turtles are associated with rain; the former provoke the clouds. Turtles maintain underground springs and purify water.

■ A scorpion is the soldier of the sun.

Scorpion

■ The Huichol depict raindrops as tiny snakes; in yarn paintings they descend to enrich the fields.

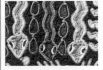

Snakes

Jose Beníctez Sánchez, (1938—) may be the elder statesman of yarn painters and has shown in Japan, Spain, the U.S., and at the Museum of Modern Art in Mexico City. His paintings sell for upward of $3,000 a piece.

6

IN FOCUS THE ART OF THE HUICHOL

TRADITION TRANSFORMED

The art of the Huichol was, for centuries, made from undyed wool, shells, stones, and other natural materials. It was not until the 1970s that the Huichol began incorporating bright, zingy colors, without sacrificing the intricate patterns and symbols used for centuries. The result is strenuously colorful, yet dignified.

YARN PAINTINGS
Dramatic and vivid yarn paintings are highly symbolic, stylized visions of life.

MASKS AND ANIMAL STATUETTES
Bead-covered wooden or ceramic masks and animal statuettes are other adaptations made for outsiders.

PRAYER ARROWS
Made for every ceremony, prayer arrows send petitions winging to God.

VOTIVE BOWLS
Ceremonious votive bowls, made from gourds, are decorated with bright, stylized beadwork.

WOVEN SHOULDER BAGS
Carried by men, the bags are decorated with traditional Huichol icons.

For years, Huichol men as well as women wore BEADED BRACELETS; today earrings and necklaces are also made.

Diamond-shape GOD'S EYES of sticks and yarn protect children from harm.

SMART SHOPPING TIPS

BEADED ITEMS: The smaller the beads, the more delicate and expensive the piece. Beads with larger holes are fine for stringed work, but if used in bowls and statuettes cheapen the piece.

Items made with iridescent beads from Japan are the priciest. Look for good-quality glass beads, definition, symmetry, and artful use of color.

Beads should fit together tightly in straight lines, with no gaps.

Bead-covered
a ram figurine

YARN PAINTINGS: Symmetry is not necessary, although there should be an overall sense of unity. Thinner thread results in finer, more costly work. Look for tightness, with no visible gaps or broken threads. Paintings should have a stamp of authenticity on the back, including artist's name and tribal affiliation.

PRAYER ARROWS: Collectors and purists should look for the traditionally made arrows of brazilwood inserted into a bamboo shaft. The most interesting ones contain embroidery work, or tiny carved icons, or are painted with copal symbols indicative of their original, intended purpose, for example protecting a child or ensuring a successful corn crop.

WHERE TO SHOP

Huichol Ethnic Art Store (✉ *Along Marina Cabo San Lucas, In the Golden Zone in Marina Fiesta Shops 23410.* ☎ *624/143–4055)* is a tiny little store that carries a variety of art forms from the Huichol people. If you're lucky they'll have some of the intricately woven bags worn by the men of the tribe; colorful and tightly woven these bags will last for decades even if you carry them everyday.

Kauyumari (✉ *Guerrero near Madero 23410.* ☎ *no phone)* is an informal co-op, operated by Huichol people, so tribal members take turns running the shop. You'll find all sorts of Huichol pieces

here, from the familiar carved wood animals covered in colorful beads and designs, to the intricately beaded earrings and necklaces with flowers and hummingbirds and butterflies.

Quality and selection range widely in here, but you know the money is going straight into the pockets of the producers, and it's a fun cultural experience.

The person minding the store might speak almost no Spanish or might have a working knowledge of English as well as Spanish. Regardless, leave any notion of rushing through at the door and enjoy the chance to learn

something about these amazing people.

Silvermoon gallery (✉ *Blvd. Mijares No. 10, 23400* ☎ *624/142–6077* ⊕ http://silvermoongallery-cabo.com) is where you'll find museum quality Huichol work, including the magnificent yarn paintings by Mexican Master Juan Silva. Señor Silva manages to create contemporary-feeling Huichol designs that are still deeply rooted in traditional imagery.

Gallery owner Armando Sanchez Icaza is a wealth of information about the Huichol art he carries.

CLOSE UP

People in Glass Houses

A beautiful glass mosaic over the entrance to **Fábrica de Vidrio Soplado** (Blown-Glass Factory) welcomes Los Cabos' most famous artisans every day. Founded in 1988 by engineer Sebastian Romo, the factory uses a glassmaking process close to the one first developed in western Asia 4,000 years ago, later refined into glass-blowing during the Roman empire. At the factory, 35 artisans produce more than 450 pieces a day from hundreds of pounds of locally recycled glass. Visitors watch while crushed recycled glass is liquefied in gas-fired ovens and, seconds later, transformed into exquisite figures. Secrets for making the thick glassware's deep blues, greens, and reds—the result of special mixtures of metals and gold—are passed from generation to generation. You are sometimes invited to make your own glassware by blowing through a hollow rod to shape a glob of molten glass at the end. The results are usually not impressive, but it's good fun nonetheless. ✉ *Lazaro Cardenas s/n Edificio Posada ✛ Drive toward San José on Av. Cárdenas, which turns into Hwy. 1; the fábrica is 2 blocks northwest of Hwy. 1, near the bypass road to Todos Santos.* ☎ *624/143–0255* ⊕ *www.glassfactory. com.mx ✛ 2:D1.*

Tutto Bene. Locals appreciate the selection of imported wines, cheeses, pâtés, and other gourmet delicacies, including organic foodstuffs, at Tutto Bene. ✉ *Plaza Nautica, at Camino del Cerro* ☎ *624/144–3300* ✛ *2:B5.*

GIFTS

Gold Duck. Gold Duck sells leather products, including handbags, belts, and wallets. ✉ *Plaza Nautica, Blvd. Marina* ☎ *624/143–2335* ✛ *2:B4.*

Mama Eli's. Mama Eli's is a three-story gallery with fine furnishings, ceramics, appliquéd clothing, and children's toys. ✉ *Av. Cabo San Lucas* ☎ *624/143–1616.*

Waboutique. Waboutique is the store associated with the funky Cabo Wabo bar. It sells memorabilia, excellent tequila, and souvenirs such as baseball hats, shot glasses, and mugs with the Cabo Wabo logo. Small bottles of tequila start at $18. ✉ *Calle Guerrero between Madero and Lazaro Cárdenas* ☎ *624/163–7400* ⊕ *www.cabowabo.com ✛ 2:B4.*

HOME FURNISHINGS

Cartes dos Lunas. Cartes dos Lunas has hand-painted pottery and tableware, pewter frames, handblown glass, and carved furniture. ✉ *Plaza Bonita, Blvd. Marina* ☎ *624/143–1770* ✛ *2:C3.*

★ **El Callejón.** El Callejón is known for the gorgeous Mexican furniture, lamps, dishes, home decor, tableware, lamps, accessories, and pottery it sells. ✉ *Miguel Hidalgo 2518 at Matamoros* ☎ *624/143–3188* ✛ *2:A4.*

★ **Galería Gattamelata.** Galería Gattamelata can be reached by walking around the marina to the quiet street east of Puerto Paraiso; the specialties here are Mexican colonial furniture and furnishings. This is a shop for antique furniture collectors, especially. The prices are commensurate to most dealers' fees. ✉ *Calle Gómez Farias, road to Hotel Hacienda* ☎ *624/143–1166* ✛ *2:D3.*

JEWELRY

Diamonds International. Diamonds International sells impressive diamonds, designer jewelry, and luxury timepieces, and has certified master jewelers on staff. ✉ *Corner of Vicente Guerrero* ☎ *624/143-3954* ⊕ *www.diamondsinternational. com* ✛ *2:C3.*

Mexico Lindo. Mexico Lindo has more than a dozen years of experience custom-designing sterling and 14k- and 18k-gold jewelry. Watch their craftsmen work at the store now located in the updated Puerto Paraíso Mall, which also sells a fair amount of Mexican artwork from around the country. ✉ *Puerto Paraíso Mall* ☎ *624/144-3868* ⊕ *www.mexicolindojewerlyloscabos. com* ✛ *2:B4.*

Ultrajewels. Ultrajewels offers all the top names in jewelry—Rolex, Cartier, Tiffany & Co. Mikimoto, TAG Heuer, Omega, Mont Blanc—at affordable prices. ✉ *Blvd. Marina and Luxury Av.* ☎ *624/163-4280* ⊕ *www.ultrajewels.com* ✛ *2:B3.*

LINENS

Cuca's Blanket Factory. Cuca's Blanket Factory displays many serapes and cotton blankets with which you can design your own and have it ready the next day. ✉ *Av. Cárdenas and Matamoros* ☎ *624/143-1913* ✛ *2:B4.*

MALLS

Golden Zone Shopping Center. Golden Zone Shopping Center is directly adjacent to Puerto Paraíso and is part of the Marina Fiesta Resort. Here you'll find the Tequila Museum, a Huichol Souvenir Shop, the All in One Aqua Market, and Presto Fast and Casual Cuisine, which offers pizzas, wraps, and pastas. ✉ *Marina San Lucas* ✛ *2:C3.*

Plaza Aramburo. Plaza Aramburo is a primarily service-oriented shopping area with a pharmacy, bank, dry cleaner, and grocery store. But it also has clothing and swimwear shops and a nice but small Internet café and inexpensive "phone home" service. ✉ *Av. Cárdenas and Zaragoza* ✛ *2:B3.*

Plaza Bonita. Plaza Bonita is a pleasant place to stroll; it's located at the western edge of the marina and has restaurants and bars catering to the cruise-ship crowd, with shops ranging from leather to clothing to local artwork and souvenirs. ✉ *Blvd. Marina and Av. Cárdenas* ✛ *2:B3.*

Plaza del Mar. Plaza del Mar, across from the Plaza Bonita Mall, sells T-shirts, tank tops, sweatshirts, and more, at its souvenir boutiques. ✉ *Av. Cárdenas.*

Plaza del Sol. Plaza del Sol Center is an open-air market with vendors selling local souvenirs like sarongs, sombreros, bathing suit cover-ups, and beaded necklaces. ✉ *Blvd. Marina* ✛ *2:C6.*

DUTY-FREE DELIGHT

Ultrafemme is the quintessential duty-free shop offering prices that can be up to 30% off designer cosmetic and perfume lines, and name-brand selection of fine jewelry and watches (Rolex, Cartier, and Omega). ✉ *Blvd. Marina at Plaza Dorada* ☎ *624/145-6090* ⊕ *www.ultrafemme.com.mx* ✛ *2:B3.*

6

Plaza Nautica. This mini-mall borders the Cabo San Lucas Marina. It's where you can find Gold Duck, Golf Pro Shop, and the Cabo Sports Center as well as other resort wear, jewelry, and furniture. ⊠ *Blvd. Marina* ✛ *2:C5.*

Puerto Paraíso. As Los Cabos continues on its upscale trajectory, it's safe to declare that this region has arrived and the shopping here has gone palatial. There is no better, or more apt, way to describe Puerto Paraíso, the city's thriving, air-conditioned, three-story marble- and glass-enclosed mall. With well more than 100 stores, boutiques, restaurants, galleries, and services, it's quickly becoming the social center of San Lucas. Paraíso offers a dizzying selection, from "A" as in **Arte de Origen,** an upscale shop selling art and local handicrafts, to "Z" as in the **Zingara Swimwear** shop. You can have a steak at **Ruth's Chris Steak House;** custom-design your own bikini; check your email at an Internet café; shop for beautiful art glass; or rent (or even buy) a Harley-Davidson motorcycle—almost anything is possible in this shopper's paradise. **Sergio Bustamante,** an acclaimed silversmith and sculptor, has recently opened a store here, and clothing shops include **Cotton Club, Tommy Bahama, Hugo Boss,** and **Nike.** Beachwear boutiques such as **Allegra, Azul, Blu Lagoon, Pacific Blue, Tropica Calipso,** and **Nautica** fulfill your beach-going needs. A 10-screen movie-theater complex provides cinematic respite, and, at the time of this writing, plans for a tennis court, outdoor park for kids, and a new food court were in the works. ⊠ *Av. Cárdenas, Marina San Lucas* ⊕ *www.puertoparaiso.com* ✛ *2:C3.*

SPAS

Auriga Spa. This spa, named for a constellation in the northern hemisphere, has a distinctive approach to wellness and beauty based on the cycles of the moon, each of which is said to impact the body in specific ways. Auriga's four signature treatments represent the varying energies of the lunar phases to align you with the rhythms of nature for enhanced well-being. The 10 treatment rooms in this body-melting spa, easily one of the best in the region, offer guests passage to the ultimate in relaxation. Cascading pools create a soothing sound track to the kneading of top technicians. Opt for the popular Full Body Massage or Full Moon Signature Treatment, or duck into the Julien Farel salon for full salon services. ⊠ *Capella Pedregal Resort, Camino Del Mar, Marina* ☎ *624/163–4300* ⊕ *www.capellahotels.com* ☞ *Body treatments: $145–$360. Facials: $175–$240* ✛ *2:A6.*

★ **The Desert Spa at Villa del Arco.** This spa on the beach in Los Cabos is also the area's largest, with 17 treatment rooms and two suites comfortably spread through three airy, sunny floors. The entire complex totals 31,000 square feet. With Los Cabos' largest hydrotherapy "wet" circuit, improve your circulation with dips in hot tubs followed by plunges in cold. The spa has the biggest fitness center in Cabo, and the beauty salon has a perfect view of the sea.

Body Treatments: *Massage:* Deep-tissue, reflexology, aromatherapy, couples. *Exfoliation:* Body scrub, fruit polish. *Wraps/baths:* Tequila wrap, fruit wrap, melon wrap, mineral bath. *Other*: Facial, hot-stone treatments, Solo pare Caballeros treatments for men.

Beauty Treatments: Facials, hair/scalp conditioning, hairstyling, mani/pedi, waxing.

✉ *Villa del Arco Beach Resort, Camino Viejo a San José, Km 0.5* ☎ *624/145–7000* ⊕ *www.villadelarcocabo.com/* ☞ *Body treatments: $52–$290. Facials: $90–$120. Mani/Pedi: $36–$46* ✛ *2:D1.*

Playa Grande Spa. Thalassotherapy comes from the practice of using seawater baths and seaweed-based treatments for prevention and curative purposes, and Playa Grande's spa is said to be the finest thalasso center in North America. Treatments may include combinations of seaweed and seawater, and the minerals in both will rejuvenate and renew your your skin like you've never experienced.

Body Treatments: *Massage*: Hot stone, shiatsu, Swedish, four hands, reflexology. *Exfoliation*: Honey body polish, sea-salt glow, cinnamon-sugar scrub, pomegranate/cran-apple scrub. *Wraps/baths*: Thalassotherapy bath, seaweed bath, hydrotherapy bath, seaweed body mask, honey/almond/buttermilk wrap. *Other*: Facials, temazcal, Vichy shower, masks.

Beauty Treatments: Hair/scalp conditioning, hair cutting/styling, manicure, pedicure, paraffin, waxing, eyebrow shaping, oxygen bar.

✉ *Playa Grande Resort, Av. Playa Grande No. 1, Playa Solmar* ☎ *624/145–7575* ⊕ *www.playagranderesort.com* ☞ *Body treatments: $175–$250. Facials: $130–$175. Hair: $30–$190. Mani/Pedi: $30–$60. Waxing: $20–$60* ✛ *2:C6.*

Spa at Pueblo Bonita Pacifica. This small, tranquil hotel on the Pacific side of Cabo is an adults-only property, filled with feng shui design, immaculately kept cactus gardens, and water, water, everywhere. Treatments at the Aromian Spa run the gamut from crystal Reiki healing to a yogurt-and-violets exfoliation, and even an intriguing temazcal (Maya sweat lodge) experience.

Body Treatments. *Massage*: Hot stone, Swedish, sports, deep-tissue, shiatsu, four hands, couples, reflexology, expectant mother, ayurveda, shirobyhanga, Thai, aromatherapy. *Exfoliation*: Honey sugar glow, green tea scrub, damiana/rosemary scrub, coconut/mango scrub, yogurt/violets scrub, chocolate/hazelnut scrub, red wine scrub, bamboo/alfalfa scrub, lavender scrub, lime scrub, sea-salt scrub. *Wraps/baths*: Bamboo/alfalfa/aloe/chamomile wrap, detox wrap, Dead Sea mud wrap, revitalizing wrap. *Other*: Shirodhara ritual, firming treatment, antioxidant treatment, Vichy shower, temazcal.

Beauty Treatments: Hair/scalp conditioning, hair cutting/styling, manicure, pedicure, waxing.

✉ *Pueblo Bonita Pacifica Resort, Predio Paraiso Escondido* ☎ *624/143–9696* ⊕ *www.pueblobonitopacifica.com* ☞ *Body treatments: $130–$330. Facials: $90–$275. Hair: $25–$110. Mani/Pedi: $35–$62. Parking: Valet (free)* ✛ *2:A6.*

The Spa at Westin Los Cabos. Massages and wraps are the specialties provided in seven treatment rooms at the Westin's Spa. Most popular is the four-hand massage, which takes guests to the peak of relaxation. Those craving body treatments can opt for the Cocolucious, which features coconut, or the Cucumber and Mint scrub. An on-site salon, barbershop, and fitness center round out the amenities. ✉ *Westin Los Cabos, Hwy. 1, Km. 22.5* ☎ *624/142–9000* ⊕ *www.westinloscabos.com* ☞ *Body Treatments: $128–$156. Facials: $119–$125* ✚ *2:D1.*

TOBACCO AND LIQUOR

J&J Casa de los Habanos. J&J Casa de los Habanos sells Cuban and international cigars, lighters, and ashtrays as well as tequila, Cuban coffee, and clothing. You can schedule a tequila tasting while you shop for cigars. ✉ *Madero and Blvd. Marina* ☎ *624/143–6160* ⊕ *www.jnjhabanos.com* ✚ *2:B4.*

Nightlife and the Arts

WORD OF MOUTH

"And for the best view perhaps in Cabo, go to the rooftop bar at the Cabo Villas, Baja Brewing, which is fantastic. It's just across from Mendano beach—by all the happening places on the beach."

—Tomsd

Updated by
Marie Elena
Martinez

Party-minded crowds roam the main strip of Cabo San Lucas every night from happy hour through last call, often staggering home or to hotel rooms just before dawn. It's not hard to see why this is *the* nightlife capital of southern Baja.

Indeed, Cabo is internationally famous (or infamous, depending on your view) for being a raucous party town, especially during spring break. On the other hand, nightlife in San José del Cabo is much more low-key: it's more about a good drink and conversation as opposed to the table-dancing chaos you'll find in some Cabo hot spots.

Between the two towns, the self-contained resorts along the Corridor have some nightlife, mainly in ever-improving restaurants and bars, which can mix up some fabulous cocktails themselves.

The lines between "bar," "nightclub," and "restaurant" are blurry here. Never forget that enjoying a fine dinner is a time-honored way to spend a Los Cabos evening. Also, don't forget that things shift into lower gear during the lowest of the low season—those slow, sweltering months of August and September when some places curtail their offerings, or may close for a few weeks altogether. Never fear though: you'll find nighttime fun here no matter what season you visit.

PLANNING

WHAT'S WHERE

San José del Cabo: Proprietors here say that you "graduate" to San José del Cabo after you sow the wild oats of your youth in Cabo San Lucas. It's quieter and more intimate here, and for a cozy, romantic evening, nothing beats San José's nightlife.

The Corridor: This sprawling strip between the two cities is the province of big resorts and their in-house bars. Expect upscale venues (and patrons). A few nightspots not affiliated with any hotel do exist here and are quite popular.

Cabo San Lucas: Had the phrase "What happens in Vegas, stays in Vegas" not already been taken, Cabo San Lucas might have snapped it up. You can experience spring break here, even if you went to college 30 years ago. Quiet Cabo nightlife does exist; you just need to look a bit harder.

WHAT TO WEAR

"Informal" is the word, although there's some wiggle room in that label. The more authentic a place is, the more likely patrons dress to impress. (Think casual-classy when taking in dance clubs such as El Squid Roe.) "Gringo" means less formal. (Shorts and T-shirts are acceptable at the Giggling Marlin.) But do keep those signs you see back home in mind: "No shoes, no shirt, no service" is always followed here.

WHAT IT COSTS

Want to drink inexpensively? Think beer, especially Baja's very own Tecate. Many places compete for the best happy-hour prices, often about $2 for a cerveza. Margaritas, the other keep-'em-coming drink, cost around $5. A glass of wine in an upscale venue should run $5 and up. Many places add a 10%–15% tip to your tab; others do not. (Look for the word "*servicio*" on your bill.) A big musical event means a nominal cover charge of a few dollars; those are rare.

WHAT'S GOING ON

You'll find copies of Los Cabos publications in hotels, restaurants, and bars all over the city. The most helpful are *Los Cabos Visitors Guide* and *Los Cabos Magazine*. Both provide a wealth of information on everything Los Cabos, from the restaurant, hotel, bar, and shopping scenes, to the many activities. The free English-language newspapers *Gringo Gazette* (⊕ *www.gringogazette.com*) and *Destino: Los Cabos* (⊕ *www.destinomagazines.com*) offer timely and cultural articles on the ever-changing scene. (We especially like the *Gringo Gazette* for its fun-loving, humorous look at expatriate life in Los Cabos.) The English-Spanish *Los Cabos News* (⊕ *www.loscabosnews.com.mx*) is also a good source for local event listings. These publications are available free at many hotels and stores or at racks on the sidewalk.

SAFETY

Nighttime is reasonably safe and secure here. Ask the bar or restaurant to call a taxi for you if you have far to go. Taxis aren't cheap, but you shouldn't put a price on getting home safely. All the standard precautions apply: Stick to well-lighted areas, where people congregate. Wandering dark, deserted streets or lonely stretches of beaches is never wise, nor is staggering home in a state of inebriation.

DRINKING AGE/SMOKING RULES

Mexico's nationwide drinking age is 18. Bars here check IDs at the door if they have any doubts about your age. Consumption of alcohol or the possession of an open beverage container is not permitted on public sidewalks, streets, or beaches (outside of licensed establishments), or in motor vehicles, whether moving or stationary.

Smoking is prohibited in all enclosed businesses, including bars and restaurants. Lighting up is allowed at outdoor-seating areas provided by such venues, but not indoors.

SAN JOSÉ DEL CABO

After-dark action in San José del Cabo caters mostly to locals and tourists seeking tranquillity and seclusion. There are no big dance clubs or discos in San José. What little nightlife there is revolves around restaurants, casual bars, and large hotels. A pre- or post-dinner stroll makes a wonderful addition to any San José evening. When night falls, people begin to fill the streets, many of them hurrying off to evening Mass when they hear the church bells peal from the central plaza.

A number of galleries hold court in central San José del Cabo, creating the **San José del Cabo Art District.** It's just north and east of the town's cathedral, primarily along Obregón, Morelos, and Guerrero streets. On Thursday nights from November through June, visit the **Art Walk,** where you can meander around about 15 galleries, sampling wine and cheese as you go.

BARS

Baja Brewing Co. The Baja Brewing Co. serves cold, on-site–microbrewed cerveza and international pub fare. You'll find entrées ranging from ahi tuna quesadillas to shepherd's pie, plus more basic pub food such as basil-and-blue-cheese burgers and pizzas. As for the seven beers, we recommend the Baja Blond Ale; the BBC also brews Cactus Wheat, Raspberry Lager, and a dark, smooth Black Scorpion. ⊠ *Morelos 1277 and Obregón* ☎ *624/146–9995* ⊕ *www.bajabrewingcompany. com* ✢ *1:C1.*

Cactus Jack's. If you feel the need to belt out *Love Shack* or *My Way,* grab the karaoke mike at Cactus Jack's, a modest, fun, open-air gringo hangout that's open until the wee hours on weekends. It has more TV screens than you normally see in a small pub, but that's why the largely American crowd comes here (football, football, and more NFL football). That, and the free pool. ⊠ *Blvd. Mijares 88* ☎ *624/142–5601* ✢ *1:C2.*

Red Martini Bar. If you know your colors, you'll easily spot the big, red, square lounge appropriately named Red Lounge down near the beach, across from Desire Resort. At night it's a stylish martini bar popular with the younger set, locals, and visitors alike. Tasty international food is served. ⊠ *Paseo de los Cabos* ☎ *624/142–3099* ⊕ *www. redmartinibar.com.mx* ☉ *Thur.–Sat. 8 pm–4 am* ✢ *1:B5.*

Shooters. For a gringo-friendly atmosphere where you're fine ordering your Bud in English, and sports blast on big-screen TVs, head to Shooters on the rooftop of the Tulip Tree restaurant. It's open until everyone leaves. Days are busy here, too, with breakfast and lunch served as well as Shooters's heavily promoted 10-peso (less than $1) beers from 9 to 4. ⊠ *Manuel Doblado at Blvd. Mijares* ☎ *624/146– 9900* ✢ *1:C2.*

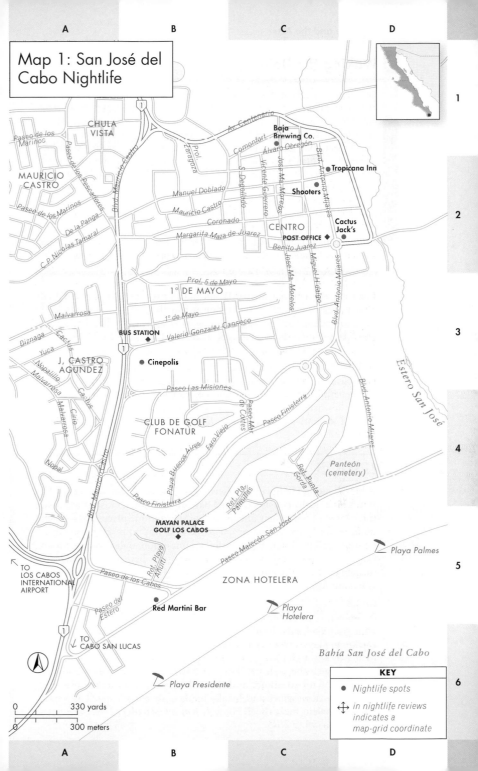

CLOSE UP

Waking the Dead

Celebrated throughout Mexico, the most important religious and indigenous festival in Los Cabos takes place November 1 and 2: All Saints' and All Souls' Day, more commonly referred to as **Día de los Muertos** (Day of the Dead). Long before Spain conquered Mexico, the festival was part of Indian culture and held during the winter equinox. In true colonial spirit, Spain changed the timing to coincide with its religious All Saints' and All Souls' Day.

Not as macabre as it sounds, the festival is a joyous celebration to welcome a visit from the souls of deceased loved ones. Family and friends prepare favorite foods and drink of the dearly departed, burn candles and incense, and place flowers in cemeteries and at memorials along the road. Shops carry candy shaped like skulls and coffins, and bread is baked to look like ghosts. No tears are to be shed, as it is said that the path back to the living world must not be made slippery by tears.

★ **Tropicana Inn.** The bar at the Tropicana Inn is a great place to mingle and enjoy live music. Conversation is usually possible on the balcony overlooking the bar and stage, though when a really hot band gets going you'll be too busy dancing to talk. ⊠ *Blvd. Mijares 30* ☎ *624/142–1580* ⊕ *www.tropicanainn.com.mx* ✛ *1:C2.*

MOVIES

Cinepolis. Cinepolis has a selection of American movies, at lower prices and generally a few weeks behind what's showing in the United States. There are usually six to eight movies playing, with the last feature starting around 11 pm. ⊠ *Hwy. 1, Plaza Cabo Ley* ☎ *624/142–3333* 🎟 *$4* ✛ *1:B3.*

THE CORRIDOR

Nightlife along Highway 1 between San José del Cabo and Cabos San Lucas historically consists of hotel bars in big resorts, most of which are frequented only by their guests. A few stand-alone places have sprung up in recent years. A taxi or car is the best way to reach these places. Because walking home is generally not an option, unless you're staying in-house or next door, nightlife ends early out here, with most places turning off the lights around 10 or 11 pm. Head to Cabo San Lucas if you want to party later.

BARS

Deckman's. If you're looking for some Miles Davis or Coltrane to pair with your cocktails, head to Deckman's, where celebrated chef Drew Deckman plays a steady sound track of classic jazz. As live bands make their way through the region, they often perform at Deckman's, so be sure to check the website. The bar has a great open-air overlook of the Costa Azul coastline, and the full bar stocks an incredible selection of Mexican wines and locally made craft beers, as well as a number of excellent mezcals. ⊠ *Hwy. 1, Km 29* ☎ *624/172–6269* ⊕ *www. deckmans.com* ✛ *2:B6.*

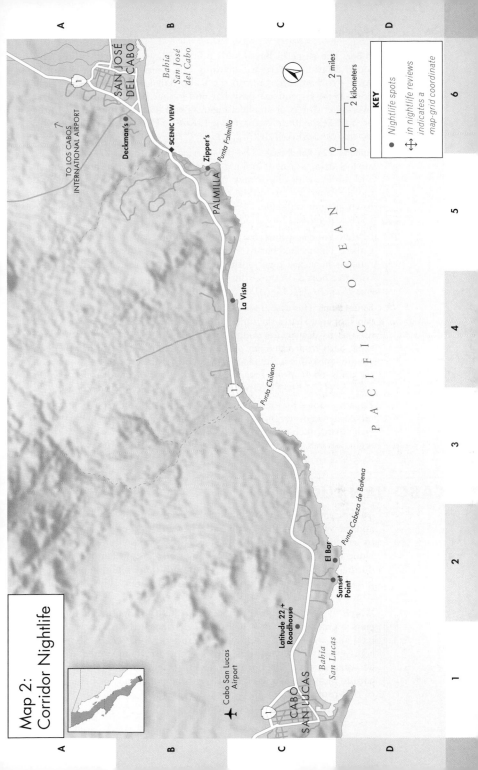

Map 2:
Corridor Nightlife

TO LOS CABOS
INTERNATIONAL AIRPORT

SAN JOSÉ
DEL CABO

Bahía
San José
del Cabo

Deckman's

SCENIC VIEW

Zipper's

PALMILLA

Punta Palmilla

La Vista

Punta Chileno

PACIFIC OCEAN

El Bar

Sunset
Point

Punta Cabezo de Ballena

Latitude 22 +
Roadhouse

Cabo San Lucas Airport

Bahía
San Lucas

CABO
SAN LUCAS

KEY

● Nightlife spots

⊕ in nightlife reviews
indicates a
map-grid coordinate

0   2 miles
0   2 kilometers

A

B

C

D

1   2   3   4   5   6

Fodor's Choice **El Bar.** The name El Bar sounds pretty utilitarian, but the dim light-
★ ing and intimacy here are anything but. Enjoy stunning views of El
Arco—you are, after all, on the Cabo San Lucas end of the Corridor—at the Esperanza's posh bar and lounge on lush couches. Linger
over quiet drinks or smoke a cigar as you listen to the sounds of the
ocean. ⊠ *Esperanza Resort, Hwy. 1, Km 3.5* 🕾 *624/145–6400* ⊕ *www.*
esperanzaresort.com ⊕ *2:C2.*

Latitude 22+ Roadhouse. The noisy, friendly Latitude 22+ Roadhouse
always attracts gringos looking to sip cold beer, down a shot of tequila,
and mingle with old or new friends. There's good, dependable, and
mostly American fare on the menu. Although Latitude 22+ is close to
town, it's not walkable. ⊠ *Hwy. 1, Km 4.5, near Costco* 🕾 *624/143–*
1516 ⊕ *www.lat22nobaddays.com* ⊕ *2:C1.*

La Vista. For classy hotel bars, it's hard to top La Vista in the Hilton Los
Cabos. The terrace bar overlooks the Sea of Cortez. There's nothing
raucous here, just quiet, intimate conversation over wine and drinks
with free hors d'oeuvres from 7 to 8 pm. ⊠ *Hilton Los Cabos, Hwy. 1,*
Km 19.5 🕾 *624/145–6500* ⊕ *www.hiltonloscabos.com* ⊕ *2:C4.*

★ **Sunset Point.** This casual wine-and-pizza lounge is a colorful, chic rooftop spot that shares the same stunning view of the famous Los Cabos
arch as its downstairs counterpart, Sunset de Mona Lisa. With free
tapas daily from 5 to 6 pm, and a selection of more than 140 wines and
champagnes, this is the place to watch the sunset with light bites and
cocktails. ⊠ *At Mona Lisa Sunset Restaurant, near Misiones Condos*
and Hotel 🕾 *624/145–8166* ⊕ *sunsetmonalisa.com* ⊕ *2:C2.*

Zipper's. Named for the nearby surf break, beachfront Zipper's attracts a
mixed crowd of surfers and nonsurfers alike. A good selection of beer, as
well as ribs and burgers, is always on hand, with live music every Friday
night. ⊠ *Hwy. 1, Km 28.5* 🕾 *624/172–6162* ⊕ *zippersbarandgrill.com*
⊕ *2:B5.*

CABO SAN LUCAS

The epicenter of Cabo San Lucas nightlife is along the Marina San Lucas
and the two streets that run parallel beyond it. You'll walk a gauntlet
of servers waving menus in your face, but the many fun sidewalk bars
along the marina between Plaza Bonita and Puerto Paraíso are great
during happy hour and late into the night. Many nightlife places do a
brisk daytime business, too, especially when cruise ships are in port,
which is several days a week.

Watch out for the tequila shooters and Jell-O shots forced upon revelers by merry waiters—they usually cost at least $5 each. Topless
bars and "gentlemen's" clubs are abundant, too. (Their "showgirls"
signs give away what—and where—they are.) Single men are often
accosted outside San Lucas bars with offers for drugs and sex. Be
careful in this area, and be aware that the police may be behind some
of these solicitations.

The bars, cantinas, clubs, and restaurants of Cabo San Lucas come alive when the sun sets.

BARS

Baja Brewing Co. The Cabo San Lucas branch of the microbrewery in San José del Cabo shares the same menu, as well as the seven beers on tap. But the partly open site here on the rooftop of a beach hotel means the vibe is decidedly different. It's a casual spot, perfect to roll right into after a day at the beach. Thursday is classic rock night, Friday means salsa, and Saturday presents reggae and soul. ⊠ *Rooftop of Cabo Villas, Médano Beach* ☎ *624/143–9199* ⊕ *www.bajabrewingcompany. com* ✢ *3:C4.*

Barómetro. Classy, tranquil, and comfortable, Barómetro gives you a peaceful panoramic view of the fishing yachts in the Marina San Lucas. Inside, a giant screen shows sports, but you can also relax outside on the couches, or across the sidewalk at a table overlooking the marina pier. Snack on taco, pizza, and fresh sashimi plates while sipping drinks during two daily happy hours. From 6 to 7 pm Corona and tequila shots are featured; from 7 to 8 pm you'll find a a rotating list of specials. ⊠ *On Marina boardwalk, near Puerto Paraíso Mall* ☎ *624/143–1466* ⊕ *www.barometro.com.mx* ✢ *3:B4.*

Billygan's Island. Twentysomethings sauntering around in revealing swimwear make up a large part of the Billygan's crowd. Spring break seems to take place year-round at this boisterous place on Médano Beach. Beer and margaritas flow to the accompaniment of bikini and dance contests. ⊠ *Médano Beach* ☎ *624/143–3435* ✢ *3:C4.*

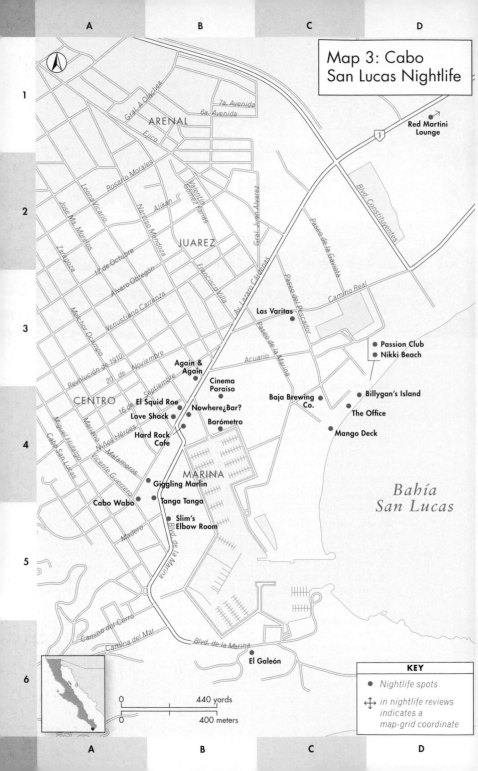

Map 3: Cabo San Lucas Nightlife

ARENAL

7a. Avenida
6a. Avenida

Elico

Red Martini Lounge

Gral. A. Olachea

Rosario Morales

Leona Vicario

Jose Ma. Morales

Zaragoza

Nardiso Mendoza

Alikan

Valentín Gómez Farías

JUAREZ

Francisco Villa

Gral. Juan Álvarez

Blvd Constituyentes

Av. Lázaro Cárdenas

Paseo de la Gaviota

Camino Real

Paseo del Pescador

Las Varitas

Paseo de la Marina

Passion Club

Nikki Beach

1ero de Octubre

Alvaro Obregón

Venustiano Carranza

Revolución de 1910

20 de Noviembre

Septiembre

Acuario

CENTRO

Again & Again

Cinema Paraíso

Melchor Ocampo

16 de Septiembre

El Squid Roe

Nowhere¿Bar?

Love Shack

Barómetro

Baja Brewing Co.

Billygan's Island

The Office

Hard Rock Cafe

Mango Deck

Niños Héroes

Matamoros

Miguel Hidalgo

Vicente Guerrero

MARINA

Giggling Marlin

Cabo Wabo

Tanga Tanga

Cabo San Lucas

Slim's Elbow Room

Madero

Blvd. de la Marina

Bahía San Lucas

Camino del Cerro

Camino del Mar

Blvd. de la Marina

El Galeón

0   440 yards

0   400 meters

KEY

● Nightlife spots

✛ in nightlife reviews indicates a map-grid coordinate

El Galeón. Ronald Valentino plays everything from *My Way* to *Bésame Mucho* at the piano at the dated El Galeón. The crowd is generally elder restaurant patrons wishing to extend their nights a little longer, and you'll find it to be a very comfortable, albeit sedate scene, with an elevated view of the Marina San Lucas. ⊠ *Blvd. Marina* 🕾 *624/143–0443* ⊕ *www.restaurantgaleon.com* ✛ *3:B6.*

Las Varitas. Las Varitas is a branch of a La Paz rock club favored by young Mexicans. One of Cabo's most popular clubs, it hosts live Mexican bands almost every night, and even boasts a house label Las Varitas tequila. ⊠ *Paseo de la Marina, about 1 block north of the entrance to the ME Cabos Hotel by Meliá, on Calle Gomez behind Puerto Paraíso* 🕾 *624/143–9999* ✛ *3:C3.*

Love Shack. If you're in the mood to spend some time in a relaxed bar just like at home, watch some American sports, shoot a couple of games of pool, or have a burger and listen to some tunes, the Love Shack is your type of casual locale. ⊠ *Morelos and Niños Héroes* 🕾 *624/143–5010* ✛ *3:B4.*

Mango Deck. Feel like getting a little bit rowdy and dancing in the sand? Overlooking the Arch, Mango Deck is a hot spot every night of the week, with DJs spinning late, and revelers partying at all hours of the day. ⊠ *At the western end of El Médano Beach, near the Casa Dorada resort* 🕾 *624/143–0901* ⊕ *www.mangodeckcabo.com* ✛ *3:C4.*

Nikki Beach. Miami meets Cabo at Nikki Beach. This restaurant, bar, and club has an over-the-top luxury feeling. If you've ever wanted to feel like you're in a music video this is your chance. White gauze canopies shade plush white sun beds and lounge chairs around swimming pools, while DJs spin all day long. Try the salmon and scallop carpaccio or cornmeal-crusted calamari. ⊠ *ME Cabo Hotel, Playa Médano* 🕾 *624/145–7800* ⊕ *www.me-cabo.com* ✛ *3:D3.*

Nowhere ¿Bar?. Local professionals loosen up over beers while exuberant tourists have too much fun at the Nowhere ¿Bar?. Two-for-one drinks and a large dance floor are big draw here. Reckless gyrating isn't strictly limited to the dance floor, though—don't be at all surprised to see people busting a move on the tables from early evening on. On weekend nights, especially over holidays and spring break, it's a madhouse scene. Sushi and tacos are served from adjacent businesses, and bartenders hand out baskets of popcorn to keep people thirsty. ⊠ *Plaza Bonita, Blvd. Marina 17* 🕾 *624/143–4493* ⊕ *www.nowherebar.com* ✛ *3:B4.*

The Office on the Beach. The Office began as a place to rent windsurfing equipment, but expanded into a bar/eatery now famous for its seafood and goblet-size margaritas. Despite the fact that the floor here is the sand, this place is a tad more upscale than the other venues on Médano Beach. Sunday and Thursday nights mean a music show with Mexican folk dances—a little touristy, but always a crowd pleaser. ⊠ *Médano Beach* 🕾 *624/143–3464* ⊕ *www.theofficeonthebeach.com* ✛ *3:C4.*

7

Fodor's Choice
★

Slim's Elbow Room. Slim's calls itself "the world's smallest bar," and you'll be lucky to get a seat at this kitschy eight-seat space that plays honky-tonk music and serves $3 beers and tequila shots. Signed dollar bills line the walls and the ceiling, and a buzzing, standing crowd loiters on the Boulevard Marina sidewalk around the bar each evening, vibing off its energy. ⊠ *Blvd. Marina, Plaza de los Mariachis* ✛ *3:B5.*

Tanga Tanga. A hot and popular spot for listening to live music, playing pool or darts, and watching sports on big-screen TVs, the sidewalk bar Tanga Tanga, has a bar outdoors and another (air-conditioned) one inside. Local reggae and rock groups play here most afternoons and nights. Margaritas are plentiful and the wings are extra spicy! ⊠ *Blvd. Marina outside Wyndham Hotel, Plaza Danza* ☎ *624/144–4501* ✛ *3:B4.*

DANCE CLUBS

Again & Again. Again & Again is one of the most popular dance clubs for locals. Two levels with pillared balconies overlook the stage and dance floor. On Thursday, the live *banda* (band) music draws a large crowd. The music, born in the 19th century in the northern state of Sinaloa, is traditional and often slow, for dancing in pairs, but very brassy. On other nights—the place is open only Thursday through Sunday—the music is a mix of dance styles, including salsa and merengue. ⊠ *Av. Cárdenas between Leona Vicario and Morelos* ☎ *624/143–6323* ✛ *3:B3.*

★ **El Squid Roe.** If you are easily offended, have a hard time letting loose, or have a heart condition, you may want to think twice before entering El Squid Roe. Just about anything goes here. Waiters dance and gyrate with female patrons, roaming waitresses pour Jell-O shots down your throat, frat-boy wannabes attempt beer-chugging contests, scantily clad dancers undulate in a makeshift penitentiary. During spring break or high season, more than 5,000 revelers come here on any given night—and many stay until sunrise. Feeling out of place? Head for one of the balconies on the third and fourth floors (which can be reached by elevator) where the scene is a bit less lurid. Around the corner stands the bar's souvenir shop with humorous T-shirts. If you need to soak up some of that alcohol before heading home, grab a taco from Billy Kitchen just at the front of the club. ⊠ *Av. Cárdenas s/n* ☎ *624/143–0655* ⊕ *www.elsquidroe.com* ✛ *3:B4.*

Giggling Marlin. Giggling Marlin has been around forever and actually predates Cabo's tourism explosion, but its gimmicks remain popular. Watch brave (and inebriated) souls be hoisted upside down at the mock fish-weighing scale, or join in an impromptu moonwalk between tables. Many fun (if a bit risqué) floor shows seem to relax people's inhibitions. The age of the clientele varies, as does the music, but the dance floor is usually jammed. A nightly two-for-one drinks special packs 'em in from 11 pm until 1 am. The bartender may place a shot of tequila in front of you the minute you sit down—you'll pay at least $5 if you drink it. ⊠ *Blvd. Marina and Matamoros* ☎ *624/143–0606* ⊕ *www.gigglingmarlin.com* ✛ *3:B4.*

A Shot of Tequila

What once was the drink of the poor Mexican farmer is now produced en masse and enjoyed internationally, with countless varieties crowding shelves across the world. Unfortunately, lower-quality brands make up the bulk of exports, so if the thought of sipping this heady liquor turns your stomach, take some time to seek out some of a higher quality while you're in Los Cabos.

Tequila must contain at least 51% blue agave, a plant related to the lily. The best tequilas are 100% blue agave. Liquid is distilled from the sap of 7- to 10-year-old plants and fermented. If you buy tequila with a worm, it was probably bottled in the United States, and is likely not a good-quality tequila.

Most of the good stuff is made in the town of Tequila, near Guadalajara. Labels bearing *reposado* indicate up to a year of aging; *añejo,* from one to three years. The longer tequila ages, the smoother it tastes.

Getting in your fill of taste-testing is an easy thing to do in Los Cabos, because every bar will have at least a couple of bottles on the shelves, but you should visit at least one establishment that specializes in the good stuff. There are a number of locations in Los Cabos to do so: **Pancho's Restaurant & Tequila Bar** (⇨ *Where to Eat chapter)* comes to mind, as does the **Tequila & Ceviche Bar** at the posh Las Ventanas al Paraíso Resort (⇨ *Where to Stay chapter).*

Pancho's might as well be a tequila museum. Hundreds of tequilas are available for tasting, and many of the colorfully named brands up on the shelves are no longer manufactured. Schedule a private tasting, at $50 per person, with Bernard Corriveau, the official "Tequila Ambassador" of Mexico, who will teach you a bit about the history, production process, and art of this complex liquor. Corriveau, appointed a "Maestro Tequilero," by the Consejo Regalador de Tequila (loosely, the industry's Tequila Board), just might be the most knowledgeable person on tequila in Los Cabos. Pancho's holds group tequila tastings in English each Tuesday night at 7 pm.

Only guests at the fantastic Las Ventanas al Paraíso Resort on the Corridor can enjoy the small, intimate Tequila & Ceviche Bar set off from its lobby. The resort's "Tequileros" conduct the lessons for several guests (a maximum of 10) where you'll learn the history, classifications, distillation process, and different types of tequila along with the appropriate way to drink it. Take note, you won't be "shooting," or tossing down these shots. Of the 95 different varieties available for sampling, some are affordable, while others—the Chinaco Emperador, aged 10 years and $180 per shot—are literally liquid gold. Other favorites include the Don Julio Real, $75 per shot; the Don Tacho Grand Reserva, $60; the Gran Centanario Reserva, $50; and the Reserva de la Familia, $35. The tequilas are served with ceviche, guacamole, baked pita crisps, and tortillas. Classes are held on Tuesday and Friday at 5 pm, at a cost of $75 per person.

Another simple, fun, and free experience is in San José del Cabo at the **Antigua Los Cabos Museum and Store**, located on the *zócalo,* town square. Here you can sample various tequilas and other interesting liquors (and even get a bit tipsy) free of charge.

7

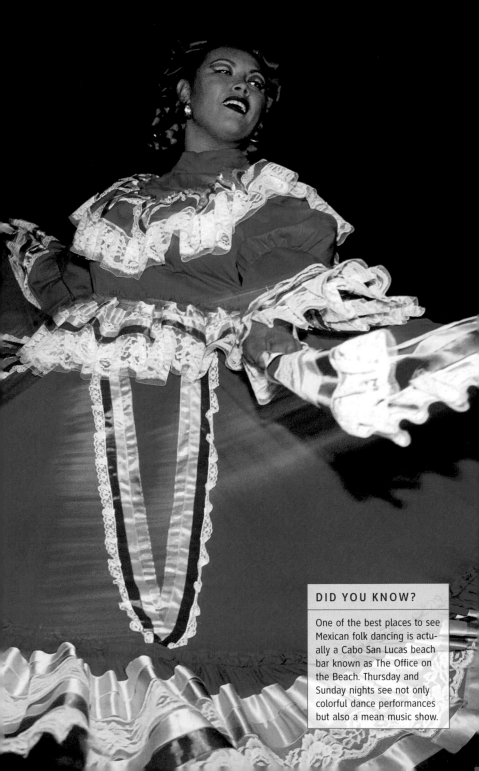

Hagar's Hangout: Cabo Wabo

According to local lore, in the mid-1980s former Van Halen lead singer Sammy Hagar and a friend were walking along the beach in Cabo San Lucas when they passed a drunk man stumbling. Hagar remarked, "Hey, he's doing the Cabo Wabo." A few years later, in 1990, Hagar and the rest of Van Halen opened the bar called Cabo Wabo—establishing one of the premier stops on the Cabo party circuit. When the group broke up in 1996, all but Hagar sold their shares in the bar.

Mexican and American rock bands perform every night. Almost always packed, the place erupts when Hagar comes to play. When he's on tour, he may only make it to the club four or five times a year. Three of those visits fall on April 22 (the bar's anniversary), October 3–4 for the bar's MELT DOWN celebration, and the week around October 13 (for Hagar's birthday celebration). When not on tour, Hagar hits Cabo Wabo up to 12 times a year. The dates are usually announced on the club's website, ⊕ *www.cabowabo.com.*

Often accompanying Hagar are some of his rock-and-roll friends. These have included Chris Isaak, Kirk Hammett of Metallica, David Crosby, Slash, Rob Zombie, the Cult, and the Sex Pistols.

Easily seen from afar due to a lighthouse replica at the main entrance, the bar was designed by architect Marco Monroy. He built high, cavernous ceilings and painted the walls with zebra stripes and psychedelic neon patterns. Hagar liked Monroy's work so much that the design of the bar was replicated for his set on the "Red Voodoo" tour.

Fodor's Choice **Passion Club.** There is no doubt that the hippest (and most expensive)
★ spot in Los Cabos is the Passion Club. Top DJs from around the world come to spin the vinyl and light up the neon, cozy club. It has a great dance floor and there are various VIP events throughout the year. ⊠ *At ME Cabo, on El Médano Beach* ☎ *624/145–7800* ⊕ *www.me-cabo. com* ✛ *3:D3.*

MOVIES

Cinema Paraíso. Cinema Paraíso has 10 screens, including a VIP screening room with reclining leather seats. First-run Hollywood movies are shown usually in English with Spanish subtitles (*subtitulada* or *versión original*), just a few weeks behind premieres in the States. Kids' movies are the exception: they will be dubbed (*doblada* or versión español) into Spanish since their very young fans don't read subtitles. ⊠ *Av. Cárdenas at Puerto Paraíso* ☎ *624/143–1515* ⊕ *www. cinemaparaiso.net* ✛ *3:B4.*

ROCK CLUBS

★ **Cabo Wabo.** American rock plays over an excellent sound system at Cabo Wabo, but the jam sessions with owner Sammy Hagar and his many music-business friends are the real highlight. Plan way in advance to attend Hagar's Birthday Bash Week—usually the second week in October—as tickets sell out. It's a large venue, with a raised stage, a tall

A CAVALCADE OF STARS

It can only be Los Cabos' proximity to Southern (upper) California: at 2½ hours by air from L.A., the southern tip of Baja has become a fabled getaway for all manner of Hollywood celebs. Stars like John Wayne and Bing Crosby vacationed here a half century ago and put Los Cabos on the map, and the area never looked back. Not all today's stars opt for the flash and glitz of Cabo San Lucas. Many prefer quieter San José del Cabo with its selection of small inns and intimate restaurants.

Sammy Hagar, formerly of the rock group Van Halen, is the celebrity most associated with Los Cabos; he's part owner of Cabo Wabo. But the list (in no particular order) of those who have vacationed here is impressive: Leonardo DiCaprio, Jennifer Lopez, George Clooney, Oprah Winfrey, Brad Pitt, Beyoncé Knowles, Michael Douglas, Catherine Zeta-Jones, Michael Jordan, Brooke Shields, Madonna, Demi Moore, Ashton Kutcher, Meg Ryan, Adam Sandler, Celine Dion, Gwyneth Paltrow, Spike Lee, Jennifer Aniston, Bono, Charlize Theron, Halle Berry, Jessica Simpson, Sarah Jessica Parker, Salma Hayek, Goldie Hawn, Kurt Russell, Sylvester Stallone—and that's just to name a few.

Many fly into a small airstrip near Cabo San Lucas that handles private jets—as does one terminal at Los Cabos International Airport. Call it a hunch, but we mere mortals probably won't be sitting next to JLo or Oprah in coach. You never know who you might see after you arrive, though, so keep your eyes peeled. Do remember that "Be cool" is one of Los Cabos' cardinal rules: gawking, staring, and taking photos are frowned upon.

ceiling resembling an auditorium, the longest bar in town, and, for VIPs, a lounge upstairs. Strong air-conditioning scores lots of points in the heat of summer. ■**TIP➔** Make dinner reservations to avoid the long lines to get in the club. Breakfast, lunch, and dinner are served with extensive menus. A taco grill cooks up tasty munchies outside if you wish to cool off after dancing. Shops on-site or at the international airport sell Cabo Wabo souvenir clothing. ⊠ *Calle Guerrero* ☎ *624/143–1901 or 624/163-7400* ⊕ *www.cabowabo.com* ✚ *3:A4.*

Hard Rock Cafe. With a '59 white Cadillac jutting through the window and dozens of rock-and-roll albums and memorabilia on the walls, this Hard Rock Cafe might be in Mexico, but is a typical member of the chain. Live rock music starts at 8 pm every Sunday through Thursday and 9:45 on Friday and Saturday with Corona drink specials. Ladies drink free from 9 pm to 11 pm on Thursday. On the first floor is the requisite shop where you can purchase your "Hard Rock Cafe Cabo San Lucas" caps and T-shirts. ⊠ *Blvd. Marina across from El Squid Roe* ☎ *624/143–3779* ⊕ *www.hardrock.com* ✚ *3:B4.*

SUNSET CRUISES

Several companies run nightly cruises for dinner or drinks that capture stunning sunsets as their vessels rounds the cape. Stands around the marina act as agents and can book excursions for you, but some manage to rope you into a time-share visit in the process. Better to book through your hotel's front desk or directly through the company.

Caborey. Caborey offers a nightly 2½-hour sunset-dinner cruise on a three-deck catamaran. Cost is $92 and includes a full prix-fixe dinner with your choice of one of six main courses, an open bar for domestic beverages, and a Las Vegas–style show of Mexican music. Departure time is 6 pm September–April, and 5 pm the rest of the year. Reserve online for 20% off. ☎ *624/143–8260, 866/460–4105 in North America* ⊕ *www.caborey.com.*

Fiesta Cabaret. Fiesta Cabaret offers two options for the nightly three-hour sunset-dinner cruise departing 6 pm September–April, and 5 pm the rest of the year: the $82 cost includes an all-you-can-eat buffet, an open bar with domestic drinks, and a tropical-music show. If just the bar interests you, you'll pay $50 for the excursion. ☎ *624/146–3563* ⊕ *www.yatefiestacabaret.com.*

Tropicat. It's jazz each evening in time for the sunset on the *Tropicat,* a 65-foot catamaran, that departs 6 pm September–April, and 4:30 pm the rest of the year. The two-hour excursion is $59 per person and includes premium wines and hors d'oeuvres. There's 10% discount if purchased online. ☎ *624/143–3797* ⊕ *www.tropicatcabo.com.*

7

Los Cabos Side Trips

TODOS SANTOS AND LA PAZ

WORD OF MOUTH

"La Paz is a great choice. I used to travel there with my family as a kid and was recently back in the area as I work with one of the hotels. It's very laid back and was nice to see that it has kept it's authentic charms—not a big party scene.

—Kyra_Dauer"

WELCOME TO LOS CABOS SIDE TRIPS

TOP REASONS TO GO

★ **Shopping Todos Santos:** An influx of artisans and craftspeople has turned Todos Santos into the region's snazziest, high-quality shopping destination.

★ **Lodging Value:** Todos Santos offers a selection of charming inns at just a fraction of the cost—but all at full quality—of Los Cabos hostelries down the coast.

★ **The Aquarium of the World:** So Jacques Cousteau christened the Sea of Cortez; La Paz makes the perfect launching point for exploring this body of water's rich marine life.

★ **The Best of Urban Baja:** La Paz is your bet for the urban pleasures of a charming, low-key Mexican city that lines a grand seaside promenade to boot.

★ **A Whale of a Time:** The annual December-through-April migration of gray whales to and from Alaska is visible from various points on the Baja coast and a guaranteed stunner.

1 Todos Santos.
Todos outgrew its surfing roots without abandoning them entirely, but you'll more likely come here for its growing number of galleries and craft shops. The arts scene has fueled a rise in gracious small inns, making this popular Los Cabos–area day trip an overnight destination in its own right.

2 La Paz. Don't let La Paz's workaday hustle and bustle fool you. This seaside state capital is one of Mexico's loveliest small cities—you'll be sold after an evening stroll on the oceanfront malecón, ice cream cone in hand—and the launching point for Baja's best diving, fishing, and whale-watching excursions.

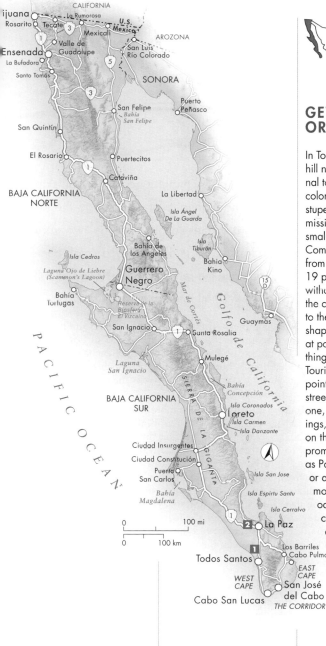

GETTING ORIENTED

In Todos Santos climb the hill north of the bus terminal to reach the original colonial town center with its stupendous views, landmark mission church, and several small inns and galleries. Coming into Todos Santos from the south, Highway 19 parallels area beaches without necessarily hugging the coastline. Roads leading to the shore are in decent shape, but twist and turn at points. Follow the signs; things are well marked. Tourist La Paz has two focal points. The dense grid of streets in the city center form one, with most sights, lodgings, and restaurants either on the malecón, the seaside promenade officially known as Paseo Alvaro Obregón, or a few blocks inland at most. (Remember: The odd curvature of the coast means that you are looking west out over the Sea of Cortez here.) The alternative to staying in the city is the 18-km (11-mile) highway leading north from La Paz to its port of Pichilingue, lined with a few small- to medium-size seaside hotels.

8

At the risk of sounding glib, we might suggest that you skip Los Cabos altogether. The highlights of your visit to the far southern tip of the Baja peninsula may include two very un-Cabo-like destinations. One is objectively a small community; the other is actually the region's largest city, but will always be an overgrown small town at heart.

Their tranquil, reverent names—Todos Santos ("all saints") and La Paz ("peace")—are the first hint that you have left the glitz of Los Cabos behind, and that it's time to shift gears and enjoy the enchantment of Mexico. As an added bonus, both are positioned in such a way on the peninsula that you can enjoy beautiful sunsets over the sea. (Los Cabos gives you only ocean sunrises.)

The appeal of Todos Santos is becoming more well known, as a growing number of expats—American and European alike—move to the area. There's a lot to love here: the surf on the Pacific, just a couple of miles west of town, is good; weather is always a bit cooler than in Los Cabos; and the lush, leisurely feel of this artsy colonial town—think a smaller version of central Mexico's San Miguel de Allende—is relatively undisturbed by the many tourists who venture up from Los Cabos for the day. Todos Santos has always been the quintessential Los Cabos day trip, especially for the myriad cruise passengers who call there. As the town's tourism offerings grow, it's becoming a destination in its own right. Break the typical pattern of day-tripping to Todos Santos and spend at least one night here amid the palms, at one of the pleasant, small inns.

La Paz plants itself firmly on the Sea of Cortez side of the Baja peninsula. A couple of hours north of Los Cabos, it remains slightly outside the Cabo orbit, and it has always attracted visitors (and an expanding expat population) who make La Paz their exclusive Baja destination. Of course, 200,000-plus Paceños view their city as being the center of the universe, thank you very much. (La Paz is the capital of the state of Baja California Sur and Los Cabos is in their orbit.) In addition to many urban trappings, La Paz offers a growing number of outdoor-travel options. This city on the water has become all about what's in the water. Sportfishing and scuba diving are big here, and La Paz is now a major launching point for whale-watching excursions.

TODOS SANTOS

73 km (44 miles) north of Cabo San Lucas, 81 km (49 miles) south of La Paz.

From the hodgepodge of signs and local businesses you see on the drive into Todos Santos, south on Highway 19, it appears that you're heading to the outskirts of a typical Baja town. But climb the hill to its old colonial center with its mission church and blocks of restored buildings, and the Todos Santos that is gaining rave reviews in tourism circles is revealed.

Todos Santos was designated one of the country's Pueblos Mágicos (Magical Towns) in 2006, joining 53 other towns around Mexico chosen for their religious or cultural significance. Pueblos Mágicos receive important financial support from the federal government for development of tourism and historical preservation. Architects and entrepreneurs have restored early 19th-century adobe-and-brick buildings around the main plaza of this former sugar town and have turned them into charming inns, whose hallmark is attentive service at prices far more reasonable than a night in Los Cabos. A good number of restaurateurs provide sophisticated, globally inspired food at hip eateries.

Todos Santos has always meant shopping, at least since about three decades ago when the first U. S. and Mexican artists began to relocate their galleries here. Day-trippers head up here from Los Cabos, enjoying lunch and a morning of shopping. The growing number of visitors who buck that trend and spend a night or two here leave feeling very satisfied indeed.

Los Cabos visitors typically take day trips here, though several small inns provide a peaceful antidote to Cabo's noise and crowds. El Pescadero, the largest settlement before Todos Santos, is home to ranchers and farmers who grow herbs and vegetables. Business hours are erratic, especially in September and October.

GETTING HERE AND AROUND

Highway 19, now upgraded to four lanes, connects Todos Santos south with Cabo San Lucas and north with La Paz, making the drive easier than ever. Nonetheless, we recommend making the trip before dark; the occasional cow or rock blocks the road. Autotransportes Aguila provides comfortable coach service 16 times a day in both directions between Los Cabos (San José and San Lucas) and La Paz with an intermediate stop in Todos Santos. Plan on an hour from La Paz or Cabo San Lucas and 90 minutes from San José del Cabo. Ecobaja Tours offers scheduled shuttle service ($20 one way) three times daily between Todos Santos and Los Cabos Airport, 90 minutes away.

Contacts Autotransportes Aguila ✉ *Zaragoza and Colegio Militar* ☎ *612/123–2157.* **Ecobaja Tours** ☎ *612/123–0000* ⊕ *www.ecobjatours.com.*

VISITOR INFORMATION

Baja California Sur State Tourist Office. The Baja California Sur State Tourist Office is in La Paz about a 10-minute drive north of the *malecón* (seaside promenade). It serves as both the state and city tourism office. There's also an information stand on the malecón (no phone) across from closed-but-hoping-to-reopen Los Arcos hotel. The booth is a more convenient spot, and it can give you info on La Paz and nearby region. Both offices and the booth are open weekdays 9–5. ⊠ *Km. 5.5, Carretera al Norte, La Paz* ☎ *866/733–5272 in U.S., 612/124–0100* ⊕ *www. explorebajasur.com.*

EXPLORING

Nuestra Señora del Pilar. Todos Santos was the second-furthest south of Baja California's 30 mission churches, a system the Spanish instituted to convert (and subdue) the peninsula's indigenous peoples. Jesuit priests established an outpost here in 1733 as a *visita* (circuit branch) of the mission in La Paz, a day's journey away on horseback. The original church north of town was sacked and pillaged twice during its existence, before being relocated in 1825 to this site in the center of town. Additions in the past two centuries have resulted in a hodgepodge of architectural styles, but the overall effect is still pleasing, and the structure serves to this day as the community's bustling parish church. ⊠ *Calle Márquez de León, between Centenario and Legaspi* ⊙ *Daily 7–7.*

Teatro Cine General Manuel Márquez de León. The mouthful of a name denotes Todos Santos's 1944 movie theater, which was quite a grand movie palace back in the day for remote, small-town Mexico. A few cultural events take place here, including the annual Todos Santos Film Festival each February. An ongoing restoration at this writing is redoing the interior to match the appearance of its 1940s heyday. It's worth a peek inside. ⊠ *Calle Legaspi s/n* ☎ *612/145–0225* ⊙ *Weekdays 8–7.*

SPORTS AND OUTDOOR ACTIVITIES

ECOTOURISM

Todos Santos Eco Adventures. Todos Santos Eco Adventures offers a number of land- and water-based adventures. Choose from cliff walks, mountain treks, or fishing trips. Friendly guides pride themselves on thorough knowledge of the area, the environment, and the culture of the region. Their weeklong Todos Santos Cooking Adventure combines Mexican lessons with local sightseeing. Whichever of the offerings you choose, you'll feel like you're traveling with a savvy friend. The Jauregui family runs the operation with great care, and it's apparent. Ask about the casitas if you need overnight accommodations. ⊠ ✛ *West on Calle Olachea, follow signs toward La Poza. (Call for detailed directions)* ☎ *612/145–0189, 619/446–6827 in U.S.* ⊕ *www.tosea.net.*

SURFING

Todos Santos offers great surfing areas for beginners to experts. The advantage here is that the crowds, including the swarming masses from the cruise ships, don't head up to these waters, which makes for a much more relaxed scene in the water and on the beach.

Los Cerritos, south of Todos Santos on Mexico 19, offers gentle waves to beginners during the summer and more challenging breaks for advanced surfers during the northwest swell from December to March. San Pedrito, also south of town, offers great surfing for experienced surfers during the winter swells, with a number of popular, low-key, surf-oriented motels along the beach. In summer, the surf is generally pretty mellow along this stretch, so locals and surfers who demand greater challenge head to the Corridor or areas along the east side of the Cape for more satisfying breaks.

Todos Santos Surf Shop. Swing by Todos Santos Surf Shop on your way out of town for board rentals, to arrange a lesson, buy gear, or get that ding in your board repaired. ⊠ *Degollado and Rangel,* ☎ *612/145–0882.*

WHERE TO EAT

Todos Santos's dining selection echoes the town—stylish expat with traditional Mexican—and makes a nice outing during any Los Cabos–area stay. Restaurants here do a brisk business at lunch, less so at dinner. It's a real treat to drive up from Los Cabos or down from La Paz for a special meal. At an hour each way, that's easier to do before dark.

$
CAFE
✕ **Baja Beans.** Although Los Cabos and Baja are not coffee-growing regions, the folks in the town of El Pescadero roast the finest beans from the Mexican states of Oaxaca, Chiapas, Puebla, and Veracruz. They turn them into the area's best gourmet coffee drinks and serve them at tables in the adjoining garden. Baked goods and light fare, such as vegetarian frittatas, round out the offerings. ⑤ *Average main: $8* ⊠ *El Pescadero, Km 64, Hwy. 19* ☎ *612/143–7138* ⊕ *www.bajabeans.com* ☺ *Closed Aug. and Sept. No dinner. No lunch July.*

$$
ITALIAN
✕ **Café Santa Fe.** The setting, with tables situated in an overgrown courtyard, is as appealing as the food, which includes salads and soups made with organic vegetables and herbs, homemade pastas, and fresh fish with light sauces. Many Cabo-area residents lunch here regularly. The marinated seafood salad is a sublime blend of shrimp, octopus, and mussels with olive oil and garlic, with plenty for two to share before dining on lobster ravioli. ⑤ *Average main: $18* ⊠ *Calle Centenario* ☎ *612/145–0340* ☺ *Closed Tues.*

$
ECLECTIC
✕ **Caffé Todos Santos.** Omelets, bagels, granola, and whole-grain breads delight the breakfast crowd at this casual small eatery; deli sandwiches, fresh salads, and an array of burritos, tamales, *flautas* (fried tortillas rolled around savory fillings), and combo plates are lunch and dinner highlights. Check for fresh seafood on the daily specials board. ⑤ *Average main: $8* ⊠ *Calle Centenario 33* ☎ *612/145–0787* ▭ *No credit cards* ☺ *No dinner Mon.*

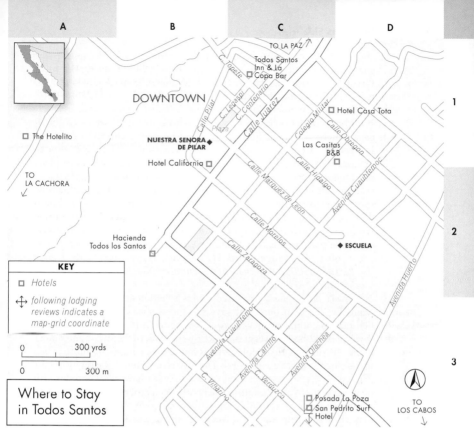

A   B   C   D

TO LA PAZ

Todos Santos
Inn & La
Copa Bar

DOWNTOWN

Hotel Casa Tota

1

The Hotelito

NUESTRA SENORA
DE PILAR

Las Casitas
B&B

Hotel California

TO
LA CACHORA

Calle Pilar
C. Topete
C. Legaspi
C. Centenario
Calle Juárez
Colegio Militar
Calle Obregon
Calle Hidalgo
Avenida Cuauhtémoc
Plaza

Calle Marquez de Leon

Hacienda
Todos los Santos

Calle Morelos

ESCUELA

2

Calle Zaragoza

Avenida Huerta

KEY

Hotels

following lodging
reviews indicates a
map-grid coordinate

0   300 yrds
0   300 m

Avenida Cuauhtémoc
Avenida Carrillo
C. Verduzco
Avenida Olachea

C. Vilarino

**Where to Stay
in Todos Santos**

Posada La Poza
San Pedrito Surf
Hotel

TO
LOS CABOS

3

$$$
ECLECTIC
Fodor's Choice
★
✕ **El Gusto!.** Even if you don't stay at the sumptuous Posada La Poza just outside town, lunch or dinner at its equally lovely restaurant will be one of the highlights of your Los Cabos vacation. Owners Jürg and Libusche Wiesendanger call their offerings "Swiss-Mex"—Mexican food with European touches, and careful attention to detail. Start with the vegetarian-based tortilla soup with three different types of dried chilies to give it just enough kick. Then sample the smoked-tuna flautas with raspberry-chipotle sauce, quesadillas with mushroom or shrimp, or marinated *arrachera* (flank steak) strips. You'll find dishes such as lamb shoulder in winter. Believe it or not, there is enough of an evening chill in the air that time of year that dining next to the fireplace feels cozy. Top your meal off with a sorbet, flan, or mousse, and possibly the best selection of wines in the region (all Mexican from northern Baja's Guadalupe Valley). Dinner is served from 6 to 8, which gives you time to catch the sunset. $ *Average main: $21* ✉ *Follow signs on Hwy. 19 and Benito Juárez to beach* ☎ *612/145–0400* ⊕ *www.lapoza. com* ⌂ *Reservations essential* ⊘ *Closed Thurs.*

$$
MEXICAN
✕ **Los Adobes.** Locals swear by the fried, cilantro-studded local cheese and the beef tenderloin with huitlacoche at this pleasant outdoor restaurant. The menu is ambitious and includes tapas and several organic, vegetarian options—rare in these parts. At night the place sparkles with

star-shape lights. Take a stroll through the adjoining landscaped desert garden while you wait for your food. If you're here during the July–October low season, make it an early dinner; the place closes at 7 on weeknights. $ *Average main: $17* ⊠ *Calle Hidalgo* ☎ *612/145–0203* ⊕ *www.losadobesdetodossantos.com* ⊘ *Closed Sun. No dinner Sat.*

$$
ASIAN
✕ **Michael's at the Gallery.** Everybody who dines here seems to know each other—the clientele is mostly the foreigners who live in town—but visitors are always welcome. The attraction at Michael's—not to be confused with Miguel's, the equally recommended Mexican place as you come into town—is the Asian menu, predominantly Vietnamese, but with a few Thai dishes, too. Share a big order of Vietnamese sweet-potato fritters and shrimp, or Vietnamese crab cakes. You'll dine on the patio behind the Galería de Todos Santos; you can browse while you wait for your food. Michael's keeps *very* limited hours, open just two evenings for a total of eight hours a week. Reservations are a must. $ *Average main: $15* ⊠ *Calle Juárez and Calle Topete* ☎ *612/145–0500* ⚓ *Reservations essential* ⊟ *No credit cards* ⊘ *Closed Sun.–Thurs. No lunch.*

$
MEXICAN
Fodor'sChoice
★
✕ **Miguel's.** Deliciously prepared chiles rellenos are the attraction at Miguel's. The sign out front says so, and it speaks the truth. Hearty bell peppers, almost any way you like them, stuffed with fish, lobster, shrimp, pork, beef, or veggies, make up the bulk of the lunch and dinner menu. Breakfast consists of burritos and eggs or Baja's ubiquitous fish tacos. A copy of *The New York Times* arrives later in the day for your perusal. Don't confuse this semi-outdoor place on the edge of town with Michael's, the Asian restaurant several blocks away near the church. Call ahead during the July–September low season as the restaurant may close one rotating day a week. $ *Average main: $9* ⊠ *Degollado at Hwy. 19* ☎ *612/145–0733* ⊟ *No credit cards.*

WHERE TO STAY

The quality of lodgings in Todos Santos is surprisingly high. It's a much better value to stay here than along the Corridor or in Los Cabos—and there isn't a megaresort to be found. In fact, some of the best lodging in the region is found right here, among the lush palm trees of this former sugarcane town.

For expanded reviews and current deals, visit Fodors.com.

$
HOTEL
▦ **Hacienda Todos los Santos.** Within each of the three *casitas* (guesthouses) here, you'll find canopied beds and antique art. **Pros:** three casitas have private terraces and fully equipped kitchens; wonderful views from upstairs rooms. **Cons:** little to do here for young children. $ *Rooms from: $125* ⊠ *End of Benito Juárez* ☎ *612/145–0547* ⊕ *www.tshacienda.com* ⥅ *4 suites, 3 casitas* ⊟ *No credit cards* ⚐ *No meals* ✣ *B2.*

$
HOTEL
▦ **Hotel California.** This handsome structure with two stories of arched terraces and rich, vibrant colors on the walls, is a testament to the artistic bent of owner Debbie Stewart. **Pros:** inn feels exotic and lush; convenient location; good value. **Cons:** some street noise; service not as smooth as other hotels in town. $ *Rooms from: $90* ⊠ *Benito Juárez at*

Todors Santos Inn

Todors Santos Inn, with a total of eight guest rooms, defines understated elegance.

Posada La Poza has spacious, stylish suites and overlooks a bird-filled lagoon.

ART WALKS IN TODOS SANTOS

The shops and galleries in the downtown area can be explored in an hour or two, or you can easily make a day of it. Start at **Nuestra Señora de Pilar** church in the morning, when it's cooler. Head up Legaspi a block to **Galería la Coronela.** Make a left out of the gallery and then make a right onto Topete to head over one block to Centenario—to the left is **Joyeria Brilanti**, and on the corner is **Manos Mexicanas.** Continue heading south on Topete and on Juarez you'll find **Galería de Todos Santos** at the intersection, and **Fénix de Todos Santos** around the corner on the right. Between the galleries mentioned you'll find dozens of additional shops to wander through, too. Satisfy your growling tummy with lunch at **Ataxcon,** a local's favorite for fantastic, very inexpensive food on Hidalgo at Camino Militar, where you'll find a chicken, beef, and vegetarian option on the menu every day.

Morelos 🕾 *612/145–0525* ⊕ *www.hotelcaliforniabaja.com* 🛏 *11 rooms* ⍥ *No meals* ✛ *B2.*

$ ⛶ **The Hotelito.** Original art is found throughout this modern lodging and
HOTEL   has been mixed with contemporary and antique Mexican decorative
Fodor's Choice   pieces; the sculptural furniture is as comfortable as it is captivating. **Pros:**
★   saltwater swimming pool is fabulous; generous breakfasts are delicious
(mangoes right off the tree!); boogie boards, beach towels and umbrellas
available for beach use; five-minute walk to the beach. **Cons:** 10-minute
walk to downtown; not recommended for families with young children.
⑤ *Rooms from: $125* ⌧ *Camino La Cachora* 🕾 *612/145–0099* ⊕ *www.
thehotelito.com* 🛏 *4 rooms* ⍥ *Breakfast* ✛ *A1.*

$ ⛶ **Las Casitas Bed & Breakfast.** Canadian artist Wendy Faith has used her
B&B/INN   talents to turn the rustic adobe-and-wood casitas on this property into
cozy, artsy lodgings set amid a lush, tropical garden. **Pros:** generous
Mexican breakfasts, with a few favorite dishes from the north, come
with house coffee; suites have private baths. **Cons:** rooms share shower;
street parking only. ⑤ *Rooms from: $85* ⌧ *Rangel between Obregón
and Hidalgo* 🕾 *612/145–0255* ⊕ *www.lascasitasbandb.com* 🛏 *3 rooms
with shared bath, 2 suites* ⊟ *No credit cards* ⍥ *Breakfast* ✛ *C2.*

$$ ⛶ **Posada La Poza.** West of town, overlooking a bird-filled lagoon that
HOTEL   gives way to the Pacific, this is the only Todos Santos property right on
Fodor's Choice   the water. **Pros:** gracious owners; very generous, delicious breakfasts; gor-
★   geous saltwater pool and hot tubs. **Cons:** no children under 12; no TV or
phones; need car to stay here. ⑤ *Rooms from: $200* ⌧ *Follow signs on
Hwy. 19 and on Benito Juárez to beach* 🕾 *612/145–0400, 855/552–7692
in U.S.* ⊕ *www.lapoza.com* 🛏 *8 suites* ⍥ *Breakfast* ✛ *C3.*

$ ⛶ **San Pedrito Surf Hotel.** Just outside Todos Santos, west of the village of
HOTEL   El Pescadero, serious surfers and anyone else in the know gather at this
cozy, family-style hotel. **Pros:** as great for families or groups as it is for
couples; fabulous beach and surfing right off the patio; laid-back but
helpful staff; big casitas, which sleep up to six people, are good value.
Cons: challenging to find—look for sign on highway; need car to stay
here; three-night minimum stay; reservations procedure can be difficult.

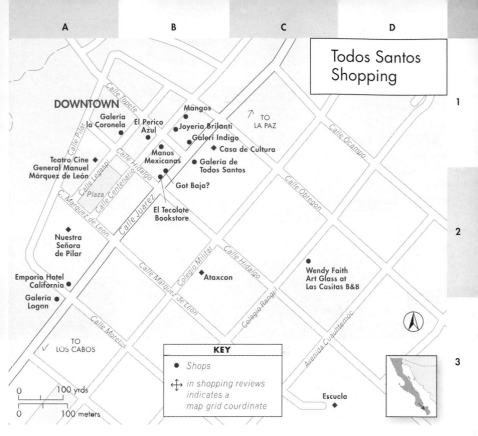

Todos Santos Shopping

DOWNTOWN

A · B · C · D

1 · 2 · 3

Calle Topete
Galería la Coronela
El Perico Azul
Mangos
Joyeria Brilanti
Galeri Indigo
↗ TO LA PAZ
Calle Ocampo
Casa de Cultura
Teatro/Cine General Manuel Márquez de León
Calle Hidalgo
Calle Legaspi
Manos Mexicanas
Galería de Todos Santos
Calle Obregon
Plaza
Calle Centenario
Got Baja?
C. Marquez de Leon
Calle Juarez
El Tecolote Bookstore
Nuestra Señora de Pilar
Calle Hidalgo
Emporio Hotel California
Calle Marquez de Leon
Colegio Militar
Ataxcon
Calle Rangel
Wendy Faith Art Glass at Las Casitas B&B
Galería Logan
Calle Morelos
Colegio Rangel
Avenida Cuauhtemoc
TO LOS CABOS

KEY
● Shops
⊕ in shopping reviews indicates a map grid coordinate

Escuela ◆

0 — 100 yrds
0 — 100 meters

$ Rooms from: $80 ⊠ Playa San Pedrito ⊕ www.sanpedritosurf.com ⤳ 6 casitas ▬ No credit cards ⊕ C3.

$ ⌨ **Todos Santos Inn.** This converted 19th-century house, with only eight guest rooms, is unparalleled in design and comfort, owing to the loving care and attention of the owners. **Pros:** traditional Mexican elegance and hospitality at its best; the interior courtyard of this property is a verdant oasis. **Cons:** street parking only; no kids under 12. $ Rooms from: $125 ⊠ Calle Legaspi 33 ☎ 612/145–0040 ⊕ www.todossantosinn.com ⤳ 4 rooms, 4 suites ✉ Breakfast ⊕ C1.

B&B/INN

Fodor's Choice

★

SHOPPING

Although Todos Santos is gaining renown in all aspects of its tourism offerings, the name still means shopping to most Los Cabos–area visitors. Artists from the U. S. Southwest (and a few from Mexico) found a haven here some two decades ago. Their galleries and shops showcase traditional and contemporary work. There is a strong Baja emphasis in the art, and you'll find beautiful jewelry and fine crafts from all over Mexico.

Colorful blankets for sale in a Todos Santos market

ART GALLERIES

Galería de Todos Santos. Five international artists living here in Baja have joined together to present their paintings in this gallery, one of the town's first and a focal point for the ever-changing local arts scene. A space in the gallery opens as an Asian restuarant, Michael's at the Gallery, on Friday and Saturday evenings. (⇨ *Where to Eat.*) ⊠ *Calle Juárez at Calle Topete* ☎ *612/145–0500* ⊕ *www.galeriadetodossantos. com* ⊗ *Mon.–Sat. 10–4* ✛ *B1.*

Galería Indigo. Local artists exhibit their works, primarily Baja-themed landscapes and abstracts, at this Belgian-owned gallery. ⊠ *Calle Juárez at Calle Topete* ☎ *612/145–0808* ⊗ *Mon.–Sat. 10–5* ✛ *B1.*

Galería La Coronela. Galería La Coronela exhibits the work of prodigious painter Victor Vega, as well as paintings by his daughter, Sofía. ⊠ *Calle Legaspi between Hidalgo and Topete* ☎ *612/149–8294* ⊗ *Daily 10–5* ✛ *A1.*

Galería Logan. The namesake gallery features the work of Jill Logan, a Southern Californian who has been in Todos Santos since 1998. Jill does bold oil-on-canvas paintings and complexly layered multimedia pieces. ⊠ *Calle Juárez and Morelos* ☎ *612/145–0151* ⊕ *www.jilllogan. com* ⊗ *Mon.–Sat. 10–5* ✛ *A3.*

Wendy Faith. Wendy Faith sells semiprecious gemstone jewelry. The art-glass studio has stained, fused, and slumped glass. ⊠ *Calle Rangel between Obregón and Hidalgo* ☎ *612/145–0255* ⊕ *www. lascasitasbandb.com* ✛ *C2.*

BOOKS

El Tecolote Bookstore. El Tecolote Bookstore is the best bookstore in Los Cabos region. Stop here for Latin American literature, poetry, children's books, current fiction and nonfiction, and books on Baja. Take a break with a coffee or juice in the back ⊠ *Calle Juárez at Calle Hidalgo* ☎ *612/145–0295* ☻ *Mon.–Sat. 9–5, Sun. noon–3* ✢ *B2.*

CLOTHING AND FOLK ART

El Perico Azul. El Perico Azul has fine handmade Mexican clothing (check out guayaberas from the Yucatán) for men and women, handwoven tablecloths, and a selection of folk art. ⊠ *Centenario at Topete* ☎ *612/145–0222* ☻ *Mon.–Sat. 10–4* ✢ *B1.*

Fodor'sChoice
★
Mangos. Mangos is filled with gorgeous Guatemalan textiles, Mexican folk art, belts, purses, wood carvings, and Day of the Dead figurines. ⊠ *Calle Centenario, between Calle Topete and Calle Obregón* ☎ *612/145–0451* ✢ *B1.*

Manos Mexicanas. Manos Mexicanas is a treasure trove of fine Mexican crafts, jewelry, decorative objects, and work by local potter Rubén Gutiérrez. Owner Alejandra Brilanti has amassed an incredible collection of affordable pieces. You are not likely to leave empty-handed. ⊠ *Topete at Centenario* ☎ *612/145–0538* ☻ *Daily 10–5* ✢ *B1.*

JEWELRY

Fodor'sChoice
★
Joyeria Brilanti. Joyeria Brilanti is a showcase for the stunning jewelry and design works of famed Taxco silversmith Ana Brilanti, in addition to a number of other contemporary-jewelry artists whose work shares the same dramatic aesthetic. Be sure to look at the silver tea services and other functional pieces. You'll also find selected stone carvings and bronzes from local artists. Prices are reasonable and the charming proprietor, José, is the deceased Ms. Brilanti's son. ⊠ *Centenario near Topete* ☎ *612/145–0799* ☻ *Mon.–Sat. 10–5* ✢ *B1.*

MARKETS

There's an informal farmers' market on Camino Militar near Hidalgo on Friday, where you can find a surprising amount of organic produce. If you get hungry while you're wandering among the stalls, don't hesitate to grab a taco or three at one of the carts by the corner.

SOUVENIRS

Got Baja?. You'll find a nice selection of Baja-themed souvenirs, including quality T-shirts, at this downtown shop. A branch is in La Paz. ⊠ *Calle Juárez s/n, between Hidalgo and Topete* ☎ *612/178–0067* ⊕ *www.gotbajamaps.com* ☻ *Daily 10–5* ✢ *B1.*

NIGHTLIFE AND THE ARTS

As tourism grows in Todos Santos, so do its nightlife options. You'll never mistake this place for Los Cabos, however, and the town is quite fine with that state of affairs, thank you very much. Lingering over dinner remains a time-honored way to spend a Todos Santos evening.

8

FESTIVALS

Todos Santos holds three annual arts-related festivals during high season, January and February. Make reservations weeks in advance if you plan to be here at those times. Visit ⊕ *www.elcalendariodetodossantos. com* for dates and details of these and other events.

Festival de Cine de Todos Santos (*Todos Santos Film Festival*). Todos Santos screens several new Latin American films during a 10-day festival in late February and early March. The 1940s-era Teatro Cine General Manuel Márquez de León serves as the venue here with a few of the films being shown at the Teatro Juárez in La Paz. ⊕ *www.todossantoscinefest.com.*

Festival del Arte Todos Santos (*Todos Santos Arts Festival*). The city goes all out to celebrate Mexican dance, music, folklore, and culture for a week in early February each year. Several of the downtown galleries hold special events in conjunction with the festival.

Todos Santos Music Festival. The town's annual music festival dates only from 2012, but reception was so phenomenal—thanks largely to an appearance by U.S. group R.E.M.—that it promises to be an annual event each January.

BARS AND WINE BARS

La Bodega de Todos Santos. Twice-weekly wine tastings at this downtown wineshop make an interesting twist on a night out in Todos Santos. Stop by Monday or Wednesday evening during the October–June high season for a taste of Baja wines—a couple of vintages are featured each time—and an appetizer supplied by a rotating selection of local restaurants. ⊠ *Calle Hidalgo, between Juárez and Colegio Militar* ☏ *612/152–0181* ⊗ *Oct.–June, Mon. and Wed. 5–8 pm* .

La Santeña. You'll find this upscale rendition of a Mexican cantina (with a restaurant, too) in the Hotel Casa Tota. It's a great place to stop for a quiet drink. ⊠ *Calle Alvaro Obregón* ☏ *612/145–0590* ⊕ *www. hotelcasatota.com* ⊗ *Daily 7 am–11 pm.*

Shut Up Frank's. Take your pick from the sporting events shown on six big-screen TVs at the consummate sports bar in Todos Santos. Enjoy the scrumptious burgers here, too. ⊠ *Degollado and Rangel, across from Pemex station* ☏ *612/145–0707* ⊕ *www.shutupfranks.com* ⊗ *Daily 10–10. Closed Mon. July–Sept.*

EN ROUTE If you're headed to La Paz on Highway 1 from San José del Cabo, a large white sphere and a shrine to the Virgin of Guadalupe at Km 93 mark 23.27° latitude north, or the Tropic of Cancer. You cross the line between the earth's temperate zone and the tropics here. Of course, Baja is Baja, and you won't detect any difference in climate no matter which side of the line you are on. Many stop for a photo posing in front of the marker, which is 2 km (1¼ miles) south of the turnoff to Santiago. You can decide how obligatory that seems.

The Tropic of Cancer also crosses Highway 19 on the West Cape, just outside Todos Santos. There is no marker there.

La Paz is the lovely and inviting capital of Baja California Sur.

LA PAZ

81 km (49 miles) north of Todos Santos, 178 km (107 miles) north of San José del Cabo (via Hwy. 1), 154 km (92 miles) north of Cabo San Lucas (via Hwy. 19).

Tidy, prosperous La Paz may be the capital of the state of Baja California Sur and home to about 220,000 residents, but it still feels like a small town in a time warp. This east-coast development could easily be the most traditional Mexican city in Baja Sur, the antithesis of the "gringolandia" developments to the south. Granted, there are plenty of foreigners in La Paz, particularly during snowbird season. But in the slowest part of the off-season, during the oppressive late-summer heat, you can easily see how La Paz aptly translates to "peace," and how its residents can be called *paceños* (peaceful ones).

Travelers use La Paz as both a destination in itself and a stopping-off point en route to Los Cabos. There's always excellent scuba diving and sportfishing in the Sea of Cortez. La Paz is the base for divers and fishermen headed for Cerralvo, La Partida, and the Espíritu Santo islands, where parrot fish, manta rays, neons, and angels blur the clear waters by the shore, and marlin, dorado, and yellowtail leap from the sea. Cruise ships are more and more often spotted sailing toward the bay as La Paz emerges as an attractive port. (Only small ships can berth at La Paz itself; most cruise liners dock at its port of Pichilingue, about 16 km [10 miles] north of town.)

La Paz officially became the state capital in 1974, and is its largest settlement (though the combined Los Cabos agglomeration is quickly

LA PAZ LANGUAGE SCHOOLS

La Paz is a laid-back city with a picturesque waterfront and some fine beaches—a great spot to work on your Spanish skills at one of the good language schools in the area. Perhaps the only drawback to learning Spanish in this area is that its large tourism industry has made English widely spoken. (It still doesn't compare to the numbers of foreigners living in Los Cabos.) Resist the temptation to hang out with other English speakers. Plunge in and practice your Spanish outside class.

Centro de Idiomas, Cultura y Comunicación. This language school offers personalized classes and immersion programs at all levels. It arranges for students to live with local families to get the maximum possible exposure to the language and daily practice. ✉ *Francisco Madero 2460* ☎ *612/125–7554* ⊕ *www.cicclapaz.com.*

Se Habla . . . La Paz. Se Habla is an American-owned language school with regular classes and home-stay programs. It also offers special programs for health-care and legal professionals. ✉ *Francisco Madero 540* ☎ *612/122–7763* ⊕ *www.sehablalapaz.com.*

catching up). All bureaucracy holds court here, and it's the site of the ferry port to Mazatlán and Topolobampo, the port of Los Mochis, on the mainland. There are few chain hotels or restaurants, but that's sure to change as resort developments come to fruition around the area.

La Paz region, including parts of the coastline south of the city, is slated as the future building site of several large-scale, high-end resort developments with golf courses, marinas, and vacation homes. Economic doldrums of recent years put brakes on those projects, but as Mexico's tourism finally, slowly, cautiously begins to rebound, plans have moved to the front burner again.

GETTING HERE AND AROUND

Aeropuerto General Manuel Márquez de León (LAP) is 11 km (7 miles) northwest of La Paz. Alaska Air partner Horizon Air flies daily from Los Angeles. Aereo Calafia connects La Paz with Los Cabos. Several airlines connect La Paz with Mexico City and various domestic airports in Mexico. Flying into the Aeropuerto Internacional de Los Cabos, two hours away near San José del Cabo, offers a far better selection of fares and itineraries. Ecobaja Tours operates shuttles five times daily between Los Cabos Airport and La Paz for $30 one way. In La Paz, taxis are readily available and inexpensive. Taxis between La Paz airport and towns are inexpensive (about $5) and convenient. A ride within town costs under $5; a trip to Pichilingue costs around $10. In La Paz the main Terminal de Autobus is on the malecón at Independencia. Bus companies offer service to Todos Santos (one hour), Los Cabos (two hours).

Baja Ferries connects La Paz with Topolobampo, the port at Los Mochis, on the mainland, with daily high-speed ferries. The trip takes seven hours and costs $73 per person. Baja Ferries also connects La Paz and Mazatlán; it's a 16-hour trip and costs $81 per person. You can buy tickets for ferries at La Paz Pichilingue terminal. The ferries

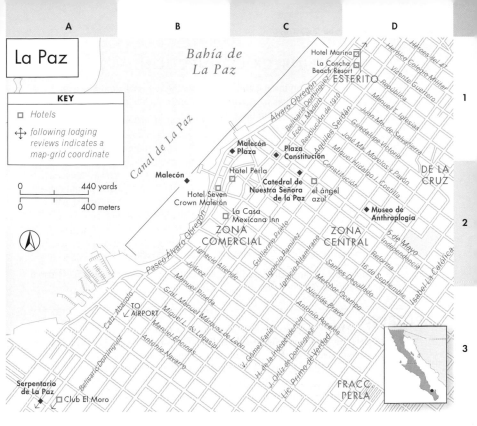

carry passengers with and without vehicles. If you're taking a car to the mainland, you must obtain a vehicle permit before boarding. Ferry officials will ask to see your Mexican auto-insurance papers and tourist card, which are obtained when crossing the U.S. border into Baja.

ESSENTIALS

Airlines Aereo Calafia ☎ 612/123-2643 ⊕ www.aerocalafia.com.mx. **Horizon Air** ☎ 800/252-7522 ⊕ www.alaskaair.com. **Aeropuerto Manuel Márquez de León** ☎ 612/124-6307 ⊕ www.aeropuertosgap.com.mx.

Bus Contacts Autotransportes Aguila ✉ Paseo Alvaro Obregón, between Independencia and 5 de Mayo ☎ 612/123-0000 ⊕ www.autotransportesaguila. net.**Ecobaja Tours** ☎ 612/123-0000 ⊕ www.ecobajatours.com.

Currency Exchange Banamex ✉ Esquerro 110 ☎ 612/122-1011 ⊕ www.banamex.com.

Emergencies (☎ Dial 065, 060, or 066). **Highway Patrol** ☎ 612/122-0369. **Police** ☎ 066.

Ferry Lines Baja Ferries ✉ La Paz Pichilingue Terminal ☎ 612/123-6600 ⊕ www.bajaferries.com.

Hospitals Centro de Especialidades Médicas ✉ Calle Delfines 110 ☎ 612/124-0400.

THE STEINBECK CONNECTION

For an account of the Baja of years past, few works beat John Steinbeck's *The Log from the Sea of Cortez*, published in 1951. It recounts a six-week voyage he took in 1940 with marine biologist Ed Ricketts for the purpose of cataloging new aquatic species on the gulf side of Baja California. (*Phialoba steinbecki*, a previously unknown species of sea anemone discovered during the excursion, was later named for the author.)

Steinbeck lamented what he was sure would one day be the inevitable tourism growth to arrive on the peninsula. The author was mistaken on one key point however: he was certain the megaboom would come to La Paz and not to then-sleepy Cabo San Lucas.

Internet Baja Net ⊠ *Av. Madero 430* ☎ *612/125–9380.*

Pharmacies Farmacia Baja California ⊠ *Calle Independencia at Calle Madero* ☎ *612/122–0240.*

EXPLORING

Catedral de Nuestra Señora de la Paz. The downtown church, Catedral de Nuestra Señora de la Paz, is a simple, unassuming stone building with a modest gilded altar but beautiful stained-glass windows. The church was built in 1860 near the site of La Paz's first mission, which no longer exists. The two towers of the present cathedral were added a half century later. ⊠ *Calle Juárez, Colonia Centro* ☎ *612/122–2596* ⊕ *www.diocesislapaz.com.*

Fodor's Choice ★ **Malecón.** Offically the Malecón Alvaro Obregón, this seaside promenade is La Paz's seawall, tourist zone, and social center all rolled into one. It runs for 5 km (3 miles) along Paseo Álvaro Obregón and has a sidewalk as well as several park areas in the sand just off it. Paceños are fond of strolling the malecón at sunset when the heat of the day finally begins to subside. Teenagers slowly cruise the street in their spiffed-up cars, couples nuzzle on park benches, and grandmothers meander along while keeping an eye on the kids. (You will see people swimming here, and the water is cleaner than it used to be, but the beaches outside town are a far surer bet in that regard.) Marina La Paz, at the malecón's southwest end, is an ever-growing development with condominiums, vacation homes, and a pleasant café-lined walkway. ⊠ *Paseo Alvaro Obregón.*

Malecón Plaza. A two-story white gazebo is the focus of Malecón Plaza, a small concrete square where musicians sometimes appear on weekend nights. An adjacent street, Calle 16 de Septiembre, leads inland to the city. ⊠ *Paseo Alvaro Obregón and Calle 16 de Septiembre.*

Museo de Antropología. La Paz's culture and heritage are well represented at the Museo de Antropología, which has re-creations of indigenous Comondu and Las Palmas villages, photos of cave paintings found in Baja, and copies of Cortés's writings on first sighting La Paz. All exhibit descriptions are labeled in Spanish only, but the museum's staff will help you translate as best they can. If you're a true Baja aficionado and want to delve into the region's history, this museum is a must; otherwise, a quick visit is all you need, if even that. ⊠ *Calle Altamirano at Calle 5 de Mayo, Centro* ☎ *612/122–0162* ✉ *$3* ⊘ *Daily 9–6.*

Plaza Constitución. Plaza Constitución, the true center of La Paz, is a traditional zócalo that also goes

SUNRISE, SUNSET

La Paz sits on the east coast of the Baja peninsula, but a convoluted curvature of the shoreline here positions the city to look out west over the Sea of Cortez. That means that you can enjoy beautiful sunsets over the water here at the end of the day.

by the name Jardín Velazco. Concerts are held in the park's gazebo and locals gather here for art shows and fairs. Day-to-day life here entails shoe shines and local bingo games. ⊠ *Bordered by Av. Independencia, Calles 5 de Mayo, Revolución de 1910, and Madero, Centro.*

Serpentario de La Paz. Better that you encounter all the creatures that slip and slither here in the safety of this serpentarium than out in the wilds of Baja. On display in the open-air exhibits are the several rattlesnake and iguana species found in the region, as well as a python and an anaconda, neither of which are native to the Baja peninsula. The focus here in La Paz's newest tourist attraction is on the importance that reptiles serve in the environment. Labeling is entirely in Spanish, but the staff offers guided tours in English with advance notice. Regardless of the language, tours are included in your admission price. ⊠ *Nueva Reforma and Guaycura, Centro* ☎ *612/122–5611* ⊕ *www.elserpentario.org* ✉ *$8* ⊘ *Tues.–Sun. 10–4.*

BEACHES

Around the malecón, stick to ambling along the sand while watching local families enjoy the sunset. Just north of town the beach experience is much better; it gets even better north of Pichilingue. Save your swimming and snorkeling energies for this area. All facilities listed here exist on the weekends. Their existence on weekdays, especially of lifeguards, may be spottier.

Playa Balandra. A rocky point shelters a clear, warm bay at Playa Balandra, 21 km (13 miles) north of La Paz. Several small coves and pristine beaches appear and disappear with the tides, but there's always a calm area where you can wade and swim. Snorkeling is fair around Balandra's south end where there's a coral reef. You may spot clams, starfish, and anemones. Kayaking and snorkeling tours usually set out from around here. If not on a tour, bring your own gear, as rentals aren't normally available. The beach has a few barbecue pits, trash cans, and palapas for shade. Camping is permitted but there are no hookups. The smallish beach gets crowded on weekends, but on a weekday morning you may have the place to yourself. Sand flies can be a nuisance here between July and October. **Amenities:** Lifeguard; toilets; showers; food concession; picnic tables; grills/fire pits; parking lot; camping. **Best for:** swimming; walking; snorkeling.

Playa Caimancito. La Concha hotel takes up some of the sand at the beach 5 km (3 miles) north of La Paz. But you can enter the beach both north and south of the hotel and enjoy a long stretch of sand facing the bay and downtown. Locals swim laps here, as the water is almost always calm and salty enough for easy buoyancy. There aren't any public facilities here, but if you wander over to the hotel for lunch or a drink you can use its restrooms and rent water toys. **Amenities:** Toilets; food concession; parking lot. **Best for:** sunsets; swimming; walking.

Playa El Tecolote. Spend a Sunday at Playa El Tecolote, 24 km (15 miles) north of La Paz, and you'll feel like you've experienced the Mexico of old. Families set up house on the soft sand, kids race after seagulls and each other, and *abuelas* (grandmothers) daintily lift their skirts to wade in the water. Vendors rent out beach chairs, umbrellas, kayaks, and small, motorized boats; a couple of restaurants serve up simple fare such as freshly grilled snapper. These eateries are usually open throughout the week, though they sometimes close on chilly days. Facilities include public restrooms, fire pits, and trash cans. Camping is permitted, but there are no hookups. **Amenities:** Lifeguard; toilets; showers; food concession; picnic tables; grills/fire pits; playground; parking lot; camping. **Best for:** sunsets; swimming; walking.

🄯 **Playa Pichilingue.** Starting in the time of Spanish invaders, Pichilingue, 16 km (10 miles) north of La Paz, was known for its preponderance of oysters bearing black pearls. In 1940 a disease killed them off, leaving the beach deserted. Today it's a pleasant place to sunbathe and watch sportfishing boats haul in their daily catches. Locals set up picnics here on weekend afternoons and linger until the blazing sun settles into the bay. Restaurants consisting of little more than a palapa over plastic tables and chairs serve oysters *diablo,* fresh clams, and plenty of cold beer. Pichilingue curves northeast along the bay to the terminals where the ferries from Mazatlán and Topolobampo arrive and many of the sportfishing boats depart. If La Paz is on your cruise itinerary, you'll likely dock at Pichilingue, too. One downside to this beach: traffic buzzes by on the nearby freeway. The water here, though not particularly clear, is calm enough for swimming. **Amenities:** Lifeguard; toilets; showers; food concession; picnic tables; fire pits; parking lot. **Best for:** sunset; walking.

SPORTS AND OUTDOOR ACTIVITIES

BOATING AND FISHING

The considerable fleet of private boats in La Paz now has room for docking at three marinas: Fidepaz Marina at the north end of town, and the Marina Palmira and Marina La Paz south of town. Most hotels can arrange trips. Fishing tournaments are held in August, September, and October.

Fishermen's Fleet. The Fishermen's Fleet has daylong fishing on pangas (skiffs), as well as multiday excursions to Magdalena Bay. 🖃 *612/122–1313, 888/642–7024 in U.S.* ⊕ *www.fishermensfleet.com.*

A diver gets up close and personal with a sea lion in the waters of the Sea of Cortez.

Mosquito Fleet. The Mosquito Fleet has cabin cruisers with charters starting around $650 per person for up to four people, and superpangas at $475 per person for two people. ☎ *612/121–6120, 877/408–6769 in U.S.* ⊕ *www.bajamosquitofleet.com.*

KAYAKING

★ The calm waters off La Paz are perfect for kayaking, and you can take multiday trips along the coast to Loreto or out to the nearby islands.

Baja Expeditions. Baja Expeditions, one of the oldest outfitters working in Baja (since 1974), offers several kayak tours, including multi-night trips between Loreto and La Paz. A support boat carries all the gear, including ingredients for great meals. The seven-day trip in the Sea of Cortez with camping on remote island beaches starts at $1,400 per person, based on double occupancy. ✉ *2625 Garnet Ave., San Diego, California, USA* ☎ *612/125–3828, 800/843–6967 in U.S.* ⊕ *www.bajaex.com.*

Fun Baja. Fun Baja offers kayak trips around the islands, scuba and snorkel excursions, and land tours. A day of kayaking and snorkeling will run about $125. ✉ *Hwy. to Pichilingue, Km 2* ☎ *612/106–7148, 800/667–5362 in U.S.* ⊕ *www.funbaja.com.*

SCUBA DIVING AND SNORKELING

Popular diving and snorkeling spots include the coral banks off Isla Espíritu Santo, the sea-lion colony off Isla Partida, and the seamount 14 km (9 miles) farther north (best for serious divers).

★ **Cortez Club.** The Cortez Club is a full-scale water-sports center with equipment rental and scuba, snorkeling, kayaking, and sportfishing tours, as well as the complete slate of PADI instructional courses. A two-tank dive costs about $125. ⊠ *Hwy. to Pichilingue, Km 5, between downtown and Pichilingue* ☏ *612/121–6120, 877/408–6769 in U.S.* ⊕ *www.cortezclub.com.*

Fun Baja. Fun Baja offers scuba and snorkel trips with the sea lions. Two-tank scuba trips start at $140. ⊠ *Hwy. to Pichilingue, Km 2* ☏ *612/106–7148, 800/667–5362 in U.S.* ⊕ *www.funbaja.com.*

TOUR OPERATORS

KAYAKING

Nichols Expeditions. Nichols Expeditions arranges kayaking tours to Isla Espíritu Santo and between Loreto and La Paz, with camping along the way. A nine-day trip costs $1,350. It also offers a combination of sea kayaking in the Sea of Cortez with whale-watching in Magdalena Bay. A nine-day trip costs $1,400. ⊠ *497 N. Main, Moab, Utah, USA* ☏ *800/648–8488 in U.S.* ⊕ *www.nicholsexpeditions.com.*

SCUBA DIVING

Baja Expeditions. Baja Expeditions runs multiday dive packages in the Sea of Cortez. Seven-day excursions aboard the 80-foot *Don José* dedicated dive boat start at $1,695 for cabin, food, and nearly unlimited diving. Live-aboard trips run from June into November. You may spot whale sharks in June. ⊠ *2625 Garnet Ave., San Diego, California, USA* ☏ *612/125–3828, 800/843–6967 in U.S.* ⊕ *www.bajaex.com.*

WHALE-WATCHING

La Paz is a good entry point for whale-watching expeditions to **Bahía Magdalena**, 266 km (165 miles) northwest of La Paz on the Pacific coast. Note, however, that such trips entail about six hours of travel from La Paz and back for two to three hours on the water. Only a few tour companies offer this as a daylong excursion, however, because of the time and distance constraints.

Many devoted whale-watchers opt to stay overnight in San Carlos, the small town by the bay. Most La Paz hotels can make arrangements for excursions, or you can head out on your own by renting a car or taking a public bus from La Paz to San Carlos, and then hire a boat captain to take you into the bay. The air and water are cold during whale season from December to April, so you'll need to bring a warm windbreaker and gloves. Captains are not allowed to "chase" whales, but that doesn't keep the whale mamas and their babies from approaching your panga so closely you can reach out and touch them.

An easier expedition is a whale-watching trip in the Sea of Cortez from La Paz, which involves boarding a boat in La Paz and motoring around until whales are spotted. They most likely won't come as close to the boats and you won't see the mothers and newborn calves at play, but it's still fabulous watching the whales breeching and spouting nearby.

Baja Expeditions. Baja Expeditions runs adventure cruises around the tip of Baja between La Paz and Magdalena Bay. The eight-day cruises start at $1,995 per person, based on double occupancy. ⊠ *2625 Garnet Ave., San Diego, California, USA* ☏ *612/125–3828, 800/843–6967 in U.S.* ⊕ *www.bajaex.com.*

Cortez Club. The water-sports center Cortez Club runs extremely popular whale-watching trips in winter. The one-day excursion costs $180 per person. ✉ *Hwy. to Pichilingue, Km 5, between downtown and Pichilingue* ☎ *612/121–6120, 877/408–6769 in U.S.* ⊕ *www.cortezclub.com.*

WHERE TO EAT

$$ ✕**Caffé Milano.** La Paz's hippest, hottest dining spot sits in a century-old
ITALIAN restored building, painted ocher on the outside with a bright blue door,
Fodor's Choice and with vaulted ceilings on the inside. Owners Lei Tam and Michele
★ Milano, natives of Hong Kong and Italy, respectively, traveled the world, gathering knowledge of the world's cuisines, before setting down in La Paz. Tam has now established herself as one of Mexico's top woman chefs. At its core, the menu is standard Italian—the pastas and breads are made fresh here daily—with local touches, such as chipotle pepper in a seafood pasta, tossed in. You can see your creation being made: the kitchen is open to view. Best of all, prices here are reasonable for what you get. ⑤ *Average main: $17* ✉ *Esquerro 15 at 16 de Septiembre, Centro* ☎ *612/125–9981* ⊕ *www.caffemilano.com.mx* ⊙ *Closed Sun.*

$ ✕**El Bismark.** The original Bismark is a bit out of the way, but it attracts
MEXICAN families who settle down for hours at long wood tables, while waitresses divide their attention between patrons and *telenovelas* (Latin American soap operas) on the TV above the bar. Tuck into seafood cocktails, enormous grilled lobsters, or carne asada served with beans, guacamole, and homemade tortillas. However, the restaurant is most loved for its seafood tacos, sold out of ice coolers that are set out in front of the restaurant before noon. The smaller Bismark on the malecón, called el Bismark-cito, is quite popular. ⑤ *Average main: $10* ✉ *Av. Degollado at Calle Altamirano, Centro* ☎ *612/122–4854* ⑤ *Average main: $10* ✉ *Alvaro Obregón s/n, at the malecón.*

$ ✕**El Quinto Sol.** El Quinto Sol's brightly painted exterior is covered with
VEGETARIAN serpent symbols and smiling suns. The all-vegetarian menu includes fresh juices and herbal elixirs. The four-course prix-fixe *comida corrida* (daily special) is a bargain; it's served from noon to 4 pm. The back half of this space is a bare-bones store stocked with natural foods. ⑤ *Average main: $5* ✉ *Blvd. Domínguez 60 at Av. Independencia, Centro* ☎ *612/122–1692* ▭ *No credit cards* ⊙ *Closed Sun.*

$$ ✕**La Pazta.** Locals rave about the excellent homemade pastas and pizzas
ITALIAN in this trattoria with a sleek black-and-white interior in the Hotel Mediterrane, a small inn popular with European visitors. Look for imported cheeses and wines and bracing espresso. La Pazta opens only for dinner, but you can enjoy the same fine imported Italian *caffe* in the hotel's adjacent café, open for breakfast and lunch. ⑤ *Average main: $13* ✉ *Hotel Mediterrane, Allende 36, Centro* ☎ *612/125–1195* ⊕ *www.hotelmed. com* ⊙ *No lunch. No dinner Tues.*

$ ✕**Los Laureles.** A small stand that looks as if it might have been rolled
SEAFOOD along the street by a vendor is just the entryway decoration for this well-established restaurant. Whether you eat at a bench at the stand outside or dine within in the air-conditioning, if you like seafood, you will enjoy Los Laureles. It offers all sorts of *fruits de mer* served in many different ways, but the seafood cocktails are notable for their freshness (you can

8

even try the shrimp raw) and variety (abalone is an option). ⑤ *Average main: $10 ✉ Paseo Alvaro Obregón s/n, Centro ☎ 612/128–8532.*

$$
SEAFOOD
★

✕ **Mar y Peña.** The freshest, tastiest seafood cocktails, ceviches, and clam tacos imaginable are served in this nautical restaurant crowded with locals. If you come with friends, go for the *mariscada,* a huge platter of shellfish and fish for four. The shrimp *albondigas* (meatballs) soup has a hearty fish stock seasoned with cilantro; and the crab *ranchero* is a savory mix of crabmeat, onions, tomatoes, and capers. Portions are huge. ⑤ *Average main: $14 ✉ Calle 16 de Septiembre, between Isabel la Católica and Albáñez, Centro ☎ 612/122–9949.*

$
BAKERY

✕ **Pan d'Les.** Fortify yourself for a morning of sightseeing—the place is open only until 2:30 pm—at Pan d'Les in La Paz's central business district. Transplanted U.S. pastry chef Les Carmona hand forms his European-style breads and pastries at his small bakery. It's all flour, water, yeast, and salt here, but no preservatives. You'll find a good selection each morning. Every day is the day for his slow-rising *rústico* sourdough bread; the specialty on individual days of the week might be focaccia or a red wine–nut bread. An extra yummy treat in this warm climate are the homemade ice cream sandwiches. ⑤ *Average main: $4 ✉ Madero, between 5 de Mayo and Constitución, Centro ☎ 612/119–8392 ▭ No credit cards ◷ Closed Sun. No dinner.*

$
MEXICAN

✕ **Rancho Viejo.** Everything is delicious, and prices are reasonable at this cheerful little restaurant painted in bright yellow and orange. Meats are the specialty here, but just about everything on the menu is good and choices are abundant. The *tacos de arrachera,* a kind of beef taco, are particularly tasty. You can pop in any time, day or night, since this restaurant is open 24 hours. ⑤ *Average main: $9 ✉ Blvd. Dominguez s/n, at M. de León 228, near the malecón ☎ 612/128–4647.*

$
MEXICAN
★

✕ **Tacos Hermanos González.** La Paz has plenty of great taco shacks, but none is better than the small stand of the González brothers who serve up hunks of fresh fish wrapped in corn tortillas and offer bowls of condiments with which to decorate your taco. The top quality draws sizable crowds of satisfied sidewalk munchers. ⑤ *Average main: $7 ✉ Mutualismo at Esquerro, Centro ▭ No credit cards.*

WHERE TO STAY

For expanded reviews and current deals, visit Fodors.com.

$
RESORT

⌂ **Club El Moro.** Possibly the best bargain on the malecón, although a bit away from the city center itself, this vacation-ownership resort has very reasonable suite rentals on a nightly and weekly basis. **Pros:** good value; shallow pool great if you don't care to swim. **Cons:** some dated decor; rooms facing pool area can be noisy. ⑤ *Rooms from: $81 ✉ Hwy. to Pichilingue, Km 2 ☎ 612/122–4084 or 866/375–2840 ⊕ www.clubelmoro.com ⌁ 18 rooms, 20 suites ❢◯❢ Breakfast ✛ A3.*

$
B&B/INN
Fodor'sChoice
★

⌂ **el ángel azul.** Owner Esther Ammann converted La Paz's historic courthouse into a bed-and-breakfast that's a comfortable retreat in the center of the city. **Pros:** lovely owner; attentive service; historic building; terrific value. **Cons:** street parking only, no kids under 12. ⑤ *Rooms from: $100 ✉ Av. Independencia 518, at Guillermo Prieto,*

Centro ☎ *612/125–5130* ⊕ *www.elangelazul.com* ⤳ *9 rooms, 1 suites* ⏐◎⏐ *Breakfast* ✛ *C2.*

$ 🖭 **Hotel Marina.** Here's a hotel with a full-service marina offering fish-
RESORT   ing, scuba diving, and kayaking. **Pros:** good value; amenities for fishing vacations. **Cons:** you may feel out of place if you're not here on a
fishing vacation. $ *Rooms from: $94* ✉ *Hwy. to Pichilingue, Km 2.5*
☎ *612/121–6254, 866/262–7187 in U.S.* ⊕ *www.hotelmarina.com.mx*
⤳ *85 rooms, 5 suites* ⏐◎⏐ *No meals* ✛ *D1.*

$ 🖭 **Hotel Perla.** The brown low-rise faces the malecón and has seen a
HOTEL   flurry of activity since 1940, due largely to its nightclub, La Cabaña.
Pros: central location; friendly staff; decent value for the price. **Cons:**
room facing street can be noisy; dated decor. $ *Rooms from: $78*
✉ *Paseo Alvaro Obregón 1570, Malecón* ☎ *612/122–0777, 888/242–
3757 in California and Arizona* ⊕ *www.hotelperlabaja.com* ⤳ *110
rooms* ⏐◎⏐ *No meals* ✛ *C2.*

$ 🖭 **Hotel Seven Crown Malecón.** This very reasonable, modern, minimal-
HOTEL   ist hotel is perfectly situated to one side of the malecón's action. **Pros:**
central location; affordable. **Cons:** very simple rooms; some rooms facing street can be noisy. $ *Rooms from: $97* ✉ *Paseo Alvaro Obregón
1710, Centro* ☎ *612/128–7787* ⊕ *www.sevencrownhotels.com* ⤳ *55
rooms, 9 suites* ⏐◎⏐ *No meals* ✛ *B2.*

$ 🖭 **La Casa Mexicana Inn.** Arlaine Cervantes has created a lovely home-
B&B/INN   like ambience in her small bed-and-breakfast just one block from the
malecón. **Pros:** central location; lovely owner; attentive service; terrific
value; exquisite art. **Cons:** closed 4½ months a year. $ *Rooms from:
$75* ✉ *Calle Nicolas Bravo 106, Centro* ☎ *612/125–2748* ⊕ *www.
casamex.com* ⤳ *6 rooms* ☽ *Closed June 1–Oct. 15* ⏐◎⏐ *No meals* ✛ *B2.*

$ 🖭 **La Concha Beach Resort.** On a long beach with calm water, this older
RESORT   resort has a water-sports center and a notable restaurant. **Pros:** ren-
♺   ovated rooms in good shape; lower priced rooms are good value.
Cons: you'll need a car to stay here. $ *Rooms from: $99* ✉ *Hwy. to
Pichilingue, Km 5* ☎ *612/121–6161, 800/999–2252 in U.S.* ⊕ *www.
laconcha.com* ⤳ *107 rooms* ⏐◎⏐ *No meals* ✛ *D1.*

SHOPPING

ART AND SOUVENIRS

Antigua California. Antigua California has the nicest selection of Mexican
folk art in La Paz, including wooden masks and lacquered boxes from
the mainland state of Guerrero. ✉ *Paseo Alvaro Obregón 220, Malecón*
☎ *612/125–5230* ☽ *Mon.–Sat. 9:30–8:30.*

Artesanía Cuauhtémoc. Artesanía Cuauhtémoc is the workshop of weaver
Fortunado Silva, who creates and sells colorful cotton place mats, rugs,
and tapestries. ✉ *Av. Abasolo, between Calles Nayarit and Oaxaca,
Centro* ☎ *612/122–4575* ☽ *Mon.–Sat. 10–5.*

Got Baja?. You'll find a nice selection of Baja-themed souvenirs, including
quality T-shirts, at this downtown shop. A branch is in Todos Santos.
✉ *Madero 1240, Centro* ☎ *612/125–5991* ⊕ *www.gotbajamaps.com.*

★   **Ibarra's Pottery.** The Ibarra family oversees the potters and painters at
their namesake shop. Their geometric designs and glazing technique

result in gorgeous mirrors, bowls, platters, and cups. ✉ *Guillermo Prieto 625, Centro* ☎ *612/122–0404* ☾ *Weekdays 9–3, Sat. 9–2.*

Mexican Designs. Unusual pottery is the hallmark of Mexican Designs. The boxes with cactus designs are particularly good souvenirs. ✉ *Calle Arreola 41, at Av. Zaragoza, Centro* ☎ *612/123–2231.*

BOOKS

Allende Books. This bookstore stocks La Paz's best selection of English-language works, mainly about Baja and Mexico, as well as laminated nature field guides. You'll also find a terrific selection of gifts here, including handcrafted jewelry, table runners, and wall hangings. ✉ *Independencia 518, between Serdán and Guillermo Prieto, Centro* ☎ *612/125–9114* ☾ *Mon.–Sat. 10–6.*

NIGHTLIFE AND THE ARTS

BARS AND DANCE CLUBS

La Terraza. The best spot for both sunset- and people-watching along the malecón is La Terraza at the Hotel Perla. The place makes killer margaritas, too. ✉ *Hotel Perla, Paseo Alvaro Obregón 1570, Malecón* ☎ *612/122–0777.*

★ **Las Varitas.** This Mexican rock club heats up after midnight. ✉ *Av. Independencia 111, at Domínguez, Centro* ☎ *612/123–1590* ☾ *Thurs.–Sat. 9 pm–3 am.*

PERFORMING ARTS

El Teatro de la Ciudad. La Paz's cultural center seats 1,500 and stages shows by visiting and local performers. ✉ *Av. Navarro 700, at Héroes de Independencia, Centro* ☎ *612/125–0486.*

UNDERSTANDING
LOS CABOS

VOCABULARY

SPANISH VOCABULARY

	ENGLISH	SPANISH	PRONUNCIATION
BASICS			
	Yes/no	Sí/no	see/no
	Please	Por favor	pore fah-**vore**
	May I?	¿Me permite?	may pair-**mee**-tay
	Thank you (very much)	(Muchas) gracias	(**moo**-chas) **grah**-see-as
	You're welcome	De nada	day **nah**-dah
	Excuse me	Con permiso	con pair-**mee**-so
	Pardon me	¿Perdón?	pair-**dohn**
	Could you tell me?	¿Podría decirme?	po-dree-ah deh-**seer**-meh
	I'm sorry	Lo siento	lo see-**en**-toh
	Good morning!	¡Buenos días!	**bway**-nohs **dee**-ahs
	Good afternoon!	¡Buenas tardes!	**bway**-nahs **tar**-dess
	Good evening!	¡Buenas noches!	**bway**-nahs **no**-chess
	Good-bye!	¡Adiós!/¡Hasta luego!	ah-dee-**ohss/ah** -stah **lwe**-go
	Mr./Mrs.	Señor/Señora	sen-**yor**/sen-**yohr**-ah
	Miss	Señorita	sen-yo-**ree**-tah
	Pleased to meet you	Mucho gusto	**moo**-cho **goose**-toh
	How are you?	¿Cómo está usted?	**ko**-mo es-**tah** oo-**sted**
	Very well, thank you.	Muy bien, gracias.	**moo**-ee bee-**en**, **grah**-see-as
	And you?	¿Y usted?	ee oos-**ted**
	Hello (on the telephone)	Diga	**dee**-gah
NUMBERS			
	1	un, uno	oon, **oo**-no
	2	dos	dos
	3	tres	tress
	4	cuatro	**kwah**-tro
	5	cinco	**sink**-oh

ENGLISH	SPANISH	PRONUNCIATION
6	seis	saice
7	siete	see-**et**-eh
8	ocho	**o**-cho
9	nueve	new-**eh**-vey
10	diez	dee-**es**
11	once	**ohn**-seh
12	doce	**doh**-seh
13	trece	**treh**-seh
14	catorce	ka-**tohr**-seh
15	quince	**keen**-seh
16	dieciséis	dee-es-ee-**saice**
17	diecisiete	dee-**es**-ee-see-**et**-eh
18	dieciocho	dee-es-ee-**o**-cho
19	diecinueve	**dee**-es-ee-new-**ev**-eh
20	veinte	**vain**-teh
21	veinte y uno/ veintiuno	**vain**-te-**oo**-noh
30	treinta	**train**-tah
32	treinta y dos	train-tay-**dohs**
40	cuarenta	kwah-**ren**-tah
43	cuarenta y tres	kwah-**ren**-tay-**tress**
50	cincuenta	seen-**kwen**-tah
54	cincuenta y cuatro	seen-**kwen**-tay **kwah**-tro
60	sesenta	sess-**en**-tah
65	sesenta y cinco	sess-**en**-tay **seen**-ko
70	setenta	set-**en**-tah
76	setenta y seis	set-en-tay **saice**
80	ochenta	oh-**chen**-tah
87	ochenta y siete	oh-**chen**-tay see-**yet**-eh
90	noventa	no-**ven**-tah

ENGLISH	SPANISH	PRONUNCIATION
98	noventa y ocho	no-**ven**-tah-**o**-choh
100	cien	see-**en**
101	ciento uno	see-**en**-toh **oo**-noh
200	doscientos	doh-see-**en**-tohss
500	quinientos	keen-**yen**-tohss
700	setecientos	set-eh-see-**en**-tohss
900	novecientos	no-veh-see-**en**-tohss
1,000	mil	meel
2,000	dos mil	dohs meel
1,000,000	un millón	oon meel-**yohn**

COLORS

black	negro	**neh**-groh
blue	azul	ah-**sool**
brown	café	kah-**feh**
green	verde	**ver**-deh
pink	rosa	**ro**-sah
purple	morado	mo-**rah**-doh
orange	naranja	na-**rahn**-hah
red	rojo	**roh**-hoh
white	blanco	**blahn**-koh
yellow	amarillo	ah-mah-**ree**-yoh

DAYS OF THE WEEK

Sunday	domingo	doe-**meen**-goh
Monday	lunes	**loo**-ness
Tuesday	martes	**mahr**-tess
Wednesday	miércoles	me-**air**-koh-less
Thursday	jueves	hoo-**ev**-ess
Friday	viernes	vee-**air**-ness
Saturday	sábado	**sah**-bah-doh

ENGLISH	SPANISH	PRONUNCIATION

MONTHS

January	enero	eh-**neh**-roh
February	febrero	feh-**breh**-roh
March	marzo	**mahr**-soh
April	abril	ah-**breel**
May	mayo	**my**-oh
June	junio	**hoo**-nee-oh
July	julio	**hoo**-lee-yoh
August	agosto	ah-**ghost**-toh
September	septiembre	sep-tee-**em**-breh
October	octubre	oak-**too**-breh
November	noviembre	no-vee-**em**-breh
December	diciembre	dee-see-**em**-breh

USEFUL PHRASES

Do you speak English?	¿Habla usted inglés?	**ah**-blah oos-**ted** in-**glehs**
I don't speak Spanish	No hablo español	no **ah**-bloh es-pahn-**yol**
I don't understand (you)	No entiendo	no en-tee-**en**-doh
I understand (you)	Entiendo	en-tee-**en**-doh
I don't know	No sé	no seh
I am American/ British	Soy americano (americana)/inglés(a)	soy ah-meh-ree-**kah**-no (ah-meh-ree- **kah**-nah)/ in-**glehs(ah)**
What's your name?	¿Cómo se llama usted?	koh-mo seh **yah**-mah oos-**ted**
My name is . . .	Me llamo . . .	may **yah**-moh
What time is it?	¿Qué hora es?	keh **o**-rah es
It is one, two, three . . . o'clock.	Es la una./Son las dos, tres . . .	es la **oo**-nah/sohnahs dohs, tress
Yes, please/ No, thank you	Sí, por favor/ No, gracias	**see** pohr fah-**vor**/ no **grah**-see-us
How?	¿Cómo?	**koh**-mo

ENGLISH	SPANISH	PRONUNCIATION
When?	¿Cuándo?	**kwahn**-doh
This/Next week	Esta semana/ la semana que entra	**es**-teh seh-**mah**- nah/ lah seh-**mah**-nah keh **en**-trah
This/Next month	Este mes/ el próximo mes	**es**-teh mehs/ el **proke**-see-mo mehs
This/Next year	Este año/el año que viene	**es**-teh **ahn**-yo/el **ahn**-yo keh vee-**yen**-ay
Yesterday/today/ tomorrow	Ayer/hoy/mañana	ah-**yehr**/oy/ mahn-**yah**-nah
This morning/ afternoon	Esta mañana/ tarde	**es**-tah mahn-**yah**- nah/ **tar**-deh
Tonight	Esta noche	**es**-tah **no**-cheh
What?	¿Qué?	keh
What is it?	¿Qué es esto?	keh es **es**-toh
Why?	¿Por qué?	pore **keh**
Who?	¿Quién?	kee-**yen**
Where is . . . ?	¿Dónde está . . . ?	**dohn**-deh es-**tah**
the train station?	la estación del tren?	la es-tah-see-on del trehn
the subway station?	la estación del tren subterráneo?	la es-ta-see-**on** del trehn la es-ta-see-**on** soob-teh-**rrahn**-eh-oh
the bus stop?	la parada del autobus?	la pah-**rah**-dah del ow-toh-**boos**
the post office?	la oficina de correos?	la oh-fee-**see**- nah deh koh-**rreh**-os
the bank?	el banco?	el **bahn**-koh
the hotel?	el hotel?	el oh-**tel**
the store?	la tienda?	la tee-**en**-dah
the cashier?	la caja?	la **kah**-hah
the museum?	el museo?	el moo-**seh**-oh
the hospital?	el hospital?	el ohss-pee-**tal**
the elevator?	el ascensor?	el ah-**sen**-sohr
the bathroom?	el baño?	el **bahn**-yoh

ENGLISH	SPANISH	PRONUNCIATION
Here/there	Aquí/allá	ah-**key**/ah-**yah**
Open/closed	Abierto/cerrado	ah-bee-**er**-toh/ ser-**ah**-doh
Left/right	Izquierda/derecha	iss-key-**er**-dah/ dare-**eh**-chah
Straight ahead	Derecho	dare-**eh**-choh
Is it near/far?	¿Está cerca/lejos?	es-**tah sehr**-kah/ **leh**-hoss
I'd like . . .	Quisiera . . .	kee-see-ehr-ah
a room	un cuarto/una habitación	oon **kwahr**-toh/ **oo**-nah ah-bee- tah-see-**on**
the key	la llave	lah **yah**-veh
a newspaper	un periódico	oon pehr-ee-**oh**- dee-koh
a stamp	un sello de correo	oon **seh**-yo deh korr-ee-oh
I'd like to buy . . .	Quisiera comprar . . .	kee-see-**ehr**-ah kohm-**prahr**
cigarettes	cigarrillos	ce-ga-**ree**-yohs
matches	cerillos	ser-**ee**-ohs
a dictionary	un diccionario	oon deek-see-oh- **nah**-ree-oh
soap	jabón	hah-**bohn**
sunglasses	gafas de sol	**ga**-fahs deh sohl
suntan lotion	Loción bronceadora	loh-see-**ohn** brohn- seh-ah-**do**-rah
a map	un mapa	oon **mah**-pah
a magazine	una revista	**oon**-ah reh-**veess**-tah
paper	papel	pah-**pel**
envelopes	sobres	**so**-brehs
a postcard	una tarjeta postal	**oon**-ah tar-**het**-ah post-**ahl**
How much is it?	¿Cuánto cuesta?	**kwahn**-toh **kwes**-tah
It's expensive/ cheap	Está caro/barato	es-**tah kah**-roh/ bah-**rah**-toh

ENGLISH	SPANISH	PRONUNCIATION
A little/a lot	Un poquito/mucho	oon poh-**kee**-toh/ **moo**-choh
More/less	Más/menos	mahss/**men**-ohss
Enough/too much/too little	Suficiente/ demasiado/ muy poco	soo-fee-see-**en**-teh/ deh-mah-see-**ah**- doh/ **moo**-ee **poh**-koh
Telephone	Teléfono	tel-**ef**-oh-no
Telegram	Telegrama	teh-leh-**grah**-mah
I am ill	Estoy enfermo(a)	es-**toy** en-**fehr**- moh(mah)
Please call a doctor	Por favor llame a un medico	pohr fah-**vor ya**-meh ah oon **med**-ee-koh

ON THE ROAD

Avenue	Avenida	ah-ven-**ee**-dah
Broad, tree-lined boulevard	Bulevar	boo-leh-**var**
Fertile plain	Vega	**veh**-gah
Highway	Carretera	car-reh-**ter**-ah
Mountain pass	Puerto	poo-**ehr**-toh
Street	Calle	**cah**-yeh
Waterfront promenade	Rambla	**rahm**-blah
Wharf	Embarcadero	em-bar-cah-**deh**-ro

IN TOWN

Cathedral	Catedral	cah-teh-**dral**
Church	Templo/Iglesia	**tem**-plo/ ee-**glehs**- see-ah
City hall	Casa de gobierno	kah-sah deh go-bee-**ehr**-no
Door, gate	Puerta portón	poo-**ehr**-tah por-**ton**
Entrance/exit	Entrada/salida	en-**trah**-dah/ sah-**lee**- dah
Inn, rustic bar, or restaurant	Taverna	tah-**vehr**-nah
Main square	Plaza principal	plah-thah prin- see-**pahl**

ENGLISH	SPANISH	PRONUNCIATION

DINING OUT

Can you recommend a good restaurant?	¿Puede recomendarme un buen restaurante?	**pweh**-deh rreh-koh-mehn-**dahr**-me oon bwehn rrehs-tow- **rahn**-teh?
Where is it located?	¿Dónde está situado?	**dohn**-deh ehs-**tah** see-**twah**-doh?
Do I need reservations?	¿Se necesita una reservación?	seh neh-seh-**see**-tah **oo**-nah rreh-sehr- bah-**syohn**?
I'd like to reserve a table . . .	Quisiera reservar una mesa . . .	kee-**syeh**-rah rreh-sehr-**bahr** oo-nah **meh**-sah . . .
for two people.	para dos personas.	**pah**-rah dohs pehr- **soh**-nahs
for this evening.	para esta noche.	**pah**-rah **ehs**-tah **noh**-cheh
for 8 pm	para las ocho de la noche.	**pah** rah lahs **oh** choh deh lah **noh**-cheh
A bottle of . . .	Una botella de . . .	**oo**-nah bo-**teh**-yah dch
A cup of . . .	Una taza de . . .	**oo**-nah **tah**-thah deh
A glass of . . .	Un vaso de . . .	oon **vah**-so deh
Ashtray	Un cenicero	oon sen-ee-**seh**-roh
Bill/check	La cuenta	lah **kwen**-tah
Bread	El pan	el pahn
Breakfast	El desayuno	el deh-sah-**yoon**-oh
Butter	La mantequilla	lah man-teh-**key**-yah
Cheers!	¡Salud!	sah-**lood**
Cocktail	Un aperitivo	oon ah-pehr-ee-**tee**-voh
Dinner	La cena	lah **seh**-nah
Dish	Un plato	oon **plah**-toh
Menu of the day	Menú del día	meh-**noo** del **dee**-ah
Enjoy!	¡Buen provecho!	bwehn pro-**veh**-cho
Fixed-price menu	Menú fijo o turistico	meh-**noo** **fee**-hoh oh too-**ree**-stee-coh

ENGLISH	SPANISH	PRONUNCIATION
Fork	El tenedor	el ten-eh-**dor**
Is the tip included?	¿Está incluida la propina?	es-**tah** in-cloo-**ee**-dah lah pro-**pee**-nah
Knife	El cuchillo	el koo-**chee**-yo
Large portion of savory snacks	Raciónes	rah-see-**oh**-nehs
Lunch	La comida	lah koh-**mee**-dah
Menu	La carta, el menú	lah **cart**-ah, el meh-**noo**
Napkin	La servilleta	lah sehr-vee-**yet**-ah
Pepper	La pimienta	lah pee-me-**en**-tah
Please give me	Por favor déme	pore fah-**vor deh**-meh
Salt	La sal	lah sahl
Savory snacks	Tapas	**tah**-pahs
Spoon	Una cuchara	**oo**-nah koo-**chah**-rah
Sugar	El azúcar	el ah-**thu**-kar
Waiter!/Waitress!	¡Por favor Señor/ Señorita!	pohr fah-**vor** sen- **yor**/ sen-yor-**ee**-tah

Travel Smart
Los Cabos

WORD OF MOUTH

"We have been in Cabo four times in last two years-November and March. The nights can be very cold—freezing even—and the wind is very stiff and cold most places. A windbreaker, warm sweater over a light top works as long as the top or sweater cover your chest up to your neck."

—clairebenson

GETTING HERE AND AROUND

■ AIR TRAVEL

You can now fly nonstop to Los Cabos from Southern California, Atlanta, Charlotte, Chicago, Dallas/Fort Worth, Denver, Houston, Las Vegas, Los Angeles, Mexico City, New York, Phoenix, Portland, Sacramento, Salt Lake City, San Diego, San Francisco, and Seattle. From most other destinations, you will have to make a connecting flight, either in the United States or in Mexico City. Via nonstop service, Los Cabos is about 2 hours from San Diego, about 2¼ hours from Houston, 3 hours from Dallas/Fort Worth, 2¼ hours from Los Angeles, and 2½ hours from Phoenix. Flying time from New York to Mexico City, where you must switch planes to continue to Los Cabos, is five hours. Los Cabos is about a 2½-hour flight from Mexico City.

Airlines and Airports Airline and Airport Links.com ⊕ *www.airlineandairportlinks.com.*

Airline Security Issues Transportation Security Administration ⊕ *www.tsa.gov.*

AIRPORTS

Aeropuerto Internacional de San José del Cabo (SJD) is 1 km (½ mile) west of the Transpeninsular Highway (Highway 1), 13 km (8 miles) north of San José del Cabo, and 48 km (30 miles) northeast of Cabo San Lucas. The airport has restaurants, duty-free shops, and car-rental agencies. Los Cabos flights increase in winter with seasonal flights from U.S. airlines, and, despite growing numbers of visitors to the area, the airport manages to keep up nicely with the crowds.

Aeropuerto General Manuel Márquez de León serves La Paz. It's 11 km (7 miles) northwest of the Baja California Sur capital, which itself is 188 km (117 miles) northwest of Los Cabos.

Airport Information Aeropuerto Internacional Los Cabos ☎ *624/146–5111* ⊕ *www.loscabos.aeropuertosgap.com.mx.*

Aeropuerto General Manuel Márquez de León ☎ *612/112–0082.*

FLIGHTS

AeroCalafia flies charter flights from Los Cabos for whale-watching. Aeroméxico has service to Los Cabos from San Diego; and to La Paz from Los Angeles, Tucson, Tijuana, and Mexico City.

Alaska Airlines flies nonstop to Los Cabos from Los Angeles, San Diego, Seattle, Portland, and San Francisco; and three times a week to La Paz from Los Angeles. Frontier flies nonstop from Denver. US Airways has nonstop service from Phoenix, San Diego, and Las Vegas. American flies nonstop from Dallas/Fort Worth, Chicago, Los Angeles, and New York JFK. British Airways and other European airlines fly to Mexico City, where connections are made for the 2½-hour flight to Los Cabos.

United has nonstop service from Houston. Delta flies to Los Cabos from Atlanta and Ontario, California, and has daily flights from Los Angeles to La Paz.

Airline Contacts AeroCalafia ☎ *624/143–4302 in Los Cabos* ⊕ *www.aereocalafia.com. mx.* **Aeroméxico** ☎ *800/237–6639 in U.S., 624/146–5097 in Los Cabos, 612/124–6366 in La Paz* ⊕ *www.aeromexico.com.* **Alaska Airlines** ☎ *800/252–7522, 624/146–5103 in Los Cabos* ⊕ *www.alaskaair.com.* **American Airlines** ☎ *800/433–7300, 624/146–5300 in Los Cabos* ⊕ *www.aa.com.* **British Airways** ☎ *800/AIRWAYS in U.S.* ⊕ *www.britishairways.com.* **Delta Airlines** ☎ *800/221–1212, 624/146–5005 in Los Cabos* ⊕ *www.delta.com.* **Frontier Airlines** ☎ *800/432–1359* ⊕ *www.flyfrontier.com.* **USAirways** ☎ *800/428–4322, 624/146–5380 in Los Cabos* ⊕ *www.usairways.com.* **United Airlines** ☎ *800/241–6522, 800/003–0777 in Mexico* ⊕ *www.united.com.*

GROUND TRANSPORTATION

If you have purchased a vacation package from an airline or travel agency, transfers are usually included. Otherwise, only the most exclusive hotels in Los Cabos offer transfers. Fares from the airport to hotels in Los Cabos are expensive. The least expensive transport is by shuttle buses that stop at various hotels along the route; fares run $12 to $25 per person. Private taxi fares run from $25 to $100. Some hotels can arrange a pickup, which is much faster and might cost about the same as a shuttle. Ask about hotel transfers, especially if you're staying in the East Cape, La Paz, or Todos Santos and not renting a car—cab fares to these areas are astronomical.

If you're renting a car and driving say, to the East Cape, make sure you get detailed directions on how to locate where you'll be staying.

Unless you want to tour a time-share or real estate property, ignore the offers for free transfers when you first come out of customs. The scene can be bewildering for first timers. Sales representatives from various time-share properties compete vociferously for clients; often you won't realize you've been suckered into a time-share presentation until you get in the van. To avoid this situation, go to the official taxi booths inside the baggage claim or just outside the final customs clearance area and pay for a ticket for a regular shuttle bus. Private taxis, often U.S. vans, are expensive and not metered, so always ask the fare before getting in. Rates change frequently, but for one to four persons, it costs about $25 per person to get to San José del Cabo, $35 to a hotel along the Corridor, and $65 to Cabo San Lucas. After the fourth passenger, it's about an additional $3 per person. Usually only vans accept more than four passengers. At the end of your trip, don't wait until the last minute to book return transport. Make arrangements a few days in advance for shuttle service, and then reconfirm the morning of your departure, or, again, at least a day in advance, sign up at your hotel's front desk to share a cab with other travelers, reconfirming the morning of your departure.

∎ BUS TRAVEL

In Los Cabos, the main Terminal de Autobus (Los Cabos Bus Terminal) is about a 10-minute drive west of Cabo San Lucas. Express buses with air-conditioning and restrooms travel frequently from the terminal to Todos Santos (one hour) and La Paz (three hours). One-way fare is $4 (payable in pesos or dollars) to Todos Santos, $14 to La Paz. From the Corridor, expect to pay about $25 for a taxi to the bus station.

SuburBaja can provide private transport for $60 between San José del Cabo and Cabo San Lucas.

In La Paz the main Terminal de Autobus is 10 blocks from the malecón.

Bus Information Los Cabos Terminal de Autobus ⊠ *Hwy. 19* ☎ *624/143–5020, 624/143–7880.* **SuburBaja** ☎ *624/146–0888.*

∎ CAR TRAVEL

Rental cars come in handy when exploring Baja. Countless paved and dirt roads branch off Highway 1 like octopus tentacles beckoning adventurers toward the mountains, ocean, and sea. Baja Sur's highways and city streets are under constant improvement, and Highway 1 is usually in good condition except during heavy rains. Four-wheel drive comes in handy for hard-core backcountry explorations, but isn't necessary most of the time. Just be aware that some car-rental companies void their insurance policies if you run into trouble off paved roads. Even if you are even slightly inclined to impromptu adventures, it's best to find out what your company's policy is before you leave the pavement.

GASOLINE

Pemex (the government petroleum monopoly) franchises all gas stations in Mexico. Stations are to be found in both towns as well as on the outskirts of San José del Cabo and Cabo San Lucas and in the Corridor, and there are also several along Highway 1. Gas is measured in liters. Gas stations in Los Cabos may not accept credit cards. Prices run higher than in the United States. Premium unleaded gas (*magna premio*) and regular unleaded gas (*magna sin*) is available nationwide, but it's still a good idea to fill up whenever you can. Fuel quality is generally lower than that in the United States and Europe. Vehicles with fuel-injected engines are likely to have problems after driving extended distances.

Gas-station attendants pump the gas for you and may also wash your windshield and check your oil and tire air pressure. A tip of 5 or 10 pesos (about 50¢ or $1) is customary depending on the number of services rendered, beyond pumping gas.

ROAD CONDITIONS

Mexico Highway 1, also known as the Carretera Transpeninsular, runs the entire 1,700 km (1,054 miles) from Tijuana to Cabo San Lucas. Do not drive the highway at high speeds or at night—it is not lighted and is very narrow much of the way.

Highway 19 runs between Cabo San Lucas and Todos Santos and is currently being widened to two lanes in each direction, albeit slowly, joining Highway 1 below La Paz. The four-lane road between San José del Cabo and Cabo San Lucas is usually in good condition. Roadwork along the highway is common and commonly frustrates locals and visitors alike. Take your time and don't act rashly if encountering delays or if you need to drive several miles out of your way to turn around and re-approach a missed turnoff.

In rural areas, roads tend to be iffy and in unpredictable condition. Use caution, especially during the rainy season, when rock slides and potholes are a problem,

and be alert for animals—cattle, goats, horses, coyotes, and dogs in particular—even on the highways. If you have a long distance to cover, start early, fill up on gas, and remember to keep your tank full as gas stations are simply not as abundant here as they are in the United States or Europe. Allow extra time for unforeseen obstacles.

Signage is not always adequate in Mexico, and the best advice is to travel with a companion and a good map. Take your time. Always lock your car, and never leave valuable items in the body of the car (the trunk will suffice for daytime outings, but be smart about stashing expensive items in there in full view of curious onlookers).

The Mexican Tourism Ministry distributes free road maps from its tourism offices outside the country. Guía Roji and Pemex publish current city, regional, and national road maps, which are available in bookstores and big supermarket chains for under $10; but stock up on every map your rental-car company has, as gas stations generally do not carry maps.

ROADSIDE EMERGENCIES

The Mexican Tourism Ministry operates a fleet of more than 350 pickup trucks, known as the Angeles Verdes, or Green Angels. Bilingual drivers provide mechanical help, first aid, radio-telephone communication, basic supplies and small parts, towing, tourist information, and protection. Services are free; spare parts, fuel, and lubricants are provided at cost. Tips are always appreciated ($5–$10 for big jobs, $2–$3 for minor repairs). The Green Angels patrol sections of the major highways daily 8–8 (later on holiday weekends). If you break down, **pull off the road as far as possible,** lift the hood of your car, hail a passing vehicle, and ask the driver to **notify the patrol.** Most bus and truck drivers will be quite helpful. If you witness an accident, do not stop to help—it could be a ploy to rob you or could get you interminably involved with the police. Instead, notify the nearest official.

Contacts **Federal Highway Patrol** ☎ *624/122–5735, 624/125–3584.* **Green Angels, La Paz** ☎ *800/987–8224 in Mexico, 078 from any Baja phone.*

SAFETY ON THE ROAD

The mythical *banditos* are not a big concern in Baja. Still, **do your very best to avoid driving at night,** especially in rural areas. Cows and burros grazing alongside the road can pose as real a danger as the ones actually *in* the road—you never know when they'll decide to wander into traffic. Other good reasons for not driving at night include potholes, cars with no working lights, road-hogging trucks, and difficulty with getting assistance. Despite the temptation of margaritas and cold *cervezas,* do not drink and drive; choose a designated driver. Plan driving times, and if night is falling, find a nearby hotel or at least slow down your speed considerably.

Though it isn't common in Los Cabos, police may pull you over for supposedly breaking the law, or for being a good prospect for a scam. If it happens to you, remember to **be polite**—displays of anger will only make matters worse—tell the officer that you would like to talk to the police captain when you get to the station. The officer will usually let you go. If you're stopped for speeding, the officer is supposed to hold your license until you pay the fine at the local police station. But he will always prefer taking a *mordida* (small bribe) to wasting his time at the police station. Corruption is a fact of life in Mexico, and the $10 or $20 it costs to get your license back is supplementary income for the officer who pulled you over with no intention of taking you to police headquarters.

RENTAL CARS

When you reserve a car, ask about cancellation penalties, taxes, drop-off charges (if you're planning to pick up the car in one city and leave it in another), and surcharges (for being under or over a certain age, for additional drivers, or for driving across state or country borders or beyond a specific distance from your point of rental). All these things can add substantially to your costs. Request car seats and extras such as GPS when you book.

Rates are sometimes—but not always—better if you book in advance or reserve through a rental agency's website. There are other reasons to book ahead, though: for popular destinations, during busy times of the year, or to ensure that you get certain types of cars (vans, SUVs, exotic sports cars). We've also found that car-rental prices are much better when reservations are made ahead of travel, from the United States. Prices can be as much as 50% more when renting a car upon arrival in Los Cabos.

■TIP➔ Make sure that a confirmed reservation guarantees you a car. Agencies sometimes overbook, particularly for busy weekends and holiday periods.

Taxi fares are especially steep in Los Cabos, and a rental car can come in handy if you'd like to dine at the Corridor hotels; travel frequently between the two towns; stay at a hotel along the Cabo Corridor; spend more than a few days in Los Cabos; or plan to see some of the sights outside Los Cabos proper, such as La Paz, Todos Santos, or even farther afield. If you don't want to rent a car, your hotel concierge or tour operator can arrange for a car with a driver or limousine service.

Convertibles and jeeps are popular rentals, but beware of sunburn and windburn and remember there's nowhere to stash your belongings out of sight. Specify whether you want air-conditioning and manual or automatic transmission. If you rent from a major U.S.-based company, you can find a car for about $40 per day ($280 per week), including automatic transmission, unlimited mileage, and 10% tax; however, having the protection of complete coverage insurance will add another $19 to $25 per day, depending on the company, so you should figure the cost of insurance into your budget. You will pay considerably more (probably double) for a larger or higher-end car. Most vendors negotiate considerably if tourism is slow; ask about special rates if you're renting by the week.

To increase the likelihood of getting the car you want and to get considerably better car-rental prices, make arrangements before you leave for your trip. You can sometimes, but not always, find cheaper rates on the Internet. No matter how you book, rates are generally much lower when you reserve a car in advance outside Mexico.

In Mexico your own driver's license is acceptable. In most cases, the minimum rental age is 25, although some companies will lower it to 22 for an extra daily charge. A valid driver's license, major credit card, and Mexican car insurance are required.

CAR-RENTAL INSURANCE

Everyone who rents a car wonders whether the insurance that the rental companies offer is worth the expense. No one—including us—has a simple answer. It all depends on how much regular insurance you have, how comfortable you are with risk, and whether or not money is an issue. Just to be on the safe side, agree to at least the minimum rental insurance. It's best to be completely covered when driving in Mexico.

If you own a car, your personal auto insurance may cover a rental to some degree, though not all policies protect you abroad; always read your policy's fine print. If you don't have auto insurance, then seriously consider buying the collision- or loss-damage waiver (CDW or LDW) from the car-rental company, which eliminates your liability for damage to the car. Some credit cards offer CDW coverage, but it's usually supplemental to your own insurance and rarely covers SUVs, minivans, luxury models, and the like. If your coverage is secondary, you may still be liable for loss-of-use costs from the car-rental company. But no credit-card insurance is valid unless you use that card for *all* transactions, from reserving to paying the final bill. All companies exclude car

rental in some countries, so be sure to find out about the destination to which you are traveling.

■**TIP➜** American Express offers primary CDW coverage on all rentals reserved and paid for with the card. This means that the American Express company—not your own car insurance—pays in case of an accident. It *doesn't* mean your car-insurance company won't raise your rates once it discovers you had an accident—but it provides a welcome amount of security for travelers.

Most rental agencies require you to have CDW coverage; many will even include it in quoted rates. All will strongly encourage you to buy CDW—making it difficult to discern whether they are recommending or requiring it—so be sure to ask about such things before renting. In most cases it's cheaper to add a supplemental CDW plan to your comprehensive travel-insurance policy than to purchase it from a rental company. That said, you don't want to pay for a supplement if you're required to buy insurance from the rental company.

▌ TAXI TRAVEL

Taxis are plentiful throughout Baja Sur, even in the smallest towns. Government-certified taxis have a license with a photo of the driver and a taxi number prominently displayed. Fares are exorbitant in Los Cabos, and the taxi union is very powerful. Some visitors have taken to boycotting taxis completely, using rental cars and buses instead, the latter of which can be most time-consuming. The fare between Cabo San Lucas and San José del Cabo runs about $50–$60—more at night. Cabs from Corridor hotels to either town run at least $30 each way. Expect to pay at least $30 from the airport to hotels in San José, and closer to $65 to Cabo.

In La Paz, taxis are readily available and inexpensive. A ride within town costs under $5; a trip to Pichilingue costs between $7 and $10. Illegal taxis aren't a problem in this region.

ESSENTIALS

■ COMMUNICATIONS

PHONES

Los Cabos is on U.S. Mountain Time. The region has good telephone service, with pay phone booths along the streets and the Corridor, and wide cell-phone reception. Most phones have Touch-Tone (digital) circuitry. Phone numbers in Mexico change frequently; a recording may offer the new number, so it's useful to learn the Spanish words for numbers 1 through 9. Beware of pay phones and hotel-room phones with signs saying "Call Home" and other enticements. Some of these phone companies charge astronomical rates.

The country code for Mexico is 52. When calling a Mexico number from abroad, dial the country code and then the area code and local number. At this writing, the area code for all of Los Cabos is 624. All local numbers now have seven digits.

CALLING WITHIN MEXICO

For local or long-distance calls, one option is to find a *caseta de larga distancia*, a telephone service usually operated out of a small business; look for the phone symbol on the door. Casetas have become less common as pay phones have begun to appear even in the smallest towns and increasing numbers of people have cell phones. Rates at casetas seem to vary widely, so shop around. Sometimes you can make collect calls from casetas, and sometimes you cannot, depending on the operator and possibly your degree of visible desperation. Casetas generally charge 50¢–$1.50 to place a collect call (some charge by the minute); it's usually better to call *por cobrar* (collect) from a pay phone.

CALLING OUTSIDE MEXICO

To make a call to the United States or Canada, dial 001 before the area code and number. For operator assistance in making an international call dial 090.

AT&T, MCI, and Sprint access codes make calling long-distance relatively convenient, but you may find the local access number blocked in many hotel rooms. First ask the hotel operator to connect you. If the hotel operator balks, ask for an international operator, or dial the international operator yourself. One way to improve your odds of getting connected to your long-distance carrier is to travel with more than one company's calling card (a hotel may block Sprint, for example, but not MCI). If all else fails, call from a pay phone.

Access Codes AT&T Direct ☎ *800/331–0500* ⊕ *www.att.com*. **MCI WorldPhone** ☎ *800/674-7000* ⊕ *www.mci.com*. **Sprint International Access** ☎ *866/866-7509* ⊕ *www.sprint.com*.

DIRECTORY AND OPERATOR ASSISTANCE

Directory assistance in Mexico is 040 nationwide. For international assistance, dial 020 first for an international operator and most likely you'll get one who speaks English; indicate in which city, state, and country you require directory assistance and you will be connected with directory assistance there.

MOBILE PHONES

If you have a multiband phone (some countries use different frequencies from what's used in the United States) and your service provider uses the world-standard GSM network (as do T-Mobile, Cingular, and Verizon), you can probably use your phone abroad. Roaming fees can be steep, however: 99¢ a minute is considered reasonable. And overseas you normally pay the toll charges for incoming calls. It's almost always cheaper to send a text message than to make a call, since text messages have a very low set fee (often less than 5¢). Verizon offers very reasonable Mexican calling plans that can be added to your existing plan.

If you just want to make local calls, consider buying a new SIM card (note that your provider may have to unlock your phone for you to use a different SIM card) and a prepaid service plan in the destination. You'll then have a local number and can make local calls at local rates. If your trip is extensive, you could also simply buy a new cell phone in your destination, as the initial cost will be offset over time.

■TIP➔ If you travel internationally frequently, save one of your old mobile phones or buy a cheap one on the Internet; ask your cell phone company to unlock it for you, and take it with you as a travel phone, buying a new SIM card with pay-as-you-go service in each destination.

There are now companies that rent cell phones (with or without SIM cards) for the duration of your trip. You get the phone, charger, and carrying case in the mail and return them in the mailer.

Contacts Cellular Abroad ☎ 800/287–5072 ⊕ www.cellularabroad.com. **Daystar** ☎ 877/820–7397 ⊕ www.daystarwireless.com. **Mobal** ☎ 888/888–9162 ⊕ www.mobalrental.com. **Planet Fone** ☎ 888/988–4777 ⊕ www.planetfone.com.

PUBLIC PHONES

Occasionally you'll see traditional black, square pay phones with push buttons or dials; although they have a coin slot on top, local calls are free. However, these coin-only pay phones are usually broken. Newer pay phones have an unmarked slot for prepaid phone cards called Telmex cards. The cards are sold in 30-, 50-, or 100-peso denominations at newsstands or pharmacies. Credit is deleted from the Telmex card as you use it, and your balance is displayed on a small screen on the phone. Some phones have two unmarked slots, one for a Telmex card and the other for a credit card. These are primarily for Mexican bank cards, but some accept Visa or MasterCard.

TOLL-FREE NUMBERS

Toll-free numbers in Mexico start with an 800 prefix. To reach them, you need to dial 01 before the number. In this guide, Mexico-only toll-free numbers appear as follows: 01–800/123–4567 (numbers have seven digits). Most of the 800 numbers in this book work in the United States only and are listed simply: 800/123–4567; you cannot access a U.S. 800 number from Mexico. Some U.S. toll-free numbers ring directly at Mexican properties. Don't be deterred if someone answers the phone in Spanish. Simply ask for someone who speaks English. Toll-free numbers that work in other countries are labeled accordingly.

■ CUSTOMS AND DUTIES

Upon entering Mexico, you'll be given a baggage declaration form and asked to itemize what you're bringing into the country. You are allowed to bring in 3 liters of spirits or wine for personal use; 400 cigarettes, 25 cigars, or 200 grams of tobacco; a reasonable amount of perfume for personal use; one video camera and one regular camera and 12 rolls of film for each; and gift items not to exceed a total of $300. If driving across the U.S. border, gift items shouldn't exceed $50, although foreigners aren't usually hassled about this. ⚠ Although the much-publicized border violence doesn't usually affect travelers, it is real. To be safe don't linger long at the border.

You aren't allowed to bring firearms, ammunition, meat, vegetables, plants, fruit, or flowers into the country. You can bring in one of each of the following items without paying taxes: a cell phone, a beeper, a radio or tape recorder, a musical instrument, a laptop computer, and portable copier or printer. Compact discs and/or audio cassettes are limited to 20 total and DVDs to five.

Mexico also allows you to bring one cat or dog, if you have two things: (1) a pet health certificate signed by a registered veterinarian in the United States and issued not more than 72 hours before the animal enters Mexico; and (2) a pet vaccination certificate showing that the animal has been treated (as applicable) for rabies, hepatitis, distemper, and leptospirosis.

For more information or information on bringing other animals or more than one type of animal, contact the Mexican consulate, which has branches in many major American cities as well as border towns. To find the consulate nearest you, check the Ministry of Foreign Affairs website (go to the "Servicios Consulares" option).

Information in Mexico Mexican Embassy ☎ *202/728-1600* ⊕ *www.embassyofmexico. org.* **Ministry of Foreign Affairs** ☎ *55/3686-5100* ⊕ *portal3.sre.qob.mx/enqlish.*

U.S. Information U.S. Customs and Border Protection ☎ *877/CBP-5511* ⊕ *www.cbp.gov.*

■ ELECTRICITY

For U.S. and Canadian travelers, electrical converters are not necessary because Mexico operates on the 60-cycle, 120-volt system; however, many Mexican outlets have not been updated to accommodate three-prong and polarized plugs (those with one larger prong), so to be safe bring an adapter. If your appliances are dual-voltage you'll need only an adapter. Don't use 110-volt outlets, marked "for shavers only," for high-wattage appliances such as blow dryers. Most laptops operate equally well on 110 and 220 volts and so require only an adapter. It is well worth bringing a small surge protector if you're going to be plugging in your laptop.

■ EMERGENCIES

The state of Baja California Sur has instituted an emergency number for police and fire: 060. A second number, 065, is available to summon medical assistance. Both numbers can be used throughout the state, and there are English-speaking operators.

For medical emergencies, Tourist Medical Assist Co. operates Balboa Hospital & Walk-In Clinic in Cabo San Lucas. Another option is air medical services—find a provider through the Association of Air Medical Services (AAMS); several of the U.S.-headquartered operations have bases around Mexico, so they can reach you more quickly.

Emergency Services AAMS ☎ *703/836-8732* ⊕ *www.aams.org.* **Highway Patrol** ☎ *624/143-0135 in Los Cabos, 612/122-0429 in La Paz.* **Police** ☎ *624/142-0361 in San José del Cabo, 624/143-3977 in Cabo San Lucas, 612/122-0477 in La Paz.* **Balboa Hospital & Walk-In Clinic** ✉ *911 Lazaro Cárdenas Av., Cabo San Lucas* ☎ *624/143-5911* ⊕ *www.hospitalbalboa.com.*

Foreign Consulates Consular Agent in Cabo San Lucas ✉ *Blvd. Marina, Local C-4, Plaza Nautica, Cabo San Lucas* ☎ *624/143-3566.*

Hospitals and Clinics AmeriMed ✉ *Av. Cárdenas at Paseo Marina, Cabo San Lucas* ☎ *624/143-9670.* **Centro de Especialidades Médicas** ✉ *Calle Delfines 110, La Paz* ☎ *612/124-0400.*

Pharmacies Farmacia Baja California ✉ *Calle Independencia at Av. Madero, La Paz* ☎ *612/122-0240.*

■ HEALTH

FOOD AND DRINK

In Mexico the biggest health risk is *turista* (traveler's diarrhea) caused by consuming contaminated fruit, vegetables, or water. To minimize risks, avoid questionable-looking street stands and bad-smelling food even in the toniest establishments; and if you're not sure of a restaurant's standards, pass up ceviche (raw fish cured in lemon juice) and raw vegetables that haven't been or can't be, peeled (e.g., lettuce and tomatoes).

In general, Los Cabos does not pose as great a health risk as other parts of Mexico. Nevertheless, watch what you eat, and drink only bottled water or water that has been boiled for a few minutes. Water in most major hotels is safe for brushing your teeth, but to avoid any risk, use bottled water. Hotels with water-purification systems will post signs to that effect in the rooms.

When ordering cold drinks at establishments that don't seem to get many tourists, skip the ice: *sin hielo*. (You can usually identify ice made commercially from purified water by its uniform shape.)

Stay away from uncooked food and unpasteurized milk and milk products. Mexicans excel at grilling meats and seafood, but be smart about where you eat—ask locals to recommend their favorite restaurants or taco stands, and if you have the slightest hesitation about cleanliness or freshness, then skip it. This caution must extend to ceviche, which is a favorite appetizer, especially at seaside resorts. The Mexican Department of Health warns that marinating in lemon juice does not constitute the "cooking" that would make the shellfish safe to eat. Fruit and *licuados* (smoothies) stands are wonderful for refreshing treats, but again, ask around, be fanatical about freshness, and watch to see how the vendor handles the food. Mexico is a food-lover's adventureland, and many travelers wouldn't dream of passing up the chance to try something new and delicious.

Mild cases of turista may respond to Imodium (known generically as loperamide), Lomotil, or Pepto-Bismol (not as strong), all of which you can buy over the counter; keep in mind, though, that these drugs can complicate more serious illnesses. You'll need to replace fluids, so drink plenty of purified water or tea.

Chamomile tea (*té de manzanilla*) and peppermint tea (*té de menta/hierbabuena*) can be good for calming upset stomachs, and they're readily available in restaurants throughout Mexico.

It's smart to bring down a few packets of drink mix, such as EmergenC, when you travel to Mexico. You can also make a salt-sugar solution (½ teaspoon salt and 4 tablespoons sugar per quart of water) to rehydrate. If your fever and diarrhea last longer than a day or two, see a doctor—you may have picked up a parasite or disease that requires prescription medication.

DIVERS' ALERT

⚠ Do not fly within 24 hours of scuba diving.

SHOTS AND MEDICATIONS

According to the U.S. National Centers for Disease Control and Prevention (CDC), there's a limited risk of dengue fever and other insect-carried or parasite-caused illnesses in some rural parts of Mexico, though Baja California Sur is not one of the major areas of concern.

Health Information National Centers for Disease Control & Prevention *(CDC)* ☎ *800/232–4636 international travelers' health line* ⊕ *www.cdc.gov/travel.* **World Health Organization *(WHO)*** ⊕ *www.who.int.*

MEDICAL INSURANCE AND ASSISTANCE

Consider buying trip insurance with medical-only coverage. Neither Medicare nor some private insurers cover medical expenses anywhere outside the United States. Medical-only policies typically reimburse you for medical care (excluding that related to pre-existing conditions) and hospitalization abroad, and provide for evacuation. You still have to pay the bills and await reimbursement from the insurer, though.

Another option is to sign up with a medical-evacuation assistance company. Membership gets you doctor referrals, emergency evacuation or repatriation, 24-hour hotlines for medical consultation, and other assistance. International SOS Assistance Emergency and AirMed International provide evacuation services and medical referrals. MedjetAssist offers medical evacuation.

Medical Assistance Companies
AirMed International ☎ 800/356-2161
in U.S., 205/443-4840 from Mexico
⊕ *www.airmed.com.* **International SOS**
Assistance Emergency ☎ 800/523-8662
⊕ *www.internationalsos.com.* **MedjetAssist**
☎ 800/527-7478 ⊕ *www.medjetassist.com.*

Medical-Only Insurers International
Medical Group ☎ 800/628-4664
⊕ *www.imglobal.com.* **Wallach & Company**
☎ 800/237-6615 or 540/687-3166
⊕ *www.wallach.com.*

HOLIDAYS

Mexico is the land of festivals; if you reserve lodging well in advance, they present a golden opportunity to have a thoroughly Mexican experience. Banks and government offices close during Holy Week (the week leading to Easter Sunday) and on Cinco de Mayo, Día de la Raza, and Independence Day. Government offices usually have reduced hours and staff from Christmas through New Year's Day. Some banks and offices close for religious holidays.

Official holidays include New Year's Day (January 1); Constitution Day (February 5); Flag Day (February 24); Benito Juárez's Birthday (March 21); Good Friday (Friday before Easter Sunday); Easter Sunday (the first Sunday after the first full moon following spring equinox); Labor Day (May 1); Cinco de Mayo (May 5); St. John the Baptist Day (June 24); Independence Day (September 16); Día de la Raza (Day of the Race; October 12); Día de los Muertos (Day of the Dead; November 2); Anniversary of the Mexican Revolution (November 20); Christmas (December 25).

Festivals include Carnaval (February and March, before Lent); Semana Santa (Holy Week; week before Easter Sunday); Día de Nuestra Señora de Guadalupe (Day of Our Lady of Guadalupe; December 12); and Las Posadas (pre-Christmas religious celebrations; December 16–25).

HOURS OF OPERATION

Banks are usually open weekdays 8:30–3 (although sometimes banks in Cabo and San José stay open until 5). Government offices are usually open to the public weekdays 8–3; they're closed—along with banks and most private offices—on national holidays. Stores are generally open weekdays and Saturday from 9 or 10 to 7 or 8. In tourist areas, some shops don't close until 10 and are open Sunday. Some shops close for a two-hour lunch break, usually from 2 to 4. Shops extend their hours when cruise ships are in town.

MAIL

Airmail letters from Baja Sur can take up to two weeks and often much longer to reach their destination. The *oficina de correos* (post office) in San José del Cabo is open 8–7 weekdays (with a possible closure for lunch) and 9–1 Saturday. Offices in Cabo San Lucas and La Paz are open 9–1 and 3–6 weekdays; La Paz and San Lucas offices are also open 9–noon on Saturday.

Post Offices Cabo San Lucas Oficina de Correo ⊠ *Av. Cárdenas s/n* ☎ *624/143-0048.* **San José del Cabo Oficina de Correo** ⊠ *Mijares and Margarita Maya de Juárez.*

SHIPPING PACKAGES

FedEx does not serve Los Cabos area. DHL has express service for letters and packages from Los Cabos to the United States and Canada; most deliveries take three to four days (overnight service is not available). To the United States, letters take three days and boxes and packages take four days. Cabo San Lucas, San José del Cabo, and La Paz have a DHL drop-off location. Mail Boxes Etc. can help with DHL and postal services.

Major Services DHL Worldwide Express ⊠ *Blvd. Mauricio Castro 1738, San José del Cabo* ☎ *800/765-6345* ⊕ *www.dhl.com* ⊠ *Plaza Los Arcos, Leona Vicario, Cabo San Lucas* ☎ *624/765-6345* ⊕ *www.dhl.com.* **Mail Boxes Etc.** ⊠ *Plaza las Palmas, Hwy. 1,*

Km 31, San José del Cabo ☎ *624/142–4355*
⊕ *www.mailboxesloscabos.com* ✉ *Plaza Bonita,*
Blvd. Marina #17, Cabo San Lucas ☎ *624/143–*
3032 ⊕ *www.mailboxesloscabos.com.*

▌ MONEY

Mexico has a reputation for being inexpensive, but Los Cabos is one of the most expensive places to visit in the country. Prices rise from 10% to 18% annually and are comparable to those in Southern California.

Prices in this book are quoted most often in U.S. dollars, which are readily accepted in Los Cabos (although you should always have pesos on you if you venture anywhere beyond the walls of a resort).
⇨ *For information on taxes, see Taxes.*

Prices throughout this guide are given for adults. Substantially reduced fees are almost always available for children, students, and senior citizens.

ATMS AND BANKS

ATMs (*cajas automáticas*) are commonplace in Los Cabos and La Paz. If you're going to a less-developed area, though, go equipped with cash. Cirrus and Plus cards are the most commonly accepted. The ATMs at Banamex, one of the oldest nationwide banks, tend to be the most reliable. Bancomer is another bank with many ATM locations.

Many Mexican ATMs cannot accept PINs with more than four digits. If yours is longer, change your PIN to four digits before you leave home. If your PIN is fine yet your transaction still can't be completed, chances are that the computer lines are busy or that the machine has run out of money or is being serviced. Don't give up.

CREDIT CARDS

When shopping, you can often get better prices if you pay with cash, particularly in small shops. But you'll receive wholesale exchange rates when you make purchases with credit cards. These exchange rates are usually better than those that banks give you for changing money. The decision to pay cash or to use a credit card might depend on whether the establishment in which you are making a purchase finds bargaining for prices acceptable, and whether you want the safety net of your card's purchase protection. To avoid fraud or errors, it's wise to make sure that "pesos" is clearly marked on all credit-card receipts.

Before you leave for Mexico, contact your credit-card company to get lost-card phone numbers that work in Mexico; the standard toll-free numbers often don't work abroad. Carry these numbers separately from your wallet so you'll have them if you need to call to report lost or stolen cards. American Express, MasterCard, and Visa note the international number for card-replacement calls on the back of their cards.

CURRENCY AND EXCHANGE

The currency in Los Cabos is the Mexican peso (MXP), though prices are often given in U.S. dollars. Mexican currency comes in denominations of 20-, 50-, 100-, 200-, and 500-peso bills. Coins come in denominations of 1, 2, 5, 10, and 20 pesos and 20 and 50 centavos (20-centavo coins are only rarely seen). Many of the coins are very similar, so check carefully; bills, however, are different colors and easily distinguished.

At this writing, US$1 was equivalent to approximately MXP 12.76.

▌ PASSPORTS AND VISAS

A passport, or other WHTI (Western Hemisphere Travel Initiative) compliant document, is now required of all visitors to Mexico, including U.S. citizens who may remember the days when only driver's licenses were needed to cross the border. Upon entering Mexico all visitors must get a tourist card. If you're arriving by plane from the United States or Canada, the standard tourist card will be given to you on the plane. They're also available through travel agents and Mexican consulates and at the border if you're entering by land.

■TIP➜ You're given a portion of the tourist card form upon entering Mexico. Keep track of this documentation throughout your trip: you will need it when you depart. You'll be asked to hand it, your ticket, and your passport to airline representatives at the gate when boarding for departure.

If you lose your tourist card, plan to spend some time (and about $60) sorting it out with Mexican officials at the airport on departure.

A tourist card costs about $20. The fee is generally tacked onto the price of your airline ticket; if you enter by land or boat you'll have to pay the fee separately. You're exempt from the fee if you enter by sea and stay less than 72 hours, or by land and do not stray past the 26- to 30-km (16- to 18-mile) checkpoint into the country's interior.

Tourist cards and visas are valid from 15 to 180 days, at the discretion of the immigration officer at your point of entry (90 days for Australians). Americans, Canadians, New Zealanders, and the British may request up to 180 days for a tourist card or visa extension. The extension fee is about $20, and the process can be time-consuming. There's no guarantee that you'll get the extension you're requesting. If you're planning an extended stay, plead with the immigration official for the maximum allowed days at the time of entry. It will save you time and money later.

■TIP➜ Mexico has some of the strictest policies about children entering the country. Minors traveling with one parent need notarized permission from the absent parent.

If you're a single parent traveling with children up to age 18, you must have a notarized letter from the other parent stating that the child has his or her permission to leave his or her home country. The child must be carrying the original letter—not a facsimile or scanned copy—as well as proof of the parent-child relationship (usually a birth certificate or court document), and an original custody decree, if applicable. If the other parent is deceased

or the child has only one legal parent, a notarized statement saying so must be obtained as proof. In addition, you must fill out a tourist card for each child over the age of 10 traveling with you.

Info Mexican Embassy ☏ *202/728-1600* ⊕ *portal.sre.gob.mx/usa.*

U.S. Passport Information
U.S. Department of State ☏ *877/487-2778* ⊕ *travel.state.gov/passport.*

■ RESTROOMS

Expect to find clean flushing toilets, toilet tissue, soap, and running water in Los Cabos. An exception may be small roadside stands or restaurants in rural areas. If there's a bucket and a large container of water sitting outside the facilities, fill the bucket and use it for the flush. Some public places, such as bus stations, charge 1 or 2 pesos for use of the facility, but toilet paper is included in the fee. Still, it's always a good idea to carry some tissue. Throw your toilet paper and any other materials into the provided waste bins rather than the toilet. Mexican plumbing simply isn't equipped to deal with the volume of paper Americans are accustomed to putting in toilets.

■ SAFETY

Although Los Cabos area is one of the safest in Mexico, it's still important to be aware of your surroundings and to follow normal safety precautions. Everyone has heard some horror story about highway assaults, pickpocketing, bribes, or foreigners languishing in Mexican jails. Reports of these crimes apply in large part to Mexico City and other large cities; in Los Cabos, pickpocketing is usually the biggest concern.

General Information and Warnings
Transportation Security Administration
(TSA) ☏ *866/289-9673* ⊕ *www.tsa.gov.*
U.S. Department of State ☏ *202/501-4444 from Mexico, 888/407-4747 from the U.S.* ⊕ *www.travel.state.gov.*

▍TAXES

Mexico charges a departure and airport tax of about US$13 and US$8.50, or the peso equivalent, respectively, when you leave the country. This tax is almost universally included in the price of your ticket, but check to be certain. Traveler's checks and credit cards are not accepted at the airport as payment for this fee.

A 2% tax on accommodations is charged in Los Cabos, with proceeds used for tourism promotion.

Baja California Sur has a value-added tax of 10%, called I.V.A. (*impuesto de valor agregado*), which is occasionally (and illegally) waived for cash purchases. Other taxes and charges apply for phone calls made from your hotel room.

▍TIME

Baja California Sur is on Mountain Standard Time, Baja California is on Pacific Standard Time. And the unofficial standard for behavior is "Mexican time"— meaning stop rushing, enjoy yourself, and practice being *tranquilo*.

▍TIPPING

When tipping in Baja, remember that the minimum wage is equivalent to a mere $4.50 a day, and that the vast majority of workers in the tourist industry of Mexico live barely above the poverty line. However, there are Mexicans who think in dollars and know, for example, that in the United States porters are tipped about $2 a bag; many of them expect the peso equivalent from foreigners but are sometimes happy to accept 5 pesos (about 50¢) a bag from Mexicans. They will complain either verbally or with a facial expression if they feel they deserve more—you and your conscience must decide. Following are some guidelines. Naturally, larger tips are always welcome.

For porters and bellboys at airports and at moderate and inexpensive hotels, $1 (about 13 pesos) per bag should be sufficient. At expensive hotels, porters expect at least $2 (about 26 pesos) per bag. Leave at least $1 (10 pesos) per night for maids at all hotels. The norm for waiters is 10% to 15% of the bill, depending on service (make sure a 10%–15% service charge hasn't already been added to the bill, although this practice is more common in resorts). Tipping taxi drivers is necessary only if the driver helps with your bags; 50¢ to $1 (6 to 13 pesos) should be enough, depending on the extent of the help. Tip tour guides and drivers at least $1 (13 pesos) per half day or 10% of the tour fee, minimum. Gas-station attendants receive 30¢ to 50¢ (4 to 6 pesos), more if they check the oil, tires, etc. Parking attendants—including those at restaurants with valet parking—should be tipped 50¢ to $1 (6 to 13 pesos).

▍TRIP INSURANCE

Comprehensive trip insurance is valuable if you're booking a very expensive or complicated trip (particularly to an isolated region) or if you're booking far in advance. Comprehensive policies typically cover trip-cancellation and interruption, letting you cancel or cut your trip short because of a personal emergency, illness, or, in some cases, acts of terrorism in your destination. Such policies also cover evacuation and medical care. (For trips abroad you should at least have medical-only coverage). Some also cover you for trip delays because of bad weather or mechanical problems as well as for lost or delayed baggage.

Another type of coverage to look for is financial default—that is, when your trip is disrupted because a tour operator, airline, or cruise line goes out of business. Generally you must buy this when you book your trip or shortly thereafter, and it's only available to you if your operator isn't on a list of excluded companies.

Always read the fine print of your policy to make sure that you are covered for the risks that are of most concern to you. Compare several policies to make sure you're getting the best price and range of coverage available.

Insurance Comparison Sites
Insure My Trip.com ☎ *800/487-4722* ⊕ *www.insuremytrip.com.* **Square Mouth.com** ☎ *800/240-0369* ⊕ *www.squaremouth.com.*

Comprehensive Travel Insurers
Allianz ☎ *800/284-8300* ⊕ *www. allianztravelinsurance.com.* **AIG Travel Guard** ☎ *800/826-4919* ⊕ *www.travelguard.com.* **CSA Travel Protection** ☎ *877/243-4135* ⊕ *www.csatravelprotection.com.* **Travelex Insurance** ☎ *800/228-9792* ⊕ *www.travelex-insurance.com.* **Travel Insured International** ☎ *800/243-3174* ⊕ *www.travelinsured.com.*

▌ VISITOR INFORMATION

Avoid tour stands on the streets; they are usually associated with time-share operations. In Todos Santos, pick up a copy of *El Calendario de Todos Santos* for information on local events. The *Gringo Gazette* newspaper and the pocket-size *Cabo Noche* are good guides for the Cabo scene. These publications are free and easy to find in hotels and restaurants throughout the region. Discover Baja, a membership club for Baja travelers, has links and info at its website. Planeta.com has information about ecotourism and environmental issues.

The Baja California Sur State Tourist Office is in La Paz about a 10-minute drive north of the *malecón*, the seaside promenade. It serves as both the state and city tourism office. There's also an information stand on the malecón (no phone) across from Los Arcos hotel. The booth is a more convenient spot, and it can give you info on La Paz, Scammon's Lagoon, Santa Rosalia, and other smaller towns. Both offices and the booth are open weekdays 9–5.

Contacts **Baja California Sur State Tourist Office** ✉ *Mariano Abasolo s/n, La Paz* ☎ *866/733-5272* ⊕ *www.vivalapaz.com.* **Discover Baja** ☎ *800/727-2252* ⊕ *www. discoverbaja.com.* ***El Calendario de Todos Santos*** ⊕ *www.elcalendariodetodossantos.com.* ***Gringo Gazette.*** ⊕ *www.gringogazette.com.* **Los Cabos Convention & Visitors Bureau** ☎ *624/143-4777 in Mexico, 866/LOS CABOS toll-free* ⊕ *www.visitloscabos.travel.* **Mexican Government Tourist Board** ☎ *800/446-3942 from U.S. and Canada* ⊕ *www.visitmexico. com.* **Planeta.com** ⊕ *www.planeta.com.* **TodosSantos-Baja.com** ⊕ *www.todossantos-baja.com.*

INDEX

234 <

PHOTO CREDITS

1, carlos sanchez pereyra/Shutterstock. 3, Jim Russi/age fotostock. Chapter 1: Experience Los Cabos: 6-7, Victor Elías/age fotostock. 8, Bruce Herman/Mexico Tourism Board. 9, Carolina K. Smith, M.D./ Shutterstock.10 (top left), Ken Ross/viestiphoto.com. 10 (top right), Michael S. Nolan/age fotostock. 10 (bottom) and 11, Bruce Herman/Mexico Tourism Board. 12, (a), Victor Elías/age fotostock. 12, (b) Katzilioness I Dreamstime.com. 12, (c), alysta/Shutterstock. 13 (top left), Visual&Written SL/Alamy. 13 (right), csp/Shutterstock. 13 (bottom left), Kim Karpeles / Alamy. 14, Bruce Herman/Mexico Tourism Board. 15 (left), Esperanza Resort. 15 (right), Adobe Guadalupe. 18, TFoxFoto/Shutterstock. 19, john hoadley/Shutterstock. 20, SuperStock/age fotostock. 21, Bruce Herman/Mexico Tourism Board. 23 (left), Pete Saloutos/Shutterstock. 23 (right), SuperStock/age fotostock. 24, Luis Garcia Photography. Chapter 2: Beaches: 25, Heeb Christian/age fotostock. 26, Brian Florky/Shutterstock. 31 and 32 (top), Jim Russi/age fotostock. 32 (center), Kato Inowe/Shutterstock. 32 (bottom), RCPPHOTO/ Shutterstock. 33, Henry William Fu/Shutterstock. 34 and 36 (top), Kato Inowe/Shutterstock. 36 (bottom), Bruce Herman/Mexico Tourism Board. 39. Victor Elías/age fotostock. 42-43, Heeb Christian/ age fotostock. Chapter 3: Sports and Outdoor Activities: 47 and 48, Bruce Herman/Mexico Tourism Board. 52-53, Ralph Hopkins/age fotostock. 58, tonobalaguerf/Shutterstock. 59, Larry Dunmire. 60 (top), Sam Woolford/iStockphoto. 60 (bottom), Larry Dunmire. 62 (top), Bruce Herman/Mexico Tourism Board. 62 (bottom), csp/Shutterstock. 63, Chris Pendleton/iStockphoto. 64, Robert Chiasson/age fotostock.68, Michele Westmorland/age fotostock. 73, Adalberto Ríos Szalay/age fotostock. 74 (illustration), Pieter Folkens. 74 (bottom), Michael S. Nolan/age fotostock. 75, Ryan Harvey/Flickr. 78, Reinhard Dirscherl/age fotostock. Chapter 4: Where to Eat in Los Cabos: 79, SIME/Grandadam Laurent/eStock Photo. 80, Matthieu Fiol. 86 (top), Rigoberto Moreno. 86 (bottom left), Casa Natalia.86 (bottom right), Frances Janisch. 93 (top), nicksan. 97 (bottom), Restaurant Sunset Da Mona Lisa. 103, Richard Cummins/age fotostock. Chapter 5: Where to Stay in Los Cabos: 107, Larry Dunmire. 108, Victor Elias. 119 (top), Hilton Los Cabos Beach & Golf Resort. 119 (bottom left), Esperanza Resort. 119 (bottom right), Small Luxury Hotels. 121 (top), Marbella en la Playa. 121 (bottom), Las Ventanas al Paraiso, A Rosewood Resort. 123 (top), One&Only Palmilla. 123 (bottom), AMResorts127 (top), Victor Elias. 127 (bottom), Pacifi ca Holistic Retreat & Spa. Chapter 6: Shopping: 131, Terrance Klassen/age fotostock. 132, Tony Hertz/Alamy. 138, Jan Butchofsky-Houser/age fotostock. 143, Greg Vaughn/Alamy.146, Richard Cummins/age fotostock. 148, John Mitchell/Alamy. 149, María Lourdes Alonso/age fotostock. 150 (top), Danita Delimont/Alamy. 150 (bottom), María Lourdes Alonso/age fotostock. 151 (top left), Ken Ross/viestiphoto.com. 151 (bottom left), Ken Ross/viestiphoto.com. 151 (bottom 2nd from left), Ken Ross/viestiphoto.com. 151 (bottom 3rd from left), Ken Ross/viestiphoto.com. 151 (right), Jane Onstott. 152 (top left), patti haskins/Flickr. 152 (bottom left), fontplaydotcom/Flickr. 152 (top right), Wonderlane/Flickr. 152 (center right), Jose Zelaya Gallery/ArtedelPueblo.com. 152 (bottom right), Jane Onstott.153, GlowImages/Alamy. Chapter 7: Nightlife and the Arts: 159, Jay Reilly/Aurora Photos. 160, Elena Koulik/Shutterstock. 167, JTB Photo/age fotostock. 172, Blaine Harrington III/Alamy. Chapter 8: Los Cabos Side Trips: 177, Photoshot/age fotostock. 178 (top), iStockphoto. 178 (bottom), William Katz/iStockphoto. 180, Sherwin McGehee/iStockphoto. 183, San Rostro/ age fotostock. 187 (top and bottom left), Todos Santos Inn. 187 (bottom right), Posada la Poza. 190, Danita Delimont/Alamy. 193, stefano lunardi/age fotostock. 199, Michael S. Nolan/age fotostock.

NOTES

NOTES

NOTES

NOTES

NOTES

NOTES

ABOUT OUR WRITERS

A New York City-based travel, food, and lifestyle writer, **Marie Elena Martinez** has contributed to a host of print publications including *The New York Times*, *Newsday*, *Boston Globe*, *Wall Street Journal*, *Miami Herald*, *Women's Adventure*, and *W* magazine, as well as online outlets like *Men's Fitness*, *The Daily Meal*, and *CNTraveler.com*. She is also the Founding Editor of *The Latin Kitchen*, an online destination about the Latin American culinary world. A regular blogger for *The Huffington Post*, she left her corporate PR job in 2005 and has been traveling the world ever since.

San José, Costa Rica–based freelance writer **Jeffrey Van Fleet** updated the Side Trips chapter for this editon. He has also contributed to Fodor's guides to Costa Rica, Guatemala, Honduras, Panama, California, Peru, Chile, Argentina, and Central and South America.